FROM MADEA TO MEDIA MOGUL

FROM MADEA TO MEDIA MOGUL

Theorizing Tyler Perry

Edited by

TreaAndrea M. Russworm, Samantha N. Sheppard, and Karen M. Bowdre

University Press of Mississippi / Jackson

www.upress.state.ms.us

The University Press of Mississippi is a member
of the Association of American University Presses.

Copyright © 2016 by University Press of Mississippi
All rights reserved

First printing 2016

∞

Library of Congress Cataloging-in-Publication Data

Names: Russworm, TreaAndrea M., editor. | Sheppard, Samantha N., editor. |
 Bowdre, Karen M., editor.
Title: From Madea to media mogul : theorizing Tyler Perry / edited by
 TreaAndrea M. Russworm, Samantha N. Sheppard, and Karen M. Bowdre ;
 foreword by Eric Pierson.
Description: Jackson : University Press of Mississippi, 2016. | Includes
 index.
Identifiers: LCCN 2015048409 (print) | LCCN 2015049985 (ebook) | ISBN
 9781496807045 (hardback) | ISBN 9781496807052 (epub single) | ISBN
 9781496807069 (epub institutional) | ISBN 9781496807076 (pdf single) |
 ISBN 9781496807083 (pdf institutional)
Subjects: LCSH: Perry, Tyler—Criticism and interpretation. | BISAC: SOCIAL
 SCIENCE / Media Studies. | PERFORMING ARTS / Film & Video / History &
 Criticism. | SOCIAL SCIENCE / Ethnic Studies / African American Studies.
Classification: LCC PN1998.3.P4575 F86 2016 (print) | LCC PN1998.3.P4575
 (ebook) | DDC 791.4302/8092—dc23
LC record available at http://lccn.loc.gov/2015048409

British Library Cataloging-in-Publication Data available

Contents

vii   **FOREWORD—CENTRALITY**
       —Eric Pierson

xi   **ACKNOWLEDGMENTS**

xiii   **INTRODUCTION—RESPECTABILITY**
       Media Studies Has Ninety-Nine Problems . . . But Tyler Perry Ain't One of Them?
       —TreaAndrea M. Russworm

3   **CHAPTER 1—PLATFORMS**
       "Tyler Perry Presents . . .": The Cultural Projects, Partnerships, and Politics of Perry's Media Platforms
       —Samantha N. Sheppard

30   **CHAPTER 2—CHITLIN**
       From the Margins to Center Stage: Tyler Perry's Popular African American Theatre
       —Rashida Z. Shaw

52   **CHAPTER 3—GOSPEL**
       Tyler Perry, T.D. Jakes, and the Birth of Gospel Cinema
       —Keith Corson

72   **CHAPTER 4—AFFECT**
       Worship at the Altar of Perry: Spectatorship and the Aesthetics of Testimony
       —Brandeise Monk-Payton

94   **CHAPTER 5—CINEPHILIA**
       "All My Life I Had to Fight": Domestic Trauma and Cinephilia in Tyler Perry's Archive of Feelings
       —Ben Raphael Sher

CHAPTER 6—DISGUISE
"Who I Am Is Conflicting with This Dress I Got On": Madea's Intimate Public and the Possibilities and Limitations of False Disguise
—Rachel Jessica Daniel
(p. 118)

CHAPTER 7—NICHE
One Man Hollywood: The Decline of Black Creative Production in Post-Network Television
—Aymar Jean Christian and Khadijah Costley White
(p. 138)

CHAPTER 8—THIRST
Bring the Payne: The Erasure of the Black Sitcom and the Emergence of *Tyler Perry's House of Payne*
—Artel Great
(p. 159)

CHAPTER 9—EXCEPTIONALISM
Spike and Tyler's Beef: Blackness, Authenticity, and Discourses of Black Exceptionalism
—Karen M. Bowdre
(p. 180)

CHAPTER 10—MOGUL
The Case for Calling George Lucas the "White Tyler Perry"
—Paul N. Reinsch
(p. 200)

CHAPTER 11—REBRAND
To Brand and Rebrand: Questioning the Futurity of Tyler Perry
—Leah Aldridge
(p. 225)

EPILOGUE—MADEA
Playing with the Changes
—Miriam J. Petty
(p. 233)

Contributors — 237

Index — 243

Foreword

We all have a Madea in our families. She is sometimes the crazy aunt with no filter who often says the first thing that comes into her head. She is the loudest and most uninhibited person in the room. A matriarch, Madea is an important element of Black life. With his plays, films, and television shows, Tyler Perry has taken what for some is a sacred cultural figure and shared it with mainstream America. In many ways, Perry's popular, politically incorrect character is viewed as all that is wrong with Black women in America. Loud, opinionated, and unapologetic about her behavior, Madea can all too easily be viewed as a stereotype. Because Hollywood films offer so very few alternatives to representation of Black women and Black life on screen, Perry's Madea and the films she appears in are often discussed without much context.

This collection will help provide readers with a rich context through which they can engage Madea and the other characters in Perry's world. The editors of this collection have done a significant service to the scholarly community in pulling together these multiple perspectives on the work and impact of Perry. The collection is not just a reflection on the significance of Perry; it is also a reflection of the complexity of questions regarding the experiences of Black folks in a world that has become increasingly influenced, manufactured, and marketed by and through the media. Normally, these essays would be spread across a series of journals and conference presentations, their relevance and importance limited to those venues.

Perry's cultural productions allow scholars from a range of disciplines and theoretical models to offer valuable contributions. Cultural Studies, Critical Race Theory, Political Economy, Film Theory, Ideological Criticism, and Rhetoric are among the available mechanisms and methods for engaging his work. Through the process of engaging Perry, these scholars have created a critical framework for examining the past and the future of racial discourse in American national and popular culture. Significantly, the analyses shared here are not just about Perry, though he is a worthy figure of critique in and of himself. The essays are also about the relationship between Black people and the social and cultural institutions that manufacture and circulate images of blackness.

I have often questioned how I could possibly take the creator of "Madea" as a serious voice in the media industry. Prior to his work as executive producer of *Precious* (Lee Daniels, 2009), Perry had only come on my radar when the latest iteration of "Madea Goes . . ." would hit the theatre. I treated his Madea films much like I treated the "Ernest Goes . . ." comedies: as a cinematic waste of time. With the release of *Precious*, however, I began to take a more serious look at the work of Perry and began to consider some of the problems and possibilities of his media empire. What became clear to me then, and has crystallized since 2009, is that Perry is a media force who is worthy of critical engagement because of his polarizing productions.

Perry's influence on Black film and media has not always been so visible, though he has clearly labored over the years to solidify his place within the media industry. For the last decade, Perry has been the dominant manufacturer of popular Black images. As America consumes these, at times, troubling images, Perry remains unapologetic to those who have issues with his offerings. In this regard, the control of the images of Black experiences have been contested spaces beginning with D. W. Griffith's *The Birth of a Nation* (1915), through the debates centering on the television version of *Amos 'n' Andy* (CBS, 1951–53) in the 1950s, then moving though the era of Blaxploitation in the 1970s, and now through the work of Perry. However, what makes the work of Perry different than the others mentioned is that he is African American and there are different expectations in this era. When whites get the Black experience wrong, we can see the ways in which roles are played by the economics and lack of cultural understandings. Perry, rightly or wrongly, will be and is held to a different set of standards. Is Perry the voice of the Black experience or is he just a businessman trafficking in the experience for profit?

In attempting to answer questions like these, it is important that we understand Perry's transition from theatre writer/actor/producer to that of multimedia mogul. During his time in the Black theatre, Perry not only honed his craft but also created a foundational relationship with his target Black audience, which became the base for his future success. Perry's theatre experience reminds us of the vitality of the Black theatrical experience. While so much of the power of Black theatre has been absorbed into the mainstream marketplace, it is easy to forget the power of theatre as a transmitter of Black culture. Importantly, the space of the Black theatre was also apart from the critique of the mainstream. In that space, Perry was free to have conversations regarding the ways in which race, class, and gender impact the Black experience with an audience that was almost always exclusively Black. These dialogues allowed for frank discussion in a safe space, analogous to the sanctuary of the Black church.

It is Perry's use of the Black church as both a setting and as a cinematic trope that causes me the greatest concern and is one of the other major problems with his representations. The Black church has always been an important and significant institution to the Black community. The power of the Black church was truly on display during the civil rights movement; it became the place where many of the leaders of the period began their sphere of influence. It has been one of the few historical places were Blacks have felt that they were safe and that they could truly express themselves. It was a site of refuge, a place where Blacks could often meet and share their most intimate feelings and fears. In much of his work, Perry has opened up the "church" so that others can look inside. The outing of Black folks and a cherished institution in the name of commerce is one reason so many seem to resist and resent Perry's work.

In many ways, Perry has taken some of the most intimate parts of Black life and turned them into profit. Because of this, Perry's voice speaks louder than others, signaling a larger void in the representation of Black experiences. It is this representation of the "Black experience" that many say is at the heart of the problems with Perry's work and speaks to the importance of this collection. He, in many ways, gets the first, last, and only word regarding important debates within Black communities, including: What counts as a "true" or "authentic" Black experience? Who gets to claim blackness and under what conditions? What it means to be Black and how does colorism play a role in that designation? What does success look like for those in the Black community and is it different than other types of success? What does it mean to be rich or poor as a Black person? What is the role of the Black father and has that role been fulfilled and if so in what ways? What relationship should Black men have with their mothers in the absence of their fathers? For better or worse, the films of Tyler Perry are controlling and shaping some of the most important debates of our time.

Perry occupies a unique space in the cultural conversation because his narratives speak so loudly and counter-narratives are absent. The debates surrounding the images of Perry's films are volatile because we are still attempting to address the lack of Black images in film and television. While there are an overall lack of Black images, the images created by Perry occupy the majority of the images that are accessible: *Meet the Browns* (TBS, 2009–11) was canceled after 140 episodes, eclipsing the 136-episode library of *Sanford and Son* (NBC, 1972–77), while *House of Payne* (TBS, 2006–12) ended its run with 254 episodes, one more than *The Jeffersons* (CBS, 1975–85). The next Madea film will be the twelfth in the series, and Perry has several film projects in various stages of development. With a series currently on BET and OWN, Perry's influence on Black culture shows no signs of decreasing in the future. With the scope and influence of Perry's work in mind, I applaud the editors for inviting us to examine and theorize the problems and possibilities of this compelling personality.

The timing of this collection is important as Perry moves into the future with new media ventures, such as *The Haves and the Have Nots* (2013–present), a prime-time soap opera for OWN, and he looks for a new film distribution partner after Lionsgate terminated their relationship as his film distributer. Often we miss the opportunity to engage in rigorous academic analyses until after the person's work has started to fade and the analysis can be more nostalgic than critical. This collection provides readers with theoretical frameworks for examining Perry through a reflective lens of history but also with a look toward his work in the future. The book speaks about Perry, and there is hope that it will speak to Perry as well.

Whether you are a fan or critic of his work, you cannot deny that in a world where mediated images can influence everything from important public policy debates to attitudes towards parenting styles, Tyler Perry has become worthy of our attention and scrutiny.

—Eric Pierson, 2015
University of San Diego

Acknowledgments

The editors are grateful for the many levels of support we have received throughout this process. At the University Press of Mississippi, we appreciate the time Leila Salisbury and Valerie Jones have devoted to the project; we also thank the anonymous readers of our manuscript for their helpful and timely comments. Additionally, many of our colleagues in the SCMS African and African American Caucus have provided encouragement, support, and feedback, including but not limited to, Anna Everett, Jacqueline Stewart, Bambi Haggins, Charlene Regester, Racquel Gates, Kristen Warner, and Beretta Shomade-Smith. Of course, this collection would not have been possible without the dedication, perseverance, and patience of all of our contributors. Their graciousness and talent made our jobs a pleasure. Finally, we each thank God for providing us the strength, fortitude, and grace to complete this project.

Individually, we extend a warm thanks to the following:

TreaAndrea would like to thank Ron'na Lytle, Mark James, Tracy Harkless, and her writing partners, colleagues, and friends: Laura Furlan, Laura Kalba, Gulru Calmak, Gina Valesquez, K. C. Nat Turner, Florence Sullivan, Michael Forbes, Jen Malkowski, and Priscilla Page. She is especially grateful for all the time spent working together on this project with Karen and Samantha. She feels younger, not older, as a result of this quality time spent together.

Samantha would like to thank Allen Holt, Amanda Rossie, Allyson Field, Jackie Thornton, Patricia Sheppard, and George Sheppard, all of whom provided rich, stimulating, and challenging conversations and feedback on Tyler Perry and support in general. She is grateful for her coeditors, TreaAndrea Russworm and Karen Bowdre, whose insight, wit, candor, and Google chats made this project come to fruition.

Karen would like to thank Cheryl and Angel, Janice and James Bowdre for their support, along with her two wonderful coeditors, Samantha and TreaAndrea, who provided stimulating conversation about Perry as well as many laughs. It was a pleasure creating and completing this project with them.

INTRODUCTION

Media Studies Has Ninety-Nine Problems . . . But Tyler Perry Ain't One of Them?

—TreaAndrea M. Russworm

My Problem(s) with Tyler Perry

I have complicated feelings about Tyler Perry. He makes me feel some kind of way, or as my students would say, I have "feels" on the matter. In fact, for a long while, whenever I mentioned to anyone (from colleagues to cab drivers to my mother) that I was working on this collection, I always found some way to distance my intellectual labor on the project from a positive endorsement of Perry's films and television shows. I'd say: "Yes. Tyler Perry. We're editing a book on him but that doesn't mean I like his stuff. I am so not a fan. I don't drink the Kool-Aid." In casual social spaces, I have used much stronger language to frame my resistance to Perry's oeuvre, and I'm not afraid to begin this collection of critical essays by repeating what I have so often said to others: I have hated every Tyler Perry movie I have ever seen (my personal viewing total is thirteen Perry-directed films and videos . . . and counting). I have stressed to anyone who broached the subject with me that every moment of watching these films has been masochistic, barely endurable. I have especially hated the fact that Tyler Perry keeps making films.

I can also say that while working on this project my personal wave of "feels," that affective torrent of powerful emotions that Tyler Perry's work seems to evoke in fans and critics alike, has shifted enough for me to now say this: I forgive Tyler Perry. I forgive him, Whoopi Goldberg, and Macy Gray for mangling Ntozake Shange's *For Colored Girls* (2010). I forgive Perry for *Madea's Family Reunion* (2006), *Madea Goes to Jail*

(2009), *Madea's Big Happy Family* (2011), and really, because there are too many Madea films to list here, I forgive him for any feature or animated film where he dons a dress and fat suit and masquerades as his signature Black female matriarch, Madea. There is room enough in my heart to forgive Tyler Perry for those weekly email reflections that his avid fans never fail to forward to me—you know, the messages where he shares with his supporters lengthy reflections about what God has told him lately. Finally, even though I like his television shows significantly less than I like Madea, I also forgive Tyler Perry for creating each of those shows, particularly the dreadful neo-minstrel sitcom *Meet the Browns* (TBS, 2009–12). Mostly, though, I forgive Tyler Perry for not making Black popular culture for *me*.

Skeptics and critics like me are a perfect and necessary audience for *From Madea to Media Mogul: Theorizing Tyler Perry*. Simply put, this book is not about drinking—or *drankin'*—the Kool-Aid or about convincing anyone to appreciate and enjoy Perry's stage plays, films, or television shows. This book does, however, aim to speak to a critical academic and wider audience that has failed to take this aspect of Black popular culture seriously, an audience that struggles to see beyond our own "feels" and blind spots, grievances and resistances, biases and problems with mainstream Black popular culture. To be clear, while there might be many "problems" when it comes to Perry's work, like his oft-discussed problems representing Black women or the problems of identification he creates for viewers who wish to see more positive imagery, with this collection we contend that one of the main problems with Tyler Perry has less to do with Perry and more to do with the limited critical attention he has garnered.

On "Disreputable" Black Objects and the Burdens of Representation

With my personal confessions about Tyler Perry now out in the open, it bears sharing how, given my obvious problems with his work, I nonetheless came to coedit this book with Karen M. Bowdre and Samantha N. Sheppard. First, some context about Perry's career is in order.

For over a decade, Tyler Perry, who is certainly best known for his drag performances as Madea, the self-proclaimed "mad Black woman" who is not afraid to brandish a gun or a scalding pot of grits in defense of herself and others, has been a lightning rod for both criticism and praise. Since his meteoric rise to fame, just as many blogs and popular headlines have led with something akin to "In Defense of Tyler Perry," "The Problem with Perry," or "Why Tyler Perry Hates Black Women" (or "Black Men," or "Black People" in general). Is this commercially successful African American actor, director, screenwriter, playwright, and producer "malt liquor for the masses," the Devil, an embarrassment to the race!, or a genius who has directed the most culturally significant American melodramas since Douglas Sirk?[1] Are his films and television shows even melodramas, or are they conservative Christian diatribes, cheeky camp, or social satires? Do Perry's flattened narratives and character tropes irresponsibly collapse important social discourses into one-dimensional tales that affirm the notion of a "post-racial" society, or is it, as a recent *Esquire* article touted, that Tyler Perry is better than the "new Obama" because his films give us one of the only occasions to talk openly about race and gender, class and stereotype, in a bipartisan, so-called "post-racial" American political climate?[2]

Whether or not we personally love or hate his productions, one thing is clear: Tyler Perry is not going anywhere. He has developed lucrative film and television partnerships with Lionsgate, TBS, and Oprah, and his films have grossed far more than any other Black filmmaker in history, including more critically acclaimed Black directors like Spike Lee, Cheryl Dunye, Kasi Lemmons, and John Singleton. While some of his films have sparked public controversies about aesthetics and respectability (or what some have described as the retrogressive and embarrassing nature of his work), Perry's influence in contemporary media culture is by now undeniable. For instance, prior to his film career, Perry generated an estimated $150 million a year by selling tickets, video recordings, and merchandise related to his popular stage performances. He has gone on to direct, produce, or star in at least one film a year since his theatre days, and his role in the television industry is increasing at a comparable rate, making him one of the most prolific television producers for Black audiences in television history. As a result of these efforts, Perry is now at the center of an influential media empire and production studio (Tyler Perry Studios) that has released over twenty commercially successful films and videos that all thematically pair representations of

Black identity with tales of betrayal, morality, incest, domestic violence, and trauma.

He has been a polarizing figure to say the least, and while there has been a lot of public rumination about the merits of his work, few opportunities have existed to examine his image and productions in scholarly venues. Before editing this collection, we were each curious about Perry's work and impact to varying degrees, but we soon discovered that it could be challenging to create a rich critical dialogue about his films, plays, and television shows in our professional spaces. For instance, in 2011, Samantha Sheppard presented a short paper, "She Ain't Heavy, She's Madea" on Perry's film *Madea's Family Reunion* on a panel about African American stars and auteurs at the Annual Society of Cinema and Media Studies conference in New Orleans.[3] Sheppard's paper was extremely well received, and I remember many members of the audience lingering to talk to her and meandering into the crowded hallways to have impromptu conversations about either the audacious scenes in Perry's film or other aspects of his work. That year's conference buzz around Tyler Perry is something that other scholars of African American media and culture noted. For instance, in their introduction to the African American Caucus's In-Focus contribution to *Cinema Journal*, editors Berretta E. Smith-Shomade, Racquel Gates, and Miriam J. Petty noted: "Interestingly, no actual panels or workshops were dedicated to the study of Perry's works that year—all the discussions about this crucial piece of black popular culture, his industrial shape-shifting, his box-office successes, his runaway brand across all media platforms, were taking place quite literally at the margins of the conference."[4] Karen Bowdre and I had a similar observation, and it was during this time that we decided to try to facilitate a larger discussion about the media mogul. We left the conference vowing to solicit papers and constitute a panel solely devoted to Perry's material for the next annual meeting.

Try as we might, however, we could never get that Tyler Perry panel accepted—not at the SCMS conferences in 2012 or 2013, nor at the annual American Studies conferences that took place during those same years. This is not to say that Tyler Perry did not come up in our papers and panels that we presented on other topics as we attended these conferences. Just as contemporary filmmakers almost obligatorily critique, parody, and otherwise acknowledge Perry's centrality in Black popular culture in their work (recent independent Black films like *Dear White People* [Justin Simien, 2014] and *Top Five* [Chris Rock, 2014], as well as mainstream films like *Hot Tub Time Machine 2* [Steve Pink, 2015], all have their moment of Perry reflection), as scholars of African American representation in media and popular culture, many of us talked about Perry incessantly.

Yet, for reasons beyond our understanding, programming committees at the conferences in our major fields did not see the usefulness in convening a full panel on him. During this time we wondered: did an entire panel on Perry seem to others redundant (since his material seemed accessible and he was such a hot topic outside the academy), frivolous, or overly indulgent (his films and shows were, after all, decidedly "lowbrow"), or tangential (perhaps Madea and *Meet the Browns* did not seem pertinent to central questions in our interdisciplinary fields)?

By this point, since I was still "so not a fan" of Perry's work, it was actually the constant rejection of the Tyler Perry panel—which we believe evinced our collective desire to think about Perry beyond the isolated individual short paper—that became the more compelling point of interest for me.

While I was beginning to realize that I needed feedback from and collaboration with a community of junior and senior scholars in my fields to begin to think more dynamically about my numerous problems with Tyler Perry, the ways in which I thought about him became inseparable from the persistent problem of exclusion and marginality that Black cultural production has long occupied in media studies, the "historical and ongoing marginalization of black media studies" in general, as Smith-Shomade and others have argued.[5]

While our inability to get a panel accepted that featured four to five papers on Tyler Perry remains both motivation and backstory for bringing together the writers in this collection, my own turning point regarding Perry's material happened because of two additional conversations: one professional, one personal. The first shift occurred in 2012 when I participated in a SCMS workshop called "Teaching the Negative Representation: Blackness and Disreputable Media." The workshop, chaired by Racquel Gates, included all early career scholars of African American media—Jacqueline Smith, Samantha Sheppard, Kristen Warner, and myself. Since this was a workshop, instead of reading formal papers, we each shared strategies for teaching material that others, especially students and colleagues at our respective universities, might deem negative, stereotypical, or otherwise unsuitable for being taken seriously in an academic context. For instance, Warner talked about Black female spectatorial practices and the less-obvious pleasures of reality television shows like *Basketball Wives* (2010–present). I introduced some ways to theorize the reception of, and voyeuristic community around, YouTube vlogs, including viral videos of Black people rapping about Kentucky Fried Chicken and confessing to drunkenness and disorderly conduct. And because Tyler Perry was still on our minds, Smith and Sheppard both talked about Perry and affect, each arguing for a deeper understanding of how attraction and repulsion often converge in complicated ways around his work.

I recall a lively conversation with the audience during this workshop, and comments and questions about Perry dominated the sixty-minute question and answer session. How could we teach his films? Was there really more than buffoonery there? Did students have a hard time taking the material seriously or seeing beyond his binaries of good and bad Black objects? As women, racial minorities, and early career scholars, did we feel particularly vulnerable centralizing the "disreputable" in our scholarship and in the classrooms at our various (predominantly white) campuses? There were, of course, no easy answers to these questions, but the conversation was the first time I saw how my interests in new media, video games, and other digital content ("disreputable" forms) had everything to do with Tyler Perry, specifically with my distaste for his material and reluctance to write about him or teach him in my film and media classes. Seeing myself from the outside in, it occurred to me that by virtue of studying Black popular culture at all, I was already "drinking the Kool-Aid." It seemed to be a significant "aha!" or "come to Jesus moment" for others in the room too, including Eric Pierson (who contributed this book's Foreword) and Christine A. Becker (who wrote a summary blog post about the panel). After our discussion on race and disreputablity, Becker reflected: "It's not easy to teach things that make us uncomfortable, right down to forgoing films we don't personally admire over ones we do in selecting course screenings, but we are likely short-changing our students (and ourselves) if we opt only to teach in areas of comfort and expertise."[6]

The second shift in my perception of Perry's relevancy happened more decisively during a conversation with my mother. It was actually my mother who introduced me to Perry's stage plays when he first came onto the cultural scene in the late 1990s. More recently, as I was doing research for this collection, my mother offered her pointed defense of Perry's films and plays, as she and many of her friends are long-standing fans. Mainly as fans, they appreciate the ways in which Perry is capable of addressing serious topics (like addiction, sexual abuse, and domestic violence) while being outrageously ridiculous at the same time. To my long list of objections about the content and the quality of Perry's productions (see the start of this introduction), she said simply: "Oh brother. We don't have the same sense of humor." My mother's comment is supported, of course, by media studies critics such as Ellen Seiter, who argues that members of an audience who most despise a given form are "often simply lacking in the cultural capital required to read the text adequately."[7] At last, my mother sighed: "Not everyone makes movies for you, you know." She was absolutely right, but therein lies the rub. Her observation that Tyler Perry simply did not make films or plays for me cut to the core of my personal dislike for Perry's material; his works offended my ideological views and personal beliefs on so many fronts, and since there is such a paucity of Black cultural production in the mainstream, I felt, above all, deeply disappointed.

This type of disappointment reflects the chronic burdens of representation that have historically faced Black cultural producers, from Black popular writers as disparate as Frances Harper (*Iola Leroy* [1892]) and Nikki Turner (*Riding Dirty on I-95: A Novel* [2003]) to Black film and televisual creators as different as Oscar Micheaux (*Within Our Gates* [1920]) and Shonda Rhimes (*Scandal* [2012–present]). For me, the comment was ultimately freeing because it reminded me that blackness as a signifier is unreliable enough that in any given popular text it does not and should not, despite my longings, have to represent who I am or what I most want to see. If truly "free," the sign of blackness might work like a soulful house music track: full of the unexpected, layered, contrapuntal. Yet the burden to produce the right type of Black popular culture in the right moment and have that work received respectfully in the right venues remains a true and steady cultural expectation—one that includes, but also extends beyond, Tyler Perry.

#OscarsSoWhite: Black Popular Culture at the Intersection of Respectability and Recognition

The academic year of 2014–15 was the year of the hashtag—a succinct, often politicized form of expression in online spaces that condenses and codes as much as it conveys meaning. This was the year when we saw #YesAllWomen (arguing that all women are affected by harassment and violence against women), #WhyIStayed (used by victims of domestic violence to narrate their experiences), #BringBackOurGirls (referencing the mass-kidnappings of Nigerian school-age children), #StopGamerGate (an attempt to expose the misogyny and racism in video game communities), #BlackLivesMatter (used to protest the police killings of unarmed Black men and women), and #IfTheyGunnedMeDown (which criticized the media's character defamation of minority victims of violent crimes). Each of these taglines went viral or "trended," playing a role in social media and public sphere conversations that were at their core about identity and the recognition of equal humanity. In the company of these other hashtags, a hashtag like #OscarsSoWhite may seem rather inconsequential, but I want to discuss it briefly in order to demonstrate how Black popular culture, including "Oscar-worthy" but "snubbed" films like *Selma* (Ava DuVernay, 2014) and apparently un-Oscar-worthy productions like Tyler Perry's *Single Moms Club* (2014), belong in the same conversation, one that points always back to the burdens of representation as well as to the politics of recognition and respectability.

The #OscarsSoWhite hashtag was started by "April," a lawyer and prolific blogger known on Twitter as @ReignOfApril, as a way to express her "frustration with the [2015] Oscar nominations."[8] To recap, while Ava DuVernay's civil rights-era drama, *Selma*, was nominated among nine other films for Best Picture, all of the Academy Award nominees for director, actor, actress, and screenwriter were white, making 2015 the year that many criticized as "the whitest Oscars in nineteen years."[9] In reaction to this, #OscarsSoWhite went viral, almost immediately, as Twitter users expressed their outrage over Hollywood's penchant for failing to recognize the achievement of Black media-makers. Some of the hashtagged tweets included: "#OscarsSoWhite they accurately represent Hollywood and its racial makeup," "#OscarsSoWhite the only time a Black person is nominated, let alone wins, is if they're in a role as a slave or the help," and "#OscarsSoWhite Denzel was mistaken for a janitor." While these tweets point obviously to critiques of industrial practices, the hashtags were also referentially loaded and (hyper)linked the lack of diversity at the Academy Awards to other social and political issues. In this vein, the hashtag also conveyed critiques of whiteness in general, like "#OscarsSoWhite it wears shorts in the winter time," and racism, as indicated in "#OscarsSoWhite it was invited to a Clippers game by Donald Sterling." Very quickly, the hashtag connected Black filmic representation and the failure to recognize Black achievement in visual culture to the larger problem of failing to recognize Black humanity in the social and political sphere. In this regard, there were other tweets including, "#OscarsSoWhite it thinks that George Zimmerman is just misunderstood" and "#OscarsSoWhite they let a grand jury decide the nominations." As the tweets that reference George Zimmerman's and Darren Wilson's acquittal and non-indictment in the murders of Trayvon Martin and Michael Brown, respectively, indicate, the hashtag connected the Hollywood awards show and Black filmic production to the systemic oppression of Black people and chronic failures of recognition on a mass scale.

Social media sites have become ready tools for fans and audiences to voice dissent or support a variety of cultural works and media personalities. As we can see with #OscarsSoWhite and the visibility of "Black Twitter" in general, such spaces have come to play a significant role in shaping the common-sense dialogue surrounding Black popular works. While Twitter and hashtag culture can be powerful platforms and tools used to express discontent, the fact that there could be such a quick slippage between emphasizing the film industry's lack of acknowledgment of Black achievement and expressing disappointment with the lack of recognition of Black humanity requires more reflection than those platforms and tools—current dominant mechanisms for shaping contemporary public discourse on race—can sustain.

Here, an interdisciplinary approach to cinema and media studies might help us make more clear Black popular culture's unique relationship to the deeply imbricated politics of respectability and recognition, on the one hand, and clarify how these things work together to inform the popular and critical reception of a Black cultural producer like Tyler Perry, on the other hand. For starters, what do the Oscars signify in the first place? While an Oscar (or Emmy or Tony Award) may increase visibility for the winners and nominees and ostensibly increase their future financial gain, such accomplishments most signify a type of recognition that is rooted in *bourgeois* aesthetic judgments. As Davies et al. argue about taste and cultural value in television programming, "the preferences and judgments of those who have the power to ascribe cultural value become the apotheosis of 'good taste'; and in this way the maintenance of aesthetic hierarchies becomes a means of perpetuating social inequities."[10] As the judges, board, or Academy set the standards for what constitutes artistic merit, these types of distinctions may indeed heighten social differences because, as Pierre Bourdieu famously insisted, "taste classifies, and it classifies the classifier."[11] Yet can the call to increase the racial and ethnic diversity of the potential winners and losers at these events enable Black cultural works that win out signal that the right type of recognition has at last been achieved for Black folk? Does it matter that these spaces will never have a "taste" for popular works that are vulgar, disreputable, or what Kristen Warner creatively defines as "ratchetness"?[12] If a film like *Selma*, which is a "respectable" and familiar drama about Black hardship, survival, hope, and American civil rights social transformations, cannot garner the type of recognition many believe it deserves at the Oscars, does it matter that a Madea film will be forever excluded from the cultural rituals that help standardize and signal inclusion?

To argue that blackness should be equally and fairly represented at award shows like the Oscars is to argue inherently that Black representation should be able to win at the game of respectability. Evelyn Brooks Higginbotham coined the phrase "politics of respectability" to describe some of the ways in which the Black Baptist women's movement "emphasized reform of individual behavior and attitudes both as a goal in itself and as a strategy for reform of the entire structural system of American race relations."[13] Higginbotham identified the acceptance of and acquiescence to middle-class behavioral norms as a strategic organizing maneuver that both "reinforced the hegemonic values of white America" and combated accusations of Black idleness and unworthiness.[14] In the current political climate, respectability politics has a slightly different indication. For instance, Fredrick C. Harris argues that respectability politics, one of the "hallmarks of black politics in the age of Obama," have been used to steer "'unrespectables' away from making demands on the state to intervene on their behalf and toward self-correction and the false belief that the market economy alone will lift them out of their plight."[15] Similarly, about affect and respectability, Michelle Smith argues that in the context of a contemporary militarized police state and the continued oppression of Black people, respectability politics have the dangerous potential for silencing and subordinating would-be Black agents and protesters who do not fit the image of what Black political leaders should look like—that is, "looters," "rioters," and "thugs" need not apply.[16]

When discussed in the context of identity politics, the annual awards circuit perpetuates hierarchies of taste through the pomp and circumstance of comparing this film to that film, this television show to that one, and thus always runs the risk of mistaking the symbolic, or simulacrum, for the real. Herman Gray, who is most often referenced in cinema and media studies for his landmark contribution, *Watching Race: Television and the Struggle for Blackness*, has argued more recently that this suture of Black representation to any aspect of the politics of recognition (to which the politics of respectability necessarily belong) may no longer serve us well in a post-civil rights and postmodern cultural and social milieu. Gray specifically rethinks the spectacle of taste-setting that televised award shows exhibit and argues that the events are neoliberal programming spectacles that "perform and sound out a normative ideal" as they instruct "viewers in the manners and morals required to belong to the nation."[17] While it may be tempting to want to play to win at the game of respectability politics that these spaces endorse, to do so also runs the risk of equating "spectacles of visibility and recognition" with political power.[18] I have argued elsewhere that while the civil rights movement needed visual media to document and sear into cultural consciousness evidence of the violent failures to recognize Black humanity, we have since consistently and compulsively relied on Black popular culture to function similarly, so that such works might evoke the type of empathy that has historically spurred action and reform.[19] Rather than create the kind of empathy and outrage that leads to systemic change, however, the ways in which our cultural works engage with the meta-project of recognition more often only compounds the problem and creates new ones. We are at a moment when we have to ask, in wedding Black popular works to the politics of respectability/recognition, to what extent are we now chasing a receding and unapproachable horizon? In this regard, Herman Gray challenges:

We presume that a corrective to the image would repair lost dignity, redress resources imbalances, and help generate recognition, empathy, and trust that might lead to more care and protection for all of us. However, getting the story straight in terms of authenticity, generating more and better facts, and telling better and more accurate representative stories seem no longer sufficient to redress injury or generate new practices of equality in the moment of racism after race.[20]

Outside of cinema and media studies there have been similar destabilizations of recognition politics, from Charles Taylor's influential inquiry to psychoanalytic theories that question whether or not individuals are even capable of "recognizing" distinct and equal others beyond brief and always fleeting moments of acknowledgment.[21] As political philosopher Patchen Markell cautions, investments in spectacles that seem to facilitate recognition risk "drawing attention away from ... some of the deeper relations of power and forms of subordination that underlie the very injustices they are meant to combat."[22] The temptation to tie Black popular culture to the protocols of respectability (and, in turn, to recognition) may not only fail to facilitate political progress, but such associations may in fact impede it, functioning as what Lauren Berlant has purposefully defined as a cruel form of optimism.[23]

The long-standing political strategy of representing in ways that are most communicable and presentable to mainstream America has without a doubt shaped how we study African American culture and media. As Kali N. Gross notes, a "strict adherence to what is socially deemed 'respectable' has resulted in African American scholars confining their scholarship on African Americans to often the most 'heroic,' and the most successful attributes in African American culture; it has also resulted in the proliferation of analyses which can be characterized as culturally defensive, patriarchal, and heterosexist."[24] Respectability politics create the double standard that insists that only certain expressions of blackness deserve to elicit outrage over the practice of exclusions, and by turn, deserve our academic attention: *The Butler* (Lee Daniels, 2013) and *Fruitvale Station* (Ryan Coogler, 2013)—yes; *The Best Man Holiday* (Malcolm D. Lee, 2013) or *A Haunted House 2* (Michael Tiddes, 2014)— not so much. In raising questions about respectability and recognition to talk about media studies, I do not mean to insist that we now ought to pay more attention to stereotypical performances or low cultural representations—say, for instance, *Flavor of Love* (VH1, 2006–08), as Racquel Gates has eloquently discussed[25]—than we do to works that adhere more closely to dominant norms of respectable art, works that use tropes of Black suffering to evoke empathy and outrage, like *12 Years a Slave* (Steve McQueen, 2013), which won the Academy Award for Best Picture. Rather than invert or create new dichotomies of good/bad, I mean to suggest that whenever representations of blackness do not fit into the cultural logic of neoliberalism, we might flag such works for at the very least requiring further, thoughtful exploration.

What does all this have to do with Tyler Perry? Perry seems to at least in part understand that being excluded from a particular set of norms offers a unique vantage point for commentary, including parody. For example, in 2011 Perry satirically marked his exclusion from the Academy Awards by creating a hilarious series of Madea posters that spoofed several of the films nominated that year for Best Picture. Instead of the official poster for *True Grit* (the Coen Brothers, 2010), Perry issued a "True Grits" poster of Madea wearing a camo dress and holding a rifle; instead of *The King's Speech* (Tom Hooper, 2010), Perry created "The Queen's Speech," a poster that featured a close-up of Madea's face before a filtered microphone. Although Perry strategically mocked one system of evaluation, his works are hardly subversive when it comes to the politics of recognition and respectability. In fact, many of his narratives, characters, and public speeches ironically reinforce the same ideological views that others use to discount and discredit his work. My point here, though, is that in overlooking his cultural contributions altogether we might not realize or fully understand ironies like this or the myriad contractions that inform his media empire.

Beyond Respectability and Recognition

"Part of the problem is that we have forgotten what sort of space the space of popular culture is."[26]

Throughout his career, Stuart Hall talked about Black popular culture in a way that offers some inspiration for distancing Black popular forms from some of its unique burdens of representation. In the example of #OscarsSoWhite, we can see how art and cultural production can quickly become overladen by the desire for the state and/or other cultural authorities, institutions, and agents to recognize Black humanity and rights. Additionally, the joining of representational culture with the politics of recognition unfortunately de-emphasizes the extent to which popular works are also so fascinatingly replete with wonky fantasies, tricky idealizations, and exhaustive contradictions. As famously theorized by Hall, these representations remain limitless and unstable iterations of a "theater of popular desires" and "popular fantasies."[27] It is no doubt easy to forget that blackness—Hall's "Black" in popular culture—is always as fantastical as it is real. Above all, Stuart Hall and the other contributors to Gina Dent's seminal 1992 anthology demonstrate that our analyses of Black popular culture are most productive when we remember to hold the many possibilities of interpretation in dialogic tension.[28]

In taking these arguments as inspiration, *From Madea to Media Mogul* makes the explicit claim that Tyler Perry must be understood as a figure at the nexus of converging factors, cultural events, and historical traditions. In doing so, we demonstrate how a critical engagement with Perry's work and media practices highlights a need for film and television criticism to grapple with developing theories and methods on disreputable media that challenge value judgment criticism and offer new insight on the industrial and formal qualities of such work. The book examines Perry's unique role in contemporary media culture but unlike the discordant popular and limited range of academic responses to Perry's work, the essays in *From Madea to Media Mogul* are engaged with neither simply celebrating nor condemning Tyler Perry. Against any temptation to displace, replace, or revere him, we situate Perry and his work at the epicenter of a rich and important interdisciplinary dialogue—one that is not happening at this moment. For example, in order to talk about Tyler Perry, to say things about the contested figure that are not apparent, we need to move beyond the singular focus on critical race studies or cinema studies or Black cultural traditions. Instead, as we demonstrate here, Perry gives us an occasion to consider how the popularity and pleasure of his texts generate discourses that are inherently political and demand an interdisciplinary attention, as I have tried to demonstrate with my methodological approach to discussing respectability and recognition.

From Madea to Media Mogul charts new ground in this regard, namely, through emphasizing creativity, theoretical savviness, and by establishing a productive fluidity between divergent fields. Throughout these pages, Tyler Perry becomes an unlikely but timely figure around which to discuss the ways in which blackness in the twenty-first century functions as Hall's theatre of desires, or, as we like to think of it, as "dark matter," a metaphor for identities that are more nebulous and shape-shifting than we often allow. This collection demonstrates that there is something inherently political about the intersection between understanding the pleasure as well as displeasure surrounding popular cultural expression. These types of intersectionalities are crucial not only to understanding Tyler Perry but also to how we think about race and identity in the twenty-first century.

As editors, we came together around our different but complementary multi- and trans-disciplinary interests. For instance, Karen Bowdre has brought to the project a background in race, genre, and performance studies that looks across multiple media platforms; several essays in the collection take into account Perry's divergent media productions. I have contributed my experience in interrogating Black popular culture's proximity to poststructuralist intellectual traditions, particularly to trauma studies and to psychoanalytic and postmodern theories. In this regard, many of the essays in the collection work with, around, and beyond familiar theories in unanticipated ways. Samantha Sheppard's training in cinema and media studies, gender studies, and Black cultural production brings an important critical focus to the politics and practices of African American representation. Accordingly, several essays in the collection critique the representational politics of Perry's work beyond the delimiting binaries of positive or negative images and provide new approaches to questions of race, gender, and representation.

Theorizing Tyler Perry: Building a Necessary Critical Vocabulary

If the hashtag represents a way of highlighting the terms of a conversation for a particular discourse community, with this collection we contend that Tyler Perry's place in media history requires a rubric—a specific set of guiding terms to establish common ground among the various critics and skeptics, fans and detractors. So, although the chapters that follow are certainly more complicated and comprehensive than the terms we have selected for them, the identifying terms and concepts give us a shared common language upon which to build further and future reflection. Unlike the hashtag or our more casual engagements with Perry, the creation of a deliberate theoretical vocabulary also invites us to rethink and expand how we use familiar terms within our fields, disciplinary terms like *cinephilia, mogul, niche, rebrand*, and *platforms* in cinema and media studies. Other concepts, like *affect, disguise, thirst*, and *exceptionalism*, engage and reference theoretical discussions of auteurs, drag performativity, Black televisual history, and the emotional culture around Perry's works, while mobilizing terms such as *chitlin* and *gospel* broaden our grasp on thematic conceits from Black cultural traditions.

The collection begins with Samantha N. Sheppard's broad and establishing consideration of how Perry functions in and across different media industries. Sheppard analyzes Perry's different "practices," "partnerships," and "politics" as she explores some of the ways in which Perry maximizes his name recognition and brand across different *platforms*, like theatre, film, television, straight to DVD, and video on demand. While Perry's brand has been instrumental in marketing his high volume of creative projects, other directors and writers now also seek an association with him so that they might leverage their own works. In this way, Sheppard theorizes that Perry has become a media platform unto himself. In complicating and destabilizing the assumption that a partnership with Perry will naturally lead to success, the chapter concludes with an analysis of the production and marketing of one of Perry's affiliated projects, Tina Gordon Chism's 2013 comedy *Tyler Perry Presents Peeples*.

If Perry now functions as a platform unto himself, his career began with seemingly much less broad, but no less significant, aspirations. In her analysis of taste, class, and the popular in Chapter Two, Rashida Z. Shaw places Tyler Perry's career within the context of a Black performance and theatre history that extends back to the nineteenth century as she centralizes the history of the "*Chitlin* Circuit" or "Urban Theatre." After establishing a literary cultural history that frames and restages the popularity, appeal, and reception of Perry's plays, Shaw's analysis more closely explores the ramifications of Perry's behind-the-scenes role and on-stage presence at the 2012 Tony Awards during a year that resulted in numerous historic successes for not only African American theatre-makers, but also for African American–centric productions in general.

Since Perry's plays share with his film production a similar thematic focus on Christian morality, Keith Corson's contribution to this collection charts the rise of regional theatre and the translation of the financial, aesthetic, and political model of "gospel theatre's" urban circuit to the multiplex. In the process of identifying the evangelical influences of some contemporary African American films, which Corson calls "*gospel* cinema," the chapter compares Perry's films with televangelist T.D. Jakes's in arguing that their films have helped reshape notions of a Black film audience. Gospel cinema narratives often function as morality tales that align closely with the rise of the Black megachurch as they express a middle-class idealism that is rooted in a doctrine of prosperity, self-help, and individualism. Yet, as Corson defines it, gospel cinema also features a unique blend of melodrama, folk humor, and camp aesthetics that complicates a simple faith-based reading.

While Shaw's and Corson's analyses of *chitlin* and *gospel* are concerned predominantly with form and genre, in "Worship at the Altar of Perry: Spectatorship and the Aesthetics of Testimony," Brandeise Monk-Payton encourages us to think more richly about the relationship between *affect* and testimony that is available to fans of Perry's content. Calling Perry's affective effect on his audiences a "cinematic ministry" that is replete with scenes of pulpit-like testimony, Monk-Payton examines faith-based affect as a type of responsiveness that characterizes intimate encounters with Perry's films. In her reading of Perry's 2012 film, *Good Deeds*, Monk-Payton theorizes that Perry, as title character Wesley Deeds, "testifies" for his fans using a mode of "cinematic address" that is predicated on the affective desire for the audience to engage in a version of African American expressivity.

In a chapter that invites us to continue thinking about Perry and affect, Ben Raphael Sher reminds us that Tyler Perry is the most prominent media personality to make a career out of representing African American women's experiences with abuse and trauma. With this fact as a starting place, Sher closely investigates Perry's cinematic representations, while simultaneously theorizing Perry's *cinephilia*, or passionate love of cinema. In making clear the relationship between domestic trauma and cinephilia in the play *Madea's Class Reunion* (2003), the film *Madea's Family Reunion* (2006), and in Perry's introduction to The 2006 Black Movie Awards, Sher addresses the widely held suspicion that Perry's work capitalizes on the traumas of Black women—the specific complaint being that Perry rehashes his traumatic past by mapping it onto the Black female characters in his scripts. This chapter complicates these criticisms by suggesting that Perry's representations of suffering Black women have less to do with a pathological desire to punish Black women and more to do with Perry's complex fantastical and personal identification with them as a trauma survivor himself. To this extent, Sher uses Perry's trauma narratives to articulate a critique of the larger cultural lack of representations of male survivors of abuse.

There is, of course, no getting around Madea—no doubt Perry's biggest signifier. In Chapter Six, Rachel Jessica Daniel commences a critical investigation of Madea by analyzing how Perry's particular style of drag performance, his use of false *disguise* enables his predominantly Christian and Black female audiences to form an intimate public around him despite the fact his performances might contradict or subvert their own personal and spiritual beliefs. In Daniel's theorization, Perry's fan base around Madea represents a powerful, critical, and vocal discourse community that has supported the media mogul and his contested character despite rampant critiques of the character's flawed presentation and of Perry's motives in constructing her.

Turning to Tyler Perry's impact on the television industry, Aymar Christian and Khadijah Costley White in "One Man Hollywood: The Decline of Black Creative Production in Post-Network Television" theorize Perry's place in the television history, explicitly in the context of his *niche* production system and industrial marketing practices. Christian and Costley White critique Perry's dominance in the televisual landscape and the numerous ways in which his direct control over his media entities has compromised not only his content but also his company's ethics and labor practices. Given that Perry's television successes occurred concomitant with the fragmentation of key media marketplaces and given the lack of structural changes surrounding his productions, Christian and Costley White's chapter ultimately questions (and redefines) the extent to which Perry has truly been a game changer in the television industry.

Continuing a television studies analysis of Perry, Artel Great argues in Chapter Eight that from both a critical and an industrial perspective the sitcom *Tyler Perry's House of Payne* (TBS, 2006–12) represents a complex but no less problematic contribution to the history of Black televisual authorship. Precisely because there has been a pronounced dearth of Black representation on television, Great demonstrates that a politics of *thirst* best characterizes how Black audiences engage the few existing images of televisual blackness. Despite several unprecedented industrial achievements (such as surpassing *The Jeffersons* [CBS, 1975–85] as the longest running Black sitcom), when considered within the context of the history and formal structure of the Black sitcom, *House of Payne* digresses as it rejuvenates the narrative conventions and visual cues of uncritical Black minstrelsy. Rife with missed opportunities for teaching complex lessons about Black subjectivity, esteem, and interiority, Perry's sitcom succeeded, then, mostly because of the continued omission of blackness on television.

Moving the conversation about Perry to a more meta-discursive level, Karen M. Bowdre's chapter features an examination of the careers of Spike Lee and Tyler Perry. The way we discuss Black Hollywood and independent directors, argues Bowdre, reinforces a (Black) American *exceptionalism* that materializes as a flawed tendency to evaluate and elevate one Black director at a time. Bowdre demonstrates that while at the onset Perry and Lee may seem worlds apart both artistically and ideologically, both directors have benefited from a similar system of exclusion.

In also comparing and contrasting Perry's media influence with that of another famous director, Paul Reinsch reframes the media discourse around Tyler Perry's work and career to consider him alongside a comparable media *mogul*: George Lucas. What might the creator of *Star Wars* and the creator of Madea possibly have in common (aside from a possible penchant for high fantasy)? In closely analyzing the critical reception, aesthetics, and ideologies of Perry's *For Colored Girls* (2010) and Lucas's *Red Tails* (2012), Reinsch exposes how each filmmaker ultimately negotiates a particular nostalgia for classical Hollywood cinema while also maintaining a particularly intrusive relationship to their creative entities and to the media complexes that pertain to them.

If Eric Pierson argues in this book's Foreword that Perry's relationship to media studies in this moment might well be thought of as a *centrality*, Leah Aldridge wonders in Chapter Eleven where things might go from here. Can we expect to see Perry *rebrand* in order to broaden his appeal to more mainstream or international markets? What might such changes mean for both his representations of blackness and for his domestic media empire?

Miriam J. Petty concludes the collection with a return to Madea by offering a brief meditation on her personal and professional engagement with Perry's controversial character. Petty's account demonstrates how, in moving forward, we might continue to deconstruct and investigate but also play with Perry's performances.

Although I have yet to come around to a personal embrace of Tyler Perry's works, as a direct result of reading, editing, and learning from this collection, I am now committed to thinking about him, to writing about his relationship to other Black cultural works, to teaching his films in my classes, and to presenting on his works at conferences (we shall not give up on this). We think this book will be valuable to media scholars and to the many different fields represented by the editors and contributors. Perhaps too it will appeal to Perry's fans and dissenters outside the academy because, as one fan wrote in a self-published guide on Tyler Perry's films: "Only after sixteen minutes of *Diary of a Mad Black Woman* does it fully sink in that you're not just watching some unsuccessful narrative. . . . You have to think in terms of the fourth dimension and parallel universes to properly label the quality of [Perry's] films."[29] Fourth dimensions and parallel universes notwithstanding, the chapters and grounding terms that follow remain productively and excitingly "dislocating in relation to one another"[30] in ways that are more invested in keepin' it dialogic than in keepin' it real. This means that chapters are free to contradict each other, including what I have said here, as they offer up examinations of the kind of polemics and problems that compel us to think more richly about how blackness travels, unravels, delights, heals, binds, and unnerves in a given moment.

Notes

1. Social commentator Touré called Perry "cinematic malt liquor for the masses" during an interview on CNN's *Newsroom* in September 2011.

2. S. T. Vanairsdale, "Why Tyler Perry Is the New Obama," *Esquire*, September 2, 2009, http://www.esquire.com/the-side/hollywood/tyler-perry-movies-and-race-090209.

3. We are pleased to note that the paper is now on its way to print. See Samantha N. Sheppard, "She Ain't Heavy, She's Madea: The Tyler Perry Discourse and the Politics of Contemporary Black Cultural Production," forthcoming in *Black Cinema Aesthetics Revisited*, eds. Michael Gillespie and Akil Houston.

4. Beretta E Smith-Shomade, Racquel Gates, and Miriam J. Perry, "Introduction: When and Where We Enter," *Cinema Journal* 53, no. 4 (2014): 126. We are also pleased to note here that two collections on Perry have been recently published. This recent scholarly attention only further demonstrates how much of a significant figure he has become. See Jamel Santa Cruze Bell and Ronald L. Jackson II, eds., *Interpreting Tyler Perry: Perspectives on Race, Class, Gender, and Sexuality* (New York and London: Routledge, 2013); LeRhonda S. Manigault-Bryant, Tamura A. Lomax, and Carol B. Duncan, eds., *Womanist and Black Feminist Responses to Tyler Perry's Productions* (New York: Palgrave Macmillan, 2014).

5. Smith-Shomade et al., 126.

6. Christine Becker, "Teaching Discomfort," *Society for Cinema and Media Studies*, March 26, 2012, http://www.cmstudies.org/blogpost/785017/140556/Teaching-Discomfort.

7. Ellen Seiter, "Qualitative Audience Research," in *The Television Studies Reader*, eds. Robert C. Allen and Annette Hill (New York: Routledge, 2004), 471.

8. @ReignOfApril, "#OscarsSoWhite," *The Reign of April*, January 15, 2015, http://www.reignofapril.com/oscarssowhite/.

9. See, for example, David Sims, "The Oscars Haven't Been This White in 19 Years," *Atlantic*, January 15, 2015, http://www.theatlantic.com/entertainment/archive/2015/01/the-oscars-havent-been-this-white-in-19-years/384550/.

10. Hannah Davies, David Buckingham, and Peter Kelley, "In the Worst Possible Taste: Children, Television, and Cultural Value," in *The Television Studies Reader*, eds. Robert C. Allen and Annette Hill (New York: Routledge, 2004), 481.

11. Pierre Bourdieu, *Distinction: A Social Critique of the Judgment of Taste*, trans. Richard Nice (Cambridge: Harvard University Press, 1984), 6.

12. Kristen J. Warner, "They Gon' Think You Loud Regardless: Ratchetness, Reality Television, and Black Womanhood," *Camera Obscura: Feminism, Culture, and Media Studies* 30, no. 88 (2015): 129–53.

13. Evelyn Brooks Higginbotham, *Righteous Discontent: The Women's Movement in the Black Baptist Church, 1880–1920* (Cambridge: Harvard University Press, 1994), 187.

14. Ibid.

15. Fredrick C. Harris, "The Rise of Respectability Politics," *Dissent* 61, no. 1 (2014): 33, 36.

16. Michelle Smith, "Affect and Respectability Politics," *Theory & Event* 17, no. 3 (2014).

17. Herman Gray, "Subject(ed) to Recognition," *American Quarterly* 65, no. 4 (2013): 788.

18. Ibid., 787.

19. TreaAndrea M. Russworm, *Blackness is Burning: Race, Popular Culture, and the Problem of Recognition* (Detroit: Wayne State University Press, 2016; forthcoming).

20. Gray, 787.

21. Charles Taylor, "The Politics of Recognition," in *Multiculturalism: Examining the Politics of Recognition*, ed. Amy Gutmann (Princeton, NJ: Princeton University Press, 1994), 25–74. For psychoanalytic theories, I'm thinking mainly of Jessica Benjamin, *The Bonds of Love: Psychoanalysis, Feminism, and the Problem of Domination* (New York: Pantheon Books, 1988).

22. Patchen Markell, *Bound by Recognition* (Princeton: Princeton University Press, 2003), 171.

23. Lauren Gail Berlant, *Cruel Optimism* (Durham: Duke University Press, 2011).

24. Kali N. Gross, "Examining the Politics of Respectability in African American Studies," *University of Pennsylvania Almanac* 43.28, April 1, 1997, http://www.upenn.edu/almanac/v43/n28/benchmark.html.

Also see Dwight A. McBride, "Straight Black Studies: On African American Studies, James Baldwin, and Black Queer Studies," in *Black Queer Studies: A Critical Anthology*, eds. E. Patrick Johnson and Mae G. Henderson (Durham: Duke University Press Books, 2005), 68–89.

25. On *Flavor of Love*, see Racquel Gates, "Keeping It Reality Television," in *Watching While Black: Centering the Television of Black Audiences*, ed. Beretta E. Smith-Shomade (New Brunswick: Rutgers University Press, 2013), 141–56.

26. Stuart Hall, "What Is This 'Black' in Black Popular Culture?" in *Black Popular Culture: A Project by Michelle Wallace*, ed. Gina Dent (Seattle: Bay Press, 1992), 21–33.

27. Ibid., 31.

28. See Gina Dent, *Black Popular Culture*.

29. Evan Saathoff, *Madea Lives!: A Film-By-Film Guide To Loving Tyler Perry*, ed. Meredith Borders (Badass Digest, 2014).

30. Hall, 32.

FROM MADEA TO MEDIA MOGUL

CHAPTER ONE

"Tyler Perry Presents...": The Cultural Projects, Partnerships, and Politics of Perry's Media Platforms

—Samantha N. Sheppard

Tyler Perry is a cultural figure entrenched in the commodification of self. Perry distinguishes his vast media empire through his ability to mold himself into a marketable persona and product, most famously the drag personality Mabel "Madea" Simmons and the theatre, film, and print work based on her character. As Madea, he successfully markets his comedic melodramas to Black women and Christian audiences. In a *USA Today* profile on Perry, one woman explained: "We trust him...It's not about being black—though it's nice to see yourself in a Hollywood movie once in a while. I know I can take my kids. I know there will be a good message. Critics can say whatever they want; he's the only one making movies about people trying to live right."[1] As this explanation demonstrates, Perry provides for his viewers both on-screen and on-stage what critic Hilton Als describes as "a lens through which to see themselves refracted, and a forum in which their religious and political beliefs would be neither challenged nor ignored."[2]

A reliable brand, Perry's success registers in two particular ways. First, as *Los Angeles Times* movie columnist Patrick Goldstein suggests, Perry's substantial box-office results have garnered him (and less so his work) critical attention, transforming him from the realm of movie mogul to that of a "movie king."[3] Second, his studio, Tyler Perry Studios, production companies, 34th Street Films and My.Te.Pe. Productions, and distribution outlet, the Tyler Perry Company, provide him with an unprecedented infrastructure to control his means of production. For these reasons alone, Perry operates as a central, albeit controversial, figure in the visibility, circulation, and exhibition of Black media in American public and popular culture.

In *Cultural Moves: African Americans and the Politics of Representation*, Herman Gray explains that "Black American cultural representations involve complex texts, discourses, and narratives that are typically expressed in multiple and overlapping sites and media."[4] As such, I consider the role of Perry's media platforms in the proliferation of Black media content and cultural production. To be clear, I am less concerned with textually analyzing Perry's specific work, meaning his films, television shows, and plays. Instead, I am interested in the projects and partnerships that use Perry and his established media convergence economy to market themselves to wider Black audiences. These projects and partnerships include his co-presentation/executive producing of Lee Daniel's *Precious: Based on the Novel "Push" by Sapphire* (2009) and the exclusive deal he struck in 2012 with the Oprah Winfrey Network (OWN) to create scripted content for the cable channel. In this regard, I analyze the ways in which Perry operates not only across multiple media platforms (e.g., theatre, film, and television) but also functions as a media platform (i.e., operates as cultural and industrial leverage for others via partnerships and co-productions). Using Gray's method of examining the politics of representation through a focus on tactics, strategies, and maneuvers, I scrutinize the cultural politics of these projects and partnerships as examples of contemporary Black cultural producers' "struggles for cultural visibility, recognition, and inclusion in the national media."[5]

With a focus on the tensions and complexities of these struggles within contemporary culture, I turn my attention to Tina Gordon Chism's 2013 comedy *Tyler Perry Presents Peeples*, which was co-produced by Perry's 34th Street Films and is a "Tyler Perry-adjacent" project. I define Chism's *Peeples* as "Tyler Perry-adjacent" in that it is related and attached to Perry's media empire but was not written or directed by him. I deliberately use the orienting term "adjacent" to highlight the diffusion of Perry's influence on contemporary media and Black representation whereby the term operates as both a site, a location in which to map the branching of Perry's ancillary media universe, of his media platforms *and* a citation, an alignment with the character, features, and aesthetic imagination of Perry's media content, of his cultural production. In my discussion of

Peeples, I examine how Perry's industrial practices and presentational aesthetic resulted in a paradoxical illumination and occlusion of Chism's directorial debut. I consider how Perry as a media platform engenders semiotic and social forces that structure "the conditions of possibility within which black cultural politics are enacted, constrained, and mediated."[6] In this regard, I address how Chism uses Perry's media platforms and Perry as a media platform to provide *Peeples* with visibility, framing, and potential commercial success, (mis)shaping her work in terms of legibility for Black audiences and, consequently, (re)shaping the creative and cultural boundaries of Perry's own work. Thus, in evaluating how he functions as a structuring agent for other Black cultural productions, I focus on the mutually constitutive relationship between Perry and his brand at work in media culture and media politics. Finally, I cast Perry, his partnerships, and his numerous "Tyler Perry-adjacent" projects within a larger social and cultural arena, examining how Perry as a Black cultural producer operates within a broader context of a contested Black cultural formation within American national and public culture.

Perry's Media Platforms

A multi-hyphenate media juggernaut, Perry operates across various media sites. Renewing, reusing, and recycling content, Perry's media conservation relies on the circulation of media across platforms and the convergence of old and new media forms. Convergence, Henry Jenkins explains, describes "the flow of content across multiple media platforms, the cooperation between multiple media industries, and the migratory behavior of media audiences who will go almost anywhere in the search of the kinds of entertainment experiences they want."[7] Perry's flow of content occurs across multiple mediums including stage, film, episodic television, and literature. This media convergence operates in conjuncture with many media industries and relies on Perry's marketability to Black audiences. In outlining Perry's media platforms, I underscore how Perry functions as a media platform. Significantly, this shift from Perry's media platforms to Perry as a media platform denotes the means by which other Black cultural producers use Perry and his brand as a way to develop, package, and elevate their media texts and themselves as media-makers. Both Perry's media platforms and Perry as a media platform widen and diversify his reach and appeal in popular media and US public culture.

Deftly commoditizing his creative texts, Perry reworks his stage plays for various mediums, including film (video and theatrical releases) and television. Most of his plays get the on-screen treatment, such as the staged version of *I Can Do Bad All by Myself* (2000) that was theatrically released on film in 2009 and starred then-recent Academy Award-nominated actress Taraji P. Henson. Additionally, some stage narratives are repurposed for the big and small screen. For example, *Why Did I Get Married* first premiered on stage in 2004 and was adapted for the silver screen in 2009. The film's commercial success made way for a sequel in 2010 that later produced a spin-off television series, *Tyler Perry's For Better or Worse* (TBS, 2011–12; OWN, 2013–present).

Moreover, before the release of his first film, *Tyler Perry's Diary of a Mad Black Woman* (Darren Grant, 2005), Perry staged six plays and released the videos on DVD. Adapting his stage catalogue for the screen with a quick-paced production style (he is known for only doing one to two takes per scene while filming), Perry released nearly two films a year from 2007 to 2013. Additionally, Perry concurrently writes and stages new gospel plays that are turned into films within a matter of months. For example, in 2010, *Madea's Big Happy Family* premiered on stage and toured the US with Perry in the title role. Perry filmed the staged play and distributed the video the same year. A year later, Lionsgate released the film adaptation *Tyler Perry's Madea's Big Happy Family* (Tyler Perry, 2011) in theatres.

There are a host of other stage-to-film-to-television combinations of his work. A skilled progenitor, Perry employs not only repetitive storylines and titles but also recognizable actors and characters. For example, gospel singers Tamela and David Mann starred in the stage play *Meet the Browns* (2004), the film adaptation *Tyler Perry's Meet the Browns* (Tyler Perry, 2009), and the television series *Tyler Perry's Meet the Browns* (TBS, 2007–2012). However, Madea stands at the center of Perry's multimedia empire as the most important of these reoccurring characters. Her character stars in nine films including an animated feature, appears in ten stage plays, guest stars on two of Perry's shows, and is the subject of his 2006 *New York Times* bestseller *Don't Make a Black Woman Take Off Her Earrings:*

Madea's Uninhibited Commentaries on Love and Life.[8] A cadre of supporting characters join in her various adventures, including Mr. Brown (David Mann), Brian (Tyler Perry), and Joe (Tyler Perry). In this regard, Perry traffics in familiar storylines and characters, providing a level of content consistency across platforms for audiences conversant in his oeuvre.

The flow of Perry's content across multiple media underscores how Perry recognizes both the affordance and limitations of each platform in relationship to his core Black audience. For instance, Perry's shift from the "Chitlin Circuit" to film and television demonstrated what Hilton Als calls Perry's pragmatism. "He understood," Als explains, "the intimacy of film and television, and the access they offer to those who are less inclined to join in the community aspect of theatre. Communities may crumble and fracture, but everybody goes to the movies."[9] Perry's flexibility and platform shifts indicate not only social forces but also the circumstances that structure reception conditions for specific Black communities. For example, in 1992, his first play, *I Know I've Been Changed* (1992), flopped, largely because of his venue choice. In 1998, Perry staged the production at a local church-turned-theatre.[10] In this case, Perry shifted his appeal to target Black, Christian, working-class people. "The audience he wanted to attract," Als explains, "thought theatergoing as a luxury. Churchgoing, on the other hand was a necessity. Perry resolved to turn his performances into an extension of their faith. He did the rounds of Atlanta's black churches, becoming a spokesman for his plays and the values it stood for."[11]

In this vein, *Tyler Perry's If Loving You Is Wrong* (OWN, 2014–present), his most recent television offering, again characterizes Perry's pragmatism regarding his audience's swaying attention span. *If Loving You Is Wrong* premiered on OWN to the network's highest ratings despite the disappointing box-office success of its source material, *Tyler Perry's The Single Mom's Club* (Tyler Perry, 2013). *The Single Mom's Club* garnered Perry his lowest box-office opening weekend and potentially indicates filmgoers' fatigue with Perry. However, *If Loving You Is Wrong*'s success points towards the migratory behavior of Perry's main audience from the big to the small screen as a viable and valuable site for Black-oriented programming. As a result, Perry's current focus on his television work, which has drastically slowed down his film production, signals his use of medium specific narrowcasting for his melodramatic imagination.

With his Madea franchise as the foundation of his mass appeal, Perry produces content across media platforms with the cooperation of multiple media industries shaped by new global markets defined by interlocking structures of ownership and complex distribution, circulation, and regulation shifts in entertainment and information technologies.[12] An impresario of the "Chitlin Circuit," Perry's media convergence begins with his theatre performances. Starting with his live shows, Perry's production company, My.Te.Pe. Productions, records them as videos and the Tyler Perry Company distributes them as DVDs (more than 25 million have been sold), a lucrative venture that helped him finance his foray into film. His theatrical films are co-produced and distributed by mini-major Lionsgate Entertainment, who struck a three-year, first-look deal with Perry in 2008.[13] The partnership ended in 2014. However, Perry's deal included being paid as much as $15 million for his above-the-line expenses, receiving 15 percent first-dollar gross and box-office bonuses, having final cut, and owning international distribution rights and 50 percent of ancillary revenue.[14]

In addition to his film and video empire, Perry and Lionsgate's television work proved lucrative with distributor Debmar-Mercury. Following a successful ten-show pilot that Perry financed himself, he sold ninety first-run syndicated episodes of his series *Tyler Perry's House of Payne* (2006–12) to TBS for $200 million. A savvy entrepreneur, Perry retained full copyright ownership of his films, video library, and television shows. With Tyler Perry Studios, an unprecedented 200,000-square-foot studio with five sound stages, a backlot, a postproduction facility, theatre, screening room, and office space located in Atlanta, Georgia, Perry successfully controls the means of production for his projects. The industrial and cultural politics of Perry's infrastructure cannot be discounted, particularly against the backdrop of Hollywood's structural and cultural racism. An innovator in Black cultural production, Perry works in the vernacular tradition of other Black pioneers, including actor and director Spencer Williams. In this mode, Perry strives to achieve legitimacy for his work and to secure his place within film history. Elsewhere, I have argued that in "naming soundstages on his studio after Sidney Poitier, Cicely Tyson, Ruby Dee, Ossie Davis, and Quincy Jones, Perry is in the business of making himself and his work matter, at the very least, by proximity alone."[15] Like those who use his name to promote themselves,

Perry's soundstage roll call is an attempt to make himself "Black film history-adjacent." I suggest that "by aligning himself with such figures, he places himself as an integral next step in the teleological history of black production and representation in American cinema, declaring that he belongs in the cultural conversation with the aforementioned figures. In doing so, he strategically makes himself legible as an important historical figure in cinematic history."[16]

Perry's strategic media convergence relies on the migratory behavior of his loyal audience who seek out his work in a variety of spaces, across mediums, and on different platforms, including on stage, screen, television, and at the bookstore. Despite claims that Perry's audience, which is resoundingly made up of Black women, does not "track well," Perry fans find traction through their loyal consumerism.[17] As Hollywood neglects Perry's older, Black, female core audience, their financial support of Perry's repetitive work demonstrates how Black audiences seek out his work and make connections among his dispersed media content. Making him a "hit" on all platforms, his fans stand in line for plays, purchase movie tickets, and watch his television series. Perry encourages viewers to follow and find pleasure in his storylines from stage to the theatre to their home televisions. In these transmedia tales, consumers interact with each text and each other in person and on his fan websites and social media, particularly his own Facebook account. Perry invites his audience to participate in shared social experiences, starting with his stage work and extending to his film and television productions all the while dialoguing with him through social media.

Perry's fans have historically rallied in defense of him and his work. They move beyond being active participants to become staunch advocates for Perry within a racially divided media universe. For example, famed film critic Roger Ebert received a deluge of responses from Black people following his scathing review of *Diary of a Mad Black Woman*, which prompted him to write a follow-up piece, "Who *Is* This Mad Black Woman," explaining: "I have received more e-mails than about any review I have ever written, outnumbering 'Fahrenheit 9/11' and 'The Passion of the Christ' put together. And they were not all the same message, generated by some website or its followers. Each manifestly came from an individual reader who felt moved to write."[18] Perry's fans' reactions did more than just indicate the intensity of his popular appeal in Black communities and proffer the assertion that "white critics don't get it"; they effectively justified Perry's circumvention of film critics as a whole. Perry eschews advanced screenings of his films, and many white critics stay away from rigorously reviewing his films. However, following the release of *Tyler Perry's Temptation: Confessions of a Marriage Counselor* (Tyler Perry, 2013), many Black and white critics professed their distaste for his repugnant drama, taking the film and Perry to task for the troubling way in which HIV is used as a punishment for the lead female character's sexual and moral transgressions.[19] Still, Perry often invokes his consumer base's spectatorial pleasure as a shield against legitimate criticism for his representations, evidenced most famously by his response to criticism from Spike Lee for his representational politics, which Karen M. Bowdre's chapter in this collection discusses in further detail.[20]

In contrast to his public friction with Lee, Perry's engagement with Black female media audiences reveals a complex relationship between him and his desired consumers. After Brittney Cooper's article "Tyler Perry Hates Black Women" went viral, Perry called Cooper and asked her to explain her conclusion that he, in fact, hates Black women, telling her: "I didn't call to try to change your mind. I simply like to hear from my critics every now and then."[21] In her article discussing the conversation, Cooper describes herself as having a love-hate relationship with Perry's films. "Around the year 2012," she explains, "I stopped going to see his movies, because I would leave the cinema feeling like I had been beaten and spat upon while being told I was loved."[22] During the call with Perry, Cooper discussed how women are punished for being assertive and ambitious. Cooper later saw Perry's newest release, *The Single Mom's Club*, and in the article expressed that he "gets a lot right in this film."[23] While much can be unfurled from him reaching out to Cooper that goes beyond his stated desire to speak to his critics once in a while, Perry's actions point toward his need to engage with (as well as resist) once-reliable and now-reluctant Black female consumers whose active participation has shifted from public support to popular critique. The example of Cooper's conversation with Perry underscores the struggles over Black representation and the cultural and political investment Black audiences have in those struggles. The tension illuminates the discursive field of media convergence "where the power of the media producer and the power of the media consumer interact in unpredictable ways" in contemporary digital culture.[24] The respective defenses and critiques by Perry's fans and foes evince the cultural, social, and political disputes over conflicting and competing claims on blackness as both a trope and a category. As blackness is always contingent, unstable, and overdetermined, Perry's work must be considered in institutional, structural, and cultural ways, allowing Black cultural production to be understood beyond negative or positive terms.

Perry as Media Platform

How does the terrain and convergence of Perry's media platforms and his ubiquitous brand function as a "platform" that elevates others' works? In this regard, the term "platform" denotes not only Perry's structural operation but also highlights the ways in which Perry is a structuring operative within the contemporary American media landscape. As a media platform, Perry's financial resources and corporate relationships benefit those associated with him. For example, he and Lionsgate explicitly designed 34th Street Films "to widen Perry's reach by developing other filmmakers' work under a 'Tyler Perry Presents...' brand."[25] Under his name-banner, Perry and industry insiders believed that "[this] move undoubtedly [would] include a broader range of storytelling and casting choices, and it [would] multiply his output given that the prolific filmmaker already writes, directs, and produces two movies a year."[26] Perry as a media platform has been used by other Black figures to gain leverage and visibility within popular US media culture and widen Perry's appeal to various audiences.

For instance, Perry's role as executive producer of Lee Daniels's 2009 critically acclaimed *Precious: Based on the Novel "Push" by Sapphire* exemplifies his position as a media platform. After seeing a rough cut of *Precious*, Perry teamed up with Oprah Winfrey and her company, Harpo Productions, to present the film. A media platform herself, Winfrey's endorsement of *Precious* benefited from the "Oprah-effect," the explosive influence her promotion has on people and products (e.g., book club recipients and her "favorite things"). The celebrity status of both Perry and Winfrey played a critical role in the promotion and wide release of the film.

While Perry's Madea fare stylistically differs from Daniels's film, *Precious*'s narrative of trauma and abuse resonates thematically with both Perry's productions and personal life, which is often cited as the source material for his own work.[27] In this collection of essays, Ben Raphael Sher explores the media and affective implications of Perry's connection to *Precious*, explaining how Perry decided to recount his own trauma on the national and public stage following his viewing of the film. Sher recounts how Perry's special "200 Men" episode on *The Oprah Winfrey Show* (ABC, 1986–2011) was "one of the most highly publicized and widely seen discussions of sexual abuse against men in media history."[28] Here, Perry as a media platform works in multiple ways. As Winfrey delivers mainstream promotion, Perry provides Daniels with "Blackstream" visibility, a form of social capital engendered by his loyal network of Black audiences. Daniels recognizes this fact in his description of Perry's success, stating: "There's only one African-American success story in movies, and that's Tyler Perry. I want to bring my DNA into that machine so I can make some money."[29] In turn, lacking a certain level of prestige attached to his own productions, Perry's connection to Daniels provides him symbolic capital, prestige, and recognizable value.[30] Because of the critical success of *Precious*, Perry attended the 82nd Academy Awards, where the film was up for several awards, including Best Picture.[31] These strategic and tactical cultural moves by both Daniels and Perry underscore the struggles for visibility, recognition, and legitimacy of Black cultural work in the contemporary period.

Daniels is not alone in partnering with Perry to "make some money." In 2012, Perry struck an exclusive deal to bring scripted content to Oprah Winfrey's fledgling network, the Oprah Winfrey Network (OWN). Prior to the deal, Perry and Lionsgate were in talks to create a network channel for Perry, tentatively titled Tyler TV by taking over the TV Guide Network.[32] That deal never went through. Instead, Perry partnered with mogul and friend Oprah Winfrey for a small equity stake in OWN and a multiyear deal with the network.[33] In this case, Perry also used OWN as a media platform, making their partnership a symbiotic relationship based on the success of each other. Both OWN and Perry were able to provide resources, status, and visibility for each other. In fact, OWN and Perry released special television advertisements to announce Perry's prime-time premieres. To promote the partnership, Perry and Winfrey reprised their famous roles as Madea and Sofia, respectively. In the promos, Madea drives up a dirt road looking for "OWN" when she comes across Sofia and asks her where she can find OWN in her local programming. In response, Sofia alters her famous lines from *The Color Purple* (Steven Spielberg, 1985): "All my life I had to fight . . ." but this time in reference to her cable channel's fight against "the press folks," "the ratings," and "dem haters."³⁴

The partnership of Perry and Winfrey highlights the means by which "institutional legitimacy and cultural authority are produced and subsequently reinforced in the press and media."³⁵ Both cultural figures and their famous personas signal how "cultural capital and social status flow in the direction of key players, spokespersons, and works because of their identification and affiliation with each other and powerful institutions."³⁶ In *Essence* magazine, Winfrey explained: "We both know how rare this is . . . Where else in the history of African American culture have two really, really successful people who can do whatever they want say, 'Let's come together and be even more powerful—let's take it to the 10th power?'"³⁷ In doing so, two of the wealthiest Black media figures in history, Perry and Winfrey, work together to lobby for cultural inclusion within the dominant US media industry while shaping Black programming on television. Perry created two new programs for OWN, including the prime-time soap opera *Tyler Perry's The Haves and the Have Nots* (2013–present) and the sitcom *Tyler Perry's Love Thy Neighbor* (2013–present). The former set records for OWN, garnering the highest ratings for a series premiere, which was later topped by Perry's second soap opera, *If Loving You Is Wrong*. Perry's dramas have fared better than his comedies for the network, setting records for OWN and cable television during their time slots. In 2013, OWN ordered a third season of Perry's *For Better or Worse*, which originally premiered on TBS in 2011 but was not renewed by the network following its second season.

Perry's partnership with the network signaled a shift in OWN's television programming. Since the network debuted on January 1, 2011, OWN struggled to find viewers for its unscripted content that included programs like *Why Not? With Shania Twain* (OWN, 2011) and *The Rosie Show* (OWN, 2011–12), both of which were canceled. Perry's scripted content, along with other Black-starring shows, including the hits *Welcome to Sweetie Pie's* (OWN, 2011–present) and *Iyanla: Fix My Life*

(OWN, 2012–present), represents a programming swing for the network. Catering to Black audiences, OWN's use of narrowcasting is reminiscent of other new networks that target Black viewership, including Fox, WB, and UPN. Kristal Brent Zook's incisive *Color by Fox: The Fox Network and the Revolution in Black Television* details the process for FOX, the "fourth network," which by 1993 "was airing the largest single crop of black-produced shows in television history."[38] While these shows were later abandoned in an attempt to "legitimize" the network with white content, Zook explains that FOX "was unique, then, in that it inadvertently fostered a space for black authorship in television."[39] In this collection of essays, Artel Great discusses this effect in relation to Perry's show *House of Payne* on TBS.[40] In a similar fashion, OWN's use of Perry's media as a means for solvency reflects the industrial impulse to capitalize on underrepresented markets.

In that process, Perry's Black-cast and Black-themed shows have helped the network get financially "in the black" and shaped the content of the network—as well as the cultural reception of the network—as "Black." Critic Tambay Obenson echoes this sentiment, explaining: "I teased that OWN would eventually become a black TV network ... So it shouldn't be a big surprise that the network has decided to nurture that viewership, expanding their options with scripted programming from a successful brand, to add to the reality-based material."[41] OWN's strategic partnership with Perry helped the network generate programming for Black audiences originally wary of Winfrey's self-help and reality fare. At the same time, Perry's shows helped to shape OWN within his aesthetic imagination, making the channel seemingly as much his as it is her own. One critic calls this brand amalgam the "Perryization of OWN," noting that industry insiders fear that "merging Winfrey's philosophy of empowerment and enlightenment that has appealed to a sophisticated, female audience with Perry's critically panned formula for low-brow humor sprinkled with what many see as cartoonish African American images smacks of desperation."[42] This fear of Perry and Oprah's partnership reflects long-standing high/low cultural debates within popular culture. The implicit class and racial critique of Perry's productions and, in turn, Perry's audiences miscasts what it means to be television's desired demographic. In terms of ratings, sophisticated (white) female audiences are not necessarily the target demographic for advertisers looking for viewers with disposable income and less brand loyalty. What Oprah and Perry understand that those industry insiders do not is that Perry's Black, women-centered programming caters to key Black demographics within OWN's targeted demographic of women between 25 and 54. Through his programming, Black viewers get a version of racial empowerment and enlightenment characteristic of Winfrey that, while at times "cartoonish," fills a huge hole in Black representation on US television.

As a visible figure with name recognition and loyal fans, Perry is a moneymaking machine for other media-makers who are associated with him. Aware of this fact, the multimedia mogul tactically deploys the self-reflexive power of himself as a media platform. For example, in 2008 and 2009, Perry premiered special one-hour episodes of *Tyler: The Tyler Perry Show* on TBS to promote his films *I Can Do Bad All by Myself* (2009) and *Why Did I Get Married Too?* (2010). In 2014, the program was revived on OWN to promote his film *The Single Mom's Club* and his hit scripted series *The Have and the Have Nots*. On the show, Perry interviews stars from his movies and series about their lives, the characters he created for them, and what it is like to work with him. However, what often happens is Perry responds to his own questions, calling attention back to himself.

Perry's use of his first name "*Tyler*" before *The Tyler Perry Show* further codifies how he uses his brand as a media platform. A kind of industrial bootstrapping, "Tyler" the host uses "Tyler Perry" the platform to launch himself. Lamenting this fact, critic Veronica Miller proclaims that *Tyler* "is merely a spruced-up press junket" for his films and shows, questioning: "How many times can one person's name show up in a title of a TV show?"[43] When discussing Tyler Perry, the answer to Miller's implicit charge of "What's in a name" is, simply, everything. Perry using his own media phenomenon as a marketing strategy demonstrates what John Caldwell calls a "quintessential form of industrial self-representation."[44] Perry's rhetorical deployment of himself as a media platform mimics how, Caldwell suggests, "the industry now constantly speaks to itself about itself, sometimes in public."[45]

Perry's move to champion his shows, actors, and films can be read as a longstanding "oppositional cultural strategy by African Americans engaged in struggles for institutional legitimacy and recognition."[46]

The tactics of self-promotion and distribution are reminiscent of early Black filmmakers, including Oscar Micheaux. For instance, film historian Jacqueline Stewart describes how Micheaux promoted his first production *The Homesteader* (1919) by staging "an elaborate premiere, with live musical performances, at the Eighth Regiment Armory on Chicago's South Side as the all-Black unit made its triumphant return from Europe."[47] Stewart explains that "Micheaux solicited African American viewer interest by cultivating pride in his achievements as a Black artist and entrepreneur and by tying *The Homesteader*'s release into Black patriotic feeling."[48] Perry cultivates pride in his financial and media achievements through his industrial self/product promotion. While there are important distinctions between Perry and Micheaux as cultural producers, both function, similarly, as interlocutors for Black audiences and content geared towards them. Therefore, as a media platform, Perry serves as a broader text and context for the creation, circulation, and reception of Black popular media.

Tyler Perry Presents . . .

In April of 2013, Perry took to Facebook to post an announcement to his followers. He wrote: "I WANNA INTRODUCE YOU TO A VERY SPECIAL LADY. I want you to meet Tina."[49] Referring to Tina Gordon Chism, Perry explained:

> For the last few years I have been looking for talented writers and directors who I could help reach their dreams. Those who have the gift but haven't had the opportunity. Those who are gifted at storytelling. Well, in my search of many I have found a few that I'm working on helping, but there was one that is so special and so unique that she is ready now. Her name is Tina Gordon Chism. She is a writer and a first-time director. She has a new movie coming out on May 10th that I'm presenting called PEEPLES. This movie is hysterical. She did such a great job. I'm so proud of her. I must tell you, it makes me feel great to be able to help usher her to her dreams. I love seeing the underdog get their shot. If y'all didn't put me in this position I couldn't help her. So thank you. I feel that there is much more room in this business and this is my first attempt at opening this door for another writer-director.

I'm excited about the possibility and I'm excited about her ... a young African-American woman getting her first shot. This is really cool.[50]

In the post, Perry promotes *Peeples*, Chism, and himself. As a "Tyler Perry-adjacent" project, Perry does not claim *Peeples* as his own; instead Perry "presents" the film in a lengthy status update that espouses support for Chism and *Peeples*. However, Perry frames his backing of Chism as a branch of his own ambition and accomplishments. Thanking his audience for putting him in the position to be a platform for others, Perry, emboldened by success, embraces his role as promoter. In a promotional video distributed by Lionsgate about *Peeples*, Perry reinforces the notion that his brand is a platform, explaining: "If I could take 34th Street to take her life, lift her and elevate her and give her a platform to do some great things then I wanted to be in."[51]

Within this discourse of support and promotion, I examine how Chism uses Perry's media platforms and Perry as a media platform to yield certain cinematic gains for *Peeples*. Situating Chism's strategy for media visibility within Perry's presentational aesthetic, I call attention to the semiotic and social forces and effects that come from having his name in the film's title. In doing so, I address how *Peeples*'s critical and cultural reception was shaped and reshaped by this process and examine the cultural struggles for Black female recognition in contemporary mainstream media.

With screenwriting credits for the films *ATL* (Chris Robinson, 2006) and *Drumline* (Charles Stone III, 2002), Chism wrote and directed *Peeples*, a comedy feature about a children's entertainer, Wade (Craig Robinson), meeting the family of his lawyer girlfriend, Grace Peeples (Kerry Washington), for the first time. Much to the chagrin of Grace's father, Virgil (David Alan Grier), Wade surprises her and her seemingly perfect family at their vacation home in Sag Harbor. As Wade tries to impress his soon-to-be in-laws, including Grace's mom, Daphne (S. Epatha Merkerson), a recovering ex-alcoholic and girl group singer; her sister, Gloria (Kali Hawk), a closeted lesbian; and her brother, Simon (Tyler James Williams), a computer genius and kleptomaniac. With his brother, Randy (Malcolm Barrett), along for the ride, Wade—following many missteps—wins over the Peepleses, including Grace's grandparents played by legendary actors Diahann Carrol and Melvin Van Peebles.

Peeples was the first non-Perry directed film produced by 34th Street Films. In describing how 34th Street acquired the film, Perry explains: "They loved it. I said, 'OK, I'm in' and to have an opportunity where I could really support her is really awesome."[52] Chism, who wrote the film "to show a family that could balance being very successful on one side and being very human on the other side," initially titled the film *We the Peeples*.[53] When 34th Street Films came on board, the title was finalized as *Tyler Perry Presents Peeples*. The film's release was pushed back by Lionsgate several times, and Chism credits Perry's support as a major facilitator in the production coming to fruition, explaining: "It helped to have Tyler Perry, because when he backed the film, it moved very quickly to a start day so I was grateful for that. But, I think because I wrote the script as well, it was a good sort of leverage to break into that glass ceiling as writer/director, and then with Tyler's support it pushed it forward."[54] Chism acknowledges Perry's role in getting the film made while also crediting her screenwriting primacy as a catalyst for her directorial turn. Her self-representation and self-fashioning as the main visionary refocuses her work onto herself. However, I argue that Chism's use of Perry's media platforms, as well as Perry as a media platform to gain visibility and recognition, resulted in both an illumination and occlusion of her role as writer-director.

Before I address how this was enacted and negotiated, I want to challenge and disrupt Perry's idealistic notion that he desires to cultivate and usher to the forefront talented writers and directors. I do this to both unsettle the possibilities and contextualize the politics of Perry's media practices. As such, I position Perry's support of Chism against the backdrop of his history of bad labor practices, which coincides with the creation of 34th Street Films.

In 2008, Perry fired four *House of Payne* writers because of their union activity, prompting protest and action from the Writers Guild of America (WGA). While Perry cited the "quality of their work" as reason for their termination, the four writers had already collaborated to pen over 100 episodes of the syndicated comedy.[55] Despite having union agreements with other organizations, including Teamsters, IATSE, SAG, and DGA, Perry's holding out from paying writers the same minimums and benefits afforded WGA members provoked outrage from WGA creators, showrunners, and executive producers. They wrote an open letter to Perry and the *House of Payne* producers asking them to "reinstate the writers and make a fair deal with WGA."[56] In a press release, the WGA explained:

> The Writers Guild of America, West is taking on the fight for justice of writers who were fired when they tried to get a union contract with Tyler Perry's production company, House of Payne, LLC. The Guild today filed unfair labor practice charges with the National Labor Relations Board (NLRB), alleging that *House of Payne* unlawfully fired four writers in retaliation for their union activity. The charge also alleges that the company bargained in bad faith with the guild, which is seeking to negotiate a contract covering the writers on Perry's cable television series *House of Payne* and *Meet the Browns*.[57]

Protestors picketed the opening of Tyler Perry Studios, making special guests such as Cicely Tyson, Will Smith, Sidney Poitier, Oprah Winfrey, and Ruby Dee cross picket lines. A month after the WGA, West filed these charges and with the help of the Hollywood Branch of the National Association for the Advancement of Colored People (NAACP), Perry and the WGA, West reached an agreement to "become a signatory to a WGA Contract."[58] None of the fired writers returned to work for Perry, and it took three years for a collective bargaining agreement to be reached with WGA, East.[59]

This labor dispute highlights the conflicting politics and power dynamics of Perry's cultural production. With his studio in Atlanta, Perry's spatial "outsider" status was strategically used to cut costs via tax breaks and circumvent guild participation. As Perry heralds the groundbreaking Black cultural workers of Hollywood at his studio's grand opening, Perry's corporate practices reify the institutional pattern of exploiting (invisible) Black labor in the film industry. In this collection, Aymar Jean Christian and Khadijah Costley White explore this particular issue in greater detail, pointing to ways in which Perry's claims to sole authorship and ownership work against the interests of building a more diverse media talent pool.[60] Nevertheless, Perry formed 34th Street Films, which was announced a month before WGA's labor filings and amidst failed union negotiations.[61]

34th Street Films was formed "to produce projects under the Tyler Perry brand while focusing on projects written and directed by outside talent."⁶² *For Colored Girls* was supposed to be the first of such produced under the company banner. Nzingha Stewart originally wrote and optioned the script adaptation of Ntozake Shange's powerful and beloved choreopoem. When Perry and Lionsgate got involved, Stewart was slated to direct the film before being ousted by Perry. Due to confidentiality agreements following a relatively quiet legal settlement with Stewart, the terms and circumstances of her dismissal from the project are not fully clear.⁶³ However, she was given the conciliatory credit as an executive producer on the film. In this regard, Perry's taking over as both (re)writer and director of *For Colored Girls* frames my debate surrounding 34th Street Films' production of Chism's *Peeples* and the ways in which he hijacks Black women's narratives vís a vís his media platforms and industry practices.

Chism's *Peeples* intended to use Perry's name for brand recognition. In this regard, the use of "Tyler Perry Presents" in *Peeples*'s title identifies Chism's work with Perry. However, this identification process blurs the associative line between being a "Tyler Perry-adjacent" project and being a Perry-created product. Take, for example, the semiotics of the film's poster. While the stars of *Peeples*—including *Scandal* (ABC, 2012–present) sensation Kerry Washington—receive top billing and have their faces on the poster, "Tyler Perry Presents" is placed prominently above the tile of the film to entice viewers. Chism's name is buried at the bottom on the billing block. Perry, known for his self-representative rhetoric on all his creative work, strategically denotes ownership through his attached possessive signature, communicating a specific style, aesthetic, and production practice. A marketing strategy, Perry's media industries rely on an affective economy that responds to "the emotional underpinnings of consumer decision-making as a driving force behind viewing and purchasing decisions."⁶⁴ Perry's name above the title was supposed to help audiences know the tone of *Peeples*. In spite of using Perry's name as such, *Peeples* flopped at the box office, making less than $10 million of its budget of $15.⁶⁵ Garnering lukewarm reviews, *Peeples* failed as counterprogramming against the blockbuster *Iron Man 3* (Shane Black, 2013) and the literary adaption *The Great Gatsby* (Baz Luhrmann, 2013).

While there are several reasons for movies to disappoint, *Peeples*'s box-office bomb can be linked to Chism's association with Perry and the disassociation of her role as writer-director. This notion becomes more evident through evaluating reviews of the film. In a positive review of the film, critic Odie Henderson explains:

> The commercials and subway posters feature producer Tyler Perry's name so prominently that, until two days ago, I thought the film was called "Tyler Perry Presents: Peeples." I don't mean to imply that Perry is some kind of Black Voldemort, but his name as a marketing device seems a disservice here. It immediately signals to much of the filmgoing public that "This film is NOT for You." "Peeples" shares Perry's penchant for gathering a great cast and mocking the "bougie," but that's where the similarities end. This is more "Meet the Parents" than "Madea Goes to Jail."[66]

While Henderson is actually incorrect and the film is called *Tyler Perry Presents Peeples* (though it is often shortened to *Peeples*), his awareness of Perry's name as a marketing device is telling of its attempt to attract Perry's fan base. "They see the title with his name on it," critic Tambay Obenson explains, "and assume it's a Tyler Perry film, even though it's not, and Chism's name (as well as those of the other 2 producers, and what they bring to the project) will get buried."[67] While attempting to focus on Chism's contributions, reviewers often wrote about *Peeples* in relation to Perry's trademark style and themes.[68]

Aligned as such, Perry frames the ways in which critics and, more importantly, audiences read Chism's work as related to his own. While Perry's name certainly does not guarantee financial success, evidenced in his unfortunate starring turn in *Alex Cross* (Rob Cohen, 2012), Chism's use of Perry as a media platform structured the reception politics surrounding her film. While Chism's directorial debut adds her to a far too small list of African American women directors, Perry's name both directly and indirectly illuminated and occluded this feat. In this regard, Chism's work with Perry emphasizes her and many others' cultural struggles for Black recognition in film. While Chism and *Peeples* gained visibility, the notion of being seen does not necessarily translate to the fact of being legible, signifying an understanding of Chism's agency and ownership. With Perry as a marketing strategy, the film ultimately was misread. One only has to turn to Perry's own website and its page for *Peeples* to understand his fans' confusion over the film.[69] While some commentators expressed their enjoyment of the film (often in terms that never signaled their knowledge that Perry did not write or direct the film), many discussed their contempt for *Peeples*'s departure from the usual Perry fare. Some lamented its "immoral message," or what others described as its "gay and lesbian messages."

Just as her use of Perry's media platform (mis)shaped her work on the national stage, Chism's association with Perry (re)shaped, in a promising way, the creative and cultural boundaries of Perry's own representation, particularly in terms of sexual politics in his films. Coming off the release of his contemptuous film *Temptation* (which fared pretty well at the box office) and his condemnation of down-low culture in *For Colored Girls*, Perry's films have a history of problematic sexual representations. In *Peeples*, Grace's sister Gloria is a gay woman struggling to come out to her family. Chism felt compelled to include this storyline based on her LGBT friends' complicated familial relationships, stating: "I didn't want to get on a soapbox about it, but I wanted to show a loving couple that really was a part of the family already."[70] Thus, Chism's *Peeples* challenges Perry's churchgoing fans who went out to see the film based on his brand approval. Despite fans' decrying of Perry going secular, as in other Hollywood films, Perry's association with *Peeples* expands the stories and subject matter associated with Perry's films. In this sense, *Peeples* fulfills 34th Street's mission to broaden Perry's range of storytelling.

Beyond the Black Voldemort

It is important to open up the all-too-narrow discussion of Perry as a media phenomenon in relation to and beyond *Peeples*. What can be learned from Perry's affinity for and co-option of Black women's subjectivities? Does Perry want his productions to be taken seriously? If so, borrowing from Henderson's cheeky reading of Perry as "some kind of Black Voldemort," what can be made of Perry operating as "he who must not be named" for "Tyler Perry-adjacent" projects and partnerships to be taken seriously? What would it look like for Perry to be a platform for others without his name affixed to the product and its promotion? And if he is a kind of Black Voldemort, why is it critically important to move beyond this designation in order to "map the social, economic and technological features of black cultural formation and to assess its political and cultural effects"?[71]

Perry has expressed on many occasions how Black women—particularly the women in his family and Oprah Winfrey—and Black women-centered cultural work have influenced him. For example, Perry often quotes or invokes Steven Spielberg's adaptation of Alice Walker's *The Color Purple* (1985) in his stage and film work. The fact that Perry draws from Spielberg's controversial adaption and not the womanist text itself underscores the problems of Perry's reverence for filtered Black women's stories. Here, Jacqueline Bobo's assessment that Spielberg's film "seeks to displace Black women at the center of the story and reinsert traditional demeaning images of them" can be extended to critique Perry's Madea-filled narratives.[72] To this point, the act of displacement also characterizes Perry's co-option of *Peeples* authorship via his "Tyler Perry Presents" imprimatur. In this regard, Perry's name shadows Chism's work, contouring the cultural reception of her film in his image (name brand) and imaginings (Madea melodramas). Taken at face value, Perry's visage over *Peeples* became the template by which the film was understood.

Perry's brand does not signal prestige. However, he does want to be taken seriously, evidenced by his dramatic work and the fact that he casts a majority of the revered Black actresses in Hollywood in his films. Elsewhere, I have explained that "some of the most celebrated black actresses—including Cicely Tyson, Maya Angelou, Lynn Whitfield, Phylicia Rashad, Whoopi Goldberg, Jennifer Lewis, Alfre Woodard, and Loretta Devine—have graced Perry's screen and supported his work. Through their black female star power, Perry's films produce their own affective economy of cultural signification. Even when a film he makes is technically and ideologically bad, his actresses are viewed as great. Their acting labor makes legible the politics of cultural visibility and erasure of black women in American cinema."[73] Moreover, as the example of *Precious* shows, Perry's name does not mean that a film cannot be taken seriously.

Therefore, despite his desire for depth, his brand does signal shallowness, ironically drowning *Peeples* in the wake of Perry's cinematic deluge. In her short essay "The Morality of Tyler Perry," Roxane Gay hits on the catch-22 of *Peeples*'s disappointing box-office returns: "I have to consider the possibility that Tyler Perry movies are successful because of their moralism and their sneering at women, not in spite of them. It's a bitter pill to swallow. He knows his audience and gives them exactly what they want, and what they have come to expect. When Perry doesn't give his audience what they want—caricatures of black men and women and broad moral messages—well, the box office doesn't lie."[74] Gay points out the complexity of *Peeples*'s abrupt failure and Perry's enduring popularity. In giving audiences what they want and have come to expect, Perry's productions and platforms highlight the quandary and boundaries in which he and "Tyler Perry-adjacent" work are positioned.

If Perry cannot be taken seriously, what would it really look like for Perry to be a platform without "Tyler Perry Presents" attached to the product? Many have called for Perry to "become an incubator of black talent."[75] In her open letter to Perry, critic Jamilah Lemieux writes: "Mr. Perry, you are in the positon now where, if you were willing, you could completely revolutionize the world of black film. You could singlehandedly develop the next crop of Tyler Perrys, Spike Lees and Julie Dashes if you want to."[76] Perry's support—both financial and promotional—of Chism and *Peeples* challenges Lemieux's charge, which places an unfair burden on Perry to be responsible for revolutionizing Black film. Chism is on the spectrum between the "Lees," "Dashes," and the "Perrys" of Black film. However, "manifesting Perry-trademarks," *Peeples* is more in the vein of Perry's popular films than that of the other independent filmmakers Lemieux mentions.[77] While a "Tyler Perry-adjacent" project without "Tyler Perry Presents" is unchartered territory, the fact that Perry might only be interested in developing the next versions of himself is a reality that must be recognized and reckoned with. In moving forward, all Lemieux and anyone else can really hope for is that Perry, if he so chooses, ushers forth better versions of himself.

I want to conclude by considering Tyler Perry's empire in broader, cultural terms. The development of Perry's multi-platform media industry illustrates a "*racing* (that is, an explicit darkening, blackening, and coloring) of American culture, at least in terms of the operation of its dominant institutions of cultural production and legitimization." [78] As such, Perry's productions, his partnerships, and "Tyler Perry-adjacent" projects must be situated within a larger, contested framework of Black cultural formation in the United States. He is part of a new generation of Black filmmakers, artists, intellectuals, athletes, actors, authors, and musicians who are "profoundly shaping the imagination of American culture."[79] The cultural politics and aesthetic ideology of Perry's work are, oftentimes, problematic and, sometimes, promising. However, in order to evaluate his institutional features and cultural representations, it is important to get beyond thinking about Perry as some kind of Black Voldemort, derisively referring to him as "you-know-who" or purposely ignoring him as "he who must not be named." Perry is not the nemesis of cinema, women, media studies, or even Black people. He is a cultural force—for good *and* bad—in representing Black lives on screen and stage. As a man so obsessed with his own name, it's important to "call on him" as much as "call him out," in order to understand the complex, complicated, creative, and contextual role he and his media platforms play in contemporary American media and popular culture.

Notes

1. Tenisha Hart, quoted in Scott Bowles, "Tyler Perry Holds Onto His Past," *USA Today*, September, 9, 2008.
2. Hilton Als, "Mama's Gun: The World of Tyler Perry," *New Yorker*, April 26, 2010, 70.
3. Patrick Goldstein, "The Kingdom of Tyler Perry," *Los Angeles Times*, February 27, 2009. While Perry's box-office dominance cannot be contested, recent Madea- and non-Madea-themed films have underperformed in relation to his previous success. Perry's 2014 film *The Single Mom's Club* had his lowest-grossing opening weekend box office to date. His films still turn profits from domestic sales but it is evident that Perry's focus is on his television shows on OWN.
4. Herman Gray, *Cultural Moves: African Americans and the Politics of Representation* (Berkeley: University of California Press, 2005), 16.
5. Ibid., 188.
6. Ibid., 3.
7. Henry Jenkins, *Convergence Culture: Where Old and New Media Collide* (New York: New York University Press, 2006), 2.
8. Tyler Perry, *Don't Make a Black Woman Take Off her Earrings: Madea's Uninhibited Commentaries on Love and Life* (New York: Riverhead Books, 2006).
9. Als, "Mama's Gun," 70.
10. "Bio," Tyler Perry.com, Tyler Perry Studios, http://www.tylerperry.com/biography/.
11. Als, "Mama's Gun," 68.
12. Gray, *Cultural Moves*, 79. Gray describes these shifting conditions, explaining: "Among the most far-reaching and consequential transformations affecting American television was passage of the 1996 Telecommunications Act, the changes in corporate ownership of media conglomerates, the emerging structure and global reach of entertainment/media/information companies, and rapid advances in new technologies and program delivery" (ibid).

13. Jay A. Fernandez, "Cross-dressed for Success: Tyler Perry Prepares to Broaden His Madea-sized empire," *Hollywood Reporter*, August 15–17, 2008, 34–35.

14. Fernandez, "Cross-dressed for Success," 35. For a further analysis of Perry's media universe, see Aymar Jean Christian and Khadijah Costley White's chapter "One Man Hollywood: The Decline of Black Creative Productions in Post-Network Television."

15. Samantha N. Sheppard, "She Ain't Heavy, She's Madea: The Tyler Perry Discourse and the Politics of Contemporary Black Cultural Production," forthcoming in *Black Cinema Aesthetics Revisited*, eds. Michael Gillespie and Akil Houston.

16. Ibid.

17. Goldstein, "The Kingdom of Tyler Perry."

18. See Roger Ebert, "Review: Diary of a Mad Black Woman," *Roger Ebert*, February 24, 2005, http://www.rogerebert.com/reviews/diary-of-a-mad-black-woman-2005; Roger Ebert, "Who *Is* That Mad Black Woman?" *Roger Ebert's Journal*, March 2, 2005, http://www.rogerebert.com/rogers-journal/who-is-that-mad-black-woman. For more on this review in relation to Perry's character of Madea, see Rachel Daniels's chapter in this collection.

19. See Joshua Alston, "Why White Critics' Fear of Engaging Tyler Perry is Stifling Honest Debate," *A.V. Club*, April 18, 2013, http://www.avclub.com/article/why-white-critics-fear-of-engaging-tyler-perry-is--96644; Louis Peitzman, "Tyler Perry's HIV: Punishment For Your Sins," *BuzzFeed*, April 3, 2013, http://www.buzzfeed.com/louispeitzman/tyler-perrys-hiv-punishment-for-your-sins#.wcEpZo6ZKV; Lindy West, "Tyler Perry Isn't Just an Artless Hack, He's a Scary Ideologue," *Jezebel*, April 3, 2013, http://jezebel.com/5993523/tyler-perry-isnt-just-an-artless-hack-hes-a-scary-ideologue.

20. In an interview on *60 Minutes*, Perry addressed Spike Lee's criticism, stating: "I would love to read that to my fan base. That pisses me off. It is so insulting. It's attitudes like that make Hollywood think that these people do not exist and that's why there's no material speaking to them." *60 Minutes*, hosted by Byron Pitts, CBS, October 25, 2009, television. See Karen Bowdre's "Spike and Tyler—Beef, Blackness, and Exceptional Negroes."

21. See Brittney Cooper, "Tyler Perry Hates Black Women: 5 Thoughts on the Haves and Have Nots," *Crunk Feminist Collective*, May 29, 2013, http://www.crunkfeministcollective.com/2013/05/29/tyler-perry-hates-black-women-5-thoughts-on-the-haves-and-have-nots/.

22. Brittney Cooper, "How I Confronted Tyler Perry: A Surprisingly Frank Phone Call Yields Real Results," *Salon*, March 18, 2014, http://www.salon.com/2014/03/18/my_surprisingly_frank_phone_call_with_tyler_perry/.

23. Ibid.

24. Jenkins, *Convergence Culture*, 2.

25. Fernandez, "Cross-dressed for Success," 35.

26. Ibid.

27. On the biography on his website, Perry explains: "Born into poverty and raised in a household scarred by abuse, Tyler fought from a young age to find the strength, faith and perseverance that would later form the foundations of his much-acclaimed plays, films, books and shows." See http://www.tylerperry.com/biography/. Also see Logan Hill, "In Support of Precious, Tyler Perry Reveals His Own History of Abuse," *Vulture*, October 6, 2009, http://www.vulture.com/2009/10/in_support_of_precious_tyler_p.html.

28. See Ben Sher, "'All My Life I Had to Fight': Trauma and Cinephilia in Tyler Perry's Archive of Feelings."

29. Lee Daniels, quoted in Lynn Hitschberg, "The Audacity of *Precious*," *New York Times Magazine*, October 25, 2009, 38.

30. I am drawing on Pierre Bourdieu's concepts of social and symbolic capital. See Pierre Bourdieu, *Distinction: A Social Critique of the Judgement of Taste* (New York: Routledge, 1984).

31. Perry and Oprah would not have been eligible to win an Oscar if the film had won (the award went to Kathryn Bigelow's 2011 *The Hurt Locker*).

32. Brian Stelter, "Tyler Perry Signs Exclusive Deal with OWN," *New York Times*, October 1, 2012.

33. Rick Kissell, "Ratings: AMC, OWN, TLC Among Notable Cable Gainers in 2014," *Variety*, April 3, 2014.

34. OWN TV, "Madea Meets Sofia: The Search for OWN-Oprah Winfrey Network," April 4, 2013, https://www.youtube.com/watch?v=7YDKYtPd3ho.

35. Gray, *Cultural Moves*, 71.

36. Ibid.

37. Oprah Winfrey, quoted in Greg Braxton and Yvonne Villarreal, "Tyler Perry-Oprah Alliance Marks a New Turn for OWN," *Los Angeles Times*, May 24, 2013.

38. Kristal Brent Zook, *Color by Fox: The Fox Network and the Revolution in Black Television* (New York: Oxford University Press, 1999), 4.

39. Ibid.

40. See Artel Great, "Bring the Payne: The Crisis of the Black Sitcom and the Emergence of Tyler Perry."

41. Tambay A. Obenson, "A Look at the Tyler Perry/Oprah Winfrey Partnership a Year After it was Announced . . ." *Shadow and Act: On Cinema of the African Diaspora*, February 6, 2014, http://blogs.indiewire.com/shadowandact/taking-a-look-at-the-tyler-perry-oprah-winfrey-partnership-over-a-year-after-it-was-announced.

42. Braxton and Villarreal, "Tyler Perry-Oprah Alliance Marks a New Turn for OWN."

43. Veronica Miller, "Can Tyler Perry Find New Success as a Talk Show Host?" *Grio*, February 20, 2014, http://thegrio.com/2014/02/20/can-tyler-perry-find-new-success-as-a-talk-show-host/.

44. John Thornton Caldwell, *Production Culture: Industrial Reflexivity and Critical Practice in Film and Television* (Durham: Duke University Press, 2008), 274.

45. Ibid., 35.

46. Gray, *Cultural Moves*, 34. I draw on this concept of oppositional strategies from Gray's analysis of Wynton Marsalis's move to institutionalize and legitimize jazz in American culture through his program at the Lincoln Center for the Performing Arts in New York City in 1991.

47. Stewart, *Migrating to the Movies*, 221.

48. Ibid., 221–22.

49. His emphasis. Tyler Perry, "I WANNA INTRODUCE YOU TO A VERY SPECIAL LADY," Tyler Perry's Facebook Page, April 23, 2013.

50. Ibid.

51. Tyler Perry, quoted in Liongsate Entertainment promotional video, *Rotten Tomatoes*.

52. Associated Press, "Tyler Perry and His 'Peeples,'" May 9, 2013, http://www.youtube.com/watch?v=ApHXfnBfLKQ.

53. Lottie Joiner, "Tina Gordon Chism: Telling Rich Black Stories One Movie at a Time," *Washington Post*, May 10, 2013.

54. Ibid.

55. Edward Wyatt, "Writers File Complaint against Tyler Perry," *New York Times*, October 3, 2008.

56. See "WGA Creators, Showrunners, and Executive Producers Submit an Open Letter to the Producers of Tyler Perry's *House of Payne*," *Writers Guild of America, West*, October 4, 2008, http://www.wga.org/content/default.aspx?id=3074.

57. Writers Guild of America, West, "Writers at Tyler Perry Studio to Take Strike Action—Will Picket Grand Opening and Ask Invited Guests Not To Attend," *Writers Guild of America, West*, October 2, 2008, http://www.wga.org/content/default.aspx?id=2970.

58. Writers Guild of America, West, "Tyler Perry Studios and Writers Guild Announce Agreement," *Writers Guild of America, West*, November 26, 2008, http://www.wga.org/content/default.aspx?id=3396.

59. Brent Lang, "Tyler Perry and WGA Reach Agreement on 'House of Payne,'" *The Wrap*, December 6, 2011, http://www.thewrap.com/tv/article/tyler-perry-studios-wga-east-reach-collective-bargaining-agreement-house-payne-33361/.

60. See Aymar Jean Christian and Khadijah Costley White's "One Man Hollywood: The Decline of Black Creative Production in Post-Network Television."

61. David McNary, "Tyler Perry Forms 34th Street Films," *Variety*, September 21, 2008.

62. Ibid.

63. Nsenga Burton, "Black Women and the Hollywood Shuffle," *The Root*, August 6, 2010, http://www.theroot.com/articles/culture/2010/08/black_women_filmmakers_struggle_in_hollywood.2.html; Tambay Obenson, "Exclusive Interview with Nzingha Stewart (Original Director of 'For Colored Girls . . .' Adaptation)," *Shadow and Act*, March 26, 2010, http://www.shadowandact.com/?p=20021.

64. Jenkins, *Convergence Culture*, 62.

65. Todd Cunningham, "Tyler Perry's 'Peeples' Starring David Alan Grier, Kerry Washington Flops," *The Wrap*, May 12, 2013, http://www.thewrap.com/movies/article/tyler-perrys-peeples-starring-kerry-washington-flops-91031/.

66. Odie Henderson, "Review: Peeples," RogerEbert.com, May 8, 2013, http://www.rogerebert.com/reviews/peeples-2013.

67. Tambay A. Obenson, "Tina Gordon Chism's 'We The Peeples' Gets a New Title + First Look Photo," *Shadow and Act*, February 19, 2013, http://blogs.indiewire.com/shadowandact/tina-gordon-chisms-we-the-peeples-gets-a-new-title-first-look-photo.

68. See, for example, Sheri Linden, "Peeples: Film Review," *Hollywood Reporter*, May 4, 2013, http://www.hollywoodreporter.com/movie/peeples/review/451731; Zachary Wigon, "*Peeples* is a Well-Meaning Farce," *Village Voice*, May 8, 2013, http://www.villagevoice

.com/2013-05-08/film/peeples/?utm_source=feedly; Leonard Maltin, "Peeples," *Leonard Maltin's Movie Crazy*, May 10, 2013, http://blogs.indiewire.com/leonardmaltin/peeples.

69. See Tyler Perry's website comment section for *Tyler Perry Present's Peeples*, Tyler Perry Studios, http://www.tylerperry.com/movies/peeples/.

70. Tina Gordon Chism, quoted in Adam B. Vary, "What The Tyler Perry-Produced 'Peeples' Has to Say About Gay Relationships," BuzzFeed, May 11, 2013, http://www.buzzfeed.com/adambvary/tyler-perry-produced-peeples-on-gay-relationships#.qvmzAJqApj.

71. Gray, *Cultural Moves*, 17. My use of the term "Black cultural formation" draws on Herman Gray, who mobilizes Michael Denning's concept of cultural formation, "as a theater and staging arena from which to explore the institutional character, features, and political implications" of Black cultural productions in the contemporary moment (ibid.)

72. Jacqueline Bobo, *Black Women as Cultural Readers* (New York: Columbia University Press, 1995), 28.

73. Sheppard, "She Ain't Heavy, She's Madea."

74. Roxane Gay, *Bad Feminist: Essays* (New York: Harper Collins, 2014), 241.

75. Ibid., 240.

76. Jamilah Lemieux, "An Open Letter to Tyler Perry," NPR, September 11, 2009, http://www.npr.org/templates/story/story.php?storyId=112760404

77. Andy Webster, "How Not to Impress Your Girlfriend's Snobby Family," *New York Times*, May 9, 2013.

78. Gray, *Cultural Moves*, 17.

79. Ibid., 13.

CHAPTER TWO

From the Margins to Center Stage: Tyler Perry's Popular African American Theatre

—Rashida Z. Shaw

In this chapter, I am interested in situating the significance of the popular within Tyler Perry's theatrical events and discussing, more broadly, his theatre's impact on the reception and perception of contemporary African American theatre. It is my view that the productions of the "Chitlin Circuit" fall squarely within the terrain of the popular and, without apology, as is the nature of the popular, they carry with them the ephemeral traces of contemporary life that are recognizable to those who happen to be in tuned in or in the know at the time of circulation, dispersion, and/or saturation. As a result, these plays contain references that may be virtually unknown to those who are less attuned to the always-already changing popular culture references within American culture and even stranger to those who are unfamiliar with the plethora of American and/or globally constituted references that have found temporal significance within African American culture. The task for the circuit outsider is not to determine the significance of a given reference, but instead to discover the ways in which circuit audiences identify with, respond to, and comprehend said references on their own terms.

Tyler Perry's African American plays are part of a unique subset of African American theatre that meld religion, comedy, African American vernacular materials, and the popular forms of Gospel, R&B, and, sometimes, jazz music into fictional narratives about urban African American life. "Chitlin Circuit" Theatre, also known as Gospel Musicals, Gospel Plays, Urban Musicals, Urban Theatre, or more recently as the Urban Circuit, has catapulted itself to a status of high recognition due to its position as a dominant, multimillion-dollar-earning entertainment form of late twentieth- and early twenty-first-century America. The contemporary "Chitlin Circuit" stands alone as a Black theatrical form that has managed to secure a prominent position in the American mainstream through its film and television offshoots that attract racially diverse consumers, despite the fact that they are created and maintained by African American popular culture interests. It would be remiss to not acknowledge how the efforts of its practitioners and the loyal support of its spectators have impacted American theatre and, even more impressively, the content and orientation of American culture.

In Consideration of Perry: Theatre's Historic Relationship to the Popular

Long before the contemporary "Chitlin Circuit" productions of Tyler Perry, American theatre has had a fraught relationship with popular entertainment. While the expansiveness of this history is too detailed to recount here, I suggest that the outside perception and popularity of Tyler Perry's theatre can be linked directly to three major historical shifts in the development of American theatre. The first transformation took place in the middle of the nineteenth century as a result of the Astor Place riot of 1849. The second moment of change occurred at the turn of the century with the rise of the segregated Black performance routes that came to be known as the "Chitlin Circuit." Third, as a result of the advent of film and a developing atmosphere of theatrical experimentation, American playwrights and audiences of the 1920s found themselves reacting to a changing aesthetic world.

First, the event that irrevocably divided audience consumption in American theatre: the notorious Astor Place riot of 1849. On May 10, what began as an evening of regular theatrical fare at New York City's Astor Place Opera House, quickly turned into a macabre scene that left over twenty people dead or fatally wounded, and over 100 people with injuries. Briefly restated here, the story is as follows: on the third night of British actor William Charles Macready's lead role in William Shakespeare's *The Tragedy of Macbeth*, the audience within and outside of the theatre house began to verbally and physically protest against the actor's performance. Responding to the growing riot, the assembled militia aimed and fired directly into the crowd. As historians have noted, accounts vary as to the exact cause of the upheaval. Included among the list of possible triggers are such factors as: an adverse reaction to Macready's home country of England; a demonstration of nationalistic pride in support of the American actor Edwin Forrest, who was also starring as Macbeth in a different production that same week;[1] or, rebellion against the new codes of conduct and upper-class strictures that were placed on the opera-house patrons by its proprietors, who were noted to be members of "New York's fashionable classes."[2] Yet, important to my discussion of the consumption of Tyler Perry's theatre with consideration of its popularity, regardless of the cause or the combination of causes, the Astor Place riot stands alone as the moment in American theatrical history in which palpable divides in theatrical entertainment occurred thereafter that were not only determined by class lines, but also by the quality, standard, and aesthetic objectives of the production at hand. As Larry Stempel recounts:

> More vividly than any other event of the period, [the riot] marked the beginning of the end of theatre in the United States as a conglomerate entertainment for a heterogeneous audience. "The Astor Place Riot intimated that this union was no longer possible," writes theatre historian David Grimstead. "The country had grown up, and grown apart. The theatre after midcentury followed this development. It expanded and divided—into legitimate drama, foreign-language drama, farce, vaudeville, circus, burlesque, minstrelsy, opera, symphony—each with its separate theater and separate audience."[3]

With the Astor Place riot and the divisions of entertainment that it helped give rise to, the indelible dye of stigmatized class-based and *low-*cultured performance had been cast. As I will discuss in the coming pages, the perception of Perry's African American theatre continues to be afflicted by the remnants of this nineteenth-century cultural fissure.

Now, in addition to the Astor Place riot history, an acknowledgment of the context in which the majority of Black performance was allowed to exist during the early twentieth century: the segregated routes of the original "Chitlin Circuit." Historically speaking, the name "Chitlin Circuit" refers to the segregated Black routes of the vaudeville circuit.[4] Like other vaudeville entertainment of the time, early "Chitlin Circuit" shows covered the gamut of popular entertainment: circus acts, melodrama, comedy, minstrelsy, and song and dance routines.[5] The word "Chitlin" is itself a derivation of the longer word chitterling. Both terms have a culinary and historical association for many African Americans because they refer to the dish that was developed by Black cooks from pig intestines during legalized slavery when African Americans had to make-do with the leftover parts of the pig. As Amiri Baraka once explained: "After the pig was stripped of its choicest parts, the feet, snout, tail, intestines, stomach, etc., were all left for the 'members,' who treated them mercilessly."[6] For business entrepreneurs like the white-partnered B. F. Keith and E. F. Albee, and the independent pursuits of African American Sherman (S. H.) Dudley, vaudeville theatre on the "Chitlin Circuit" was able to capture the attention of a nationwide audience that was divided along class, ethnic, gender, and racial lines.

After the Astor Place riot and before the inception of vaudeville in the 1880s, American entertainment was performed in multifarious venues across the country—anywhere from saloons and burlesque houses to small theatres and music halls. These performance spaces did not cater to diverse audiences nor were acts able to move to new locations with any consistency or wide recognition.[7] However, with the introduction of Keith and Albee's vaudeville theatre agency, known as the Theater Owners Booking Association or TOBA, vaudevillian spectators were figuratively "lifted ... out of [their] intimate communities and placed ... [with] in a mass audience."[8] Keith and Albee centralized their booking agencies in two major locations: Chicago and New York, giving them access to the East and West Coasts as well as parts of the south. These circuits catered to almost all subgroups of America's population and divided themselves between top-billing and beginner venues and routes. Out of these two major offices flowed acts originating from variety theatres,[9] Blackface minstrelsy, dramatic theatre houses,[10] and circuses.

In 1916, the African American actor, producer, and writer Sherman (S. H.) Dudley created his own company, the Dudley Theatrical Enterprise, through which he owned several theatres across the south and Midwest as well as in Washington, DC, Virginia, and Philadelphia.[11] Soon after, Dudley and his partners created the Southern Consolidated Circuit or the SCC, which had a far-reaching impact on Black American touring entertainment in the south, southeast, northeast (excluding

New York City), and Midwestern portions of the country.[12] According to David Krasner and the respective coauthored discussions of Errol Hill and James Hatch, it was not until the early 1920s that the white-owned TOBA became interested in Black performers and Black performance routes. Once the TOBA owners realized that there was a competitive market for Black entertainment, they decided to revive their fledgling agency, which had come to a halt a few years after its inception in 1909. Recognizing a lucrative opportunity, Keith and Albee declared that they would "'save the colored theatrical industry.'"[13] With the return of TOBA, Black theatre producers, booking agents, and managers were now forced to reckon with this competitive entertainment giant. As a result, a National Managers Protective Agency was organized on May 26–27, 1920, and Dudley created the Colored Actor's Union, which focused on the rights of African American artists.[14] Unfortunately, none of these efforts were able to withstand the eventual takeover of smaller booking agencies by TOBA before it too dismantled in the 1930s. As Krasner notes, although Dudley's own musicals and performances catered to white as well as Black audiences (because Black audiences were less accessible), and the modes of many of his performances were Blackface minstrelsy and comedy, his work and touring routes should be considered "forerunners of the 'Chitlin Circuit,'" we are still encountering today.[15]

From the respective histories of Keith, Albee, and Dudley, we gain an understanding of not only the historical context in which the original "Chitlin Circuit" was birthed, but also a glimpse into the financial motivations that were involved in harnessing lucrative Black entertainment that catered to all-Black audiences. Paralleled with this is an acknowledgment of the perceived quality and status of this kind of Black entertainment, not only because it was vaudeville, but significantly because its artists and their spectators were Black. In other words, despite the performance innovations and artistic growth that may have occurred on these traveling stages, these presentations of Black vaudeville were understood to serve a devalued and lowly segment of America's population. As African American artists, they would never rise to the heights of their white counterparts; as African American spectators, their interests would never be considered by the mainstream entertainment world. Symptomatic of the same low-culture designation that maligns Tyler Perry's African American theatre, turn-of-the-century African

American entertainment was considered popular yet unfit, and so were the choices of its spectators.

Of course, when the words "popular" and "theatre" are usually discussed in conjunction with one another, they are most commonly mentioned within conversations about musical theatre. In his article, "Toward a Historiography of the Popular," David Savran remarks upon the last historical shift that I would like to shed light on: the changing environment of 1920s theatre, vaudeville notwithstanding, and the burgeoning motion picture industry that was rapidly developing alongside it. As Savran explains, "in the United States ... theatre and popular culture have largely gone their separate ways since the 1920s. As the so-called legitimate theatre became increasingly and irrevocably literary, high modernist and haut bourgeois, to distinguish itself from motion pictures, the theatrical forms categorized as popular have declined or expired – with the important exception of the Broadway musical."[16] In this quote, Savran comments not only on the literary experimentation in form that dramatists were undertaking during the 1920s that caused a fissure within theatrical entertainment due to modernist and experimental leanings, but also on the adverse influence and effect that the rise of the American film product was having on theatre consumption. Thus, with contemporary "Chitlin Circuit" theatre holding a classification as musical theatre and, as has been discussed by Warren Burdine's writings on the gospel musical,[17] carrying a distinct Black musical lineage, it should be of no surprise then that, despite its popularity, it shares with the Broadway musical the benefits, rewards, and disdain of being regarded as "throwaway entertainment."[18] In walks Tyler Perry.

Taking the Tonys: A Day of "Legitimate" Reckoning

Taking his cue from a practitioner produced tradition of African American musical theatre, Tyler Perry, like his Black dramatist counterparts on the contemporary "Chitlin Circuit" scene, infuses religion, comedy, and popular African American music into narratives about urban African American life, set within fictional inner-city environments. To be clear, this specific kind of self-produced Black American theatre has been touring the country and performing before large and predominantly

Black spectators since the beauty shop-, barbershop-, and gospel-based African American plays of the 1980s. During that early wave, playwrights such as Vy Higgensen and Ken Wydro, the creators of the musical *Mama, I Want to Sing* (1983), and Shelly Garrett, the author of *Beauty Shop* (1989), achieved commercial success based on the popularity of one play that in turn helped to catapult their names into recognition among African Americans and secure loyal audiences for extended runs and additional tour bookings. Due to the independent, sometimes community-based nature of these productions during their nascent stages, it was common to see these playwrights serving as their own directors and producers. Financial support often came from the pockets of the playwrights themselves as well as family, friends, and interested members of the community.

In the 1990s, a new wave of "Chitlin Circuit" theatre emerged that improved upon the content and marketing skills of the previous decade. Religion, comedy, music, and African American culture still loomed large within this second generation, yet, unlike their predecessors, these younger playwrights were interested in creating a repertoire of hit productions rather than relying solely on the successes of one or two box-office successes. Although there were many African American playwrights and producers staging productions randomly throughout the country, by the twenty-first century four men in particular emerged as the leaders of the pack and quickly gained financial and commercial success by writing, producing, and directing their own circuit plays. Listed among the game-changers, Tyler Perry, along with David Talbert and the playwriting duo of Je'Caryous Johnson and Gary Guidry, respectively, became self-made millionaires due to their successful and often sold-out theatrical productions catering to African American audiences. With the marked and continued successes of the "Chitlin Circuit," the Broadway musical no longer stood alone as the sole proprietor of American popular theatre.

It is a large and inescapable fact of theatre that the success and duration of a production depends on its ability to engage with its spectators. Nowhere is this fact more evident than on Broadway stages where, each season, shows are continuously canceled or extended based on audience inclinations, preferences, and reactions. Thus, while the monetary gains of Perry and his peers are remarkable, it is significant to note that their consistent triumphs marked a turning point in the relationship between Black theatre and Black audiences. With the advent of the *new* "Chitlin Circuit" in a desegregated America, Black spectators had become discriminating consumers of theatre who were willingly spending their money according to their interests and pleasures. Not to be understated, the cultural and historic phenomenon of Black patrons choosing "Chitlin Circuit" theatre as an entertainment form and paying ticket prices that are on par with a typical Broadway show remains so profound that it continues to leave many American critics, academics, and practitioners dumbfounded and wondering: how have these artists been able to develop such a loyal Black fan base when, historically speaking, past the days of segregated entertainment, theatre producers have struggled to get Black patrons into the seats, even when the featured event is a Black-authored play that focuses on Black experiences? To be sure, the quality, nature, and sustainability of this kind of Black theatrical spectatorship had never before been seen even in response to America's most celebrated Black playwrights.

Case in point, the 1986–87 and 1987–88 Broadway seasons provide historical insight on just how difficult it has been to secure Black audiences, even for the country's most celebrated Black playwright, August Wilson. In March of 1987, near the end of the 1986–87 season, *Fences*, the third theatrical installment of August Wilson's "Pittsburgh Cycle," opened on Broadway to huge acclaim. Prior to *Fences*, Wilson had garnered reputable success on Broadway with *Ma Rainey's Black Bottom*, his play set in the 1920s, so there was already considerable interest in his work. Years before, the playwright had set out to capture the African American experience of the twentieth century, decade-by-decade, within ten plays that were fictionally set within either the Hill District of Pittsburgh or Chicago, Illinois. In *Fences*, Wilson presented his fictionalized version of the 1950s African American experience within a tightly wound narrative that focused on the rights of Black sanitation workers, father-son dynamics, infidelity, the legacies of segregation, and sports. Later that year, the play earned Wilson his first Pulitzer Prize in drama and the Tony Award for best play. Broadway audiences followed suit by flocking to the theatre and encouraging an extended run of the play that continued well into the next season. By the spring of 1988, Wilson had achieved a success that is still considered rare for any playwright on the

American stage: two of his plays were being simultaneously produced on Broadway, his 1987 play *Fences* and his newly opened play, set in the 1910s, *Joe Turner's Come and Gone*.

Even during the heyday of America's most celebrated African American playwright, August Wilson, Broadway producers and financial backers undertook major audience outreach initiatives in order to attract Black New Yorkers to the landmark productions of *Fences* and *Joe Turner's Come and Gone*. Notably, by the time *Joe Turner* opened, with *Fences* still running, it helped mark the pinnacle of Black theatrical presence both on and off Broadway. On Broadway, the South African-inspired musical *Sarafina!* was also being featured, as was Lee Breuer's Black gospel-inspired musical *The Gospel at Colonus*. Regarding *The Gospel at Colonus*, I should note that this musical presented an all-Black cast within a gospel musical adaptation of Sophocles' *Oedipus at Colonus*, created by two white Americans, director Lee Breuer and composer Bob Telson.[19] Taken together, this unprecedented offering of Black performance encouraged Black audiences to come out in record numbers to Broadway. As journalist Jeremy Gerard put it: "Broadway ha[d] more offerings for Black theatergoers than any other time in memory."[20] Although *Sarafina!* alone boasted Black audience numbers of almost 85 percent, for the most part, instead of creating Black majority audiences, the increased Black participation resulted in more balanced and diverse audiences for Black productions.[21]

Contributing to the increase in Black spectatorship during this time were the targeted efforts made by the producers of these shows to ensure high attendance. During many weeks, ticket prices were reduced to as low as $8, and the encouragement offered to Black patrons did not stop there. Producers also enlisted marketing specialists to reach out to the Black community and advertise these Black-oriented productions. Many of these specialists, who were African American themselves, had prior experience advertising Black dramatic and musical shows produced in Harlem. (I suspect that many of these Harlem-rooted productions were themselves part of the 1980s wing of the touring contemporary "Chitlin Circuit.") Schools, leisure clubs, Black-owned businesses, Black radio stations, and even churches became targets. Numerous arrangements were made for various community groups to take part in discounted trips.[22] The specialists even tried to encourage Black ministers and preachers to mention information about productions in their sermons. In the case of *The Gospel at Colonus*, for example, ministers were sent information about the production that was cross-referenced with passages of the Bible so they would be encouraged to build entire sermons around the production. With time, many of the specialists discovered that after the first few waves of new Black participants came to the shows, instead of advertising, word of mouth became the most solidifying factor that encouraged Black community participation.[23]

Fences and *Joe Turner's Come and Gone* benefited from these various recruiting efforts in varying degrees. The latter arrived on the scene with a New York Drama Critics' Circle Award for best play of the year, huge fanfare because of *Fences*' continuing success, and thousands of dollars spent on advertising.[24] Taking these factors together, the producers believed that they would have no problem encouraging audiences to attend the show, especially African American audiences. Yet, after only a few weeks after *Joe Turner*'s opening, the cost of keeping the production running with low ticket sales had already depleted most of the show's $300,000 reserve budget. Not even half of the Ethel Barrymore Theatre's 1,100 seats were being filled. The show was in danger of closing after its first month and, then, it was only able to hold on for another two months after heavy advertising.[25] On June 24, 1988, *Joe Turner's Come and Gone* closed on the very same weekend of *Fences*' closing, leaving the newcomer with a production run of only three months and the former with a run of fifteen months.[26] For reasons that have not yet been deeply considered, the low audience attendance by African Americans contributed to the short three-month run of *Joe Turner* just as much as the low white attendance. As history would document, despite colossal recruiting efforts, many African Americans still chose not to support the show. Thus, even for a celebrated American playwright like August Wilson, there were dire consequences for not capturing the interests of potential patrons, especially those who were African Americans. Conversely, by the apex of Tyler Perry's career, almost two decades later, it was clear that if you considered his Black audience satisfaction rate in addition to his crossover appeal, Perry had achieved heights—by way of popularity and thereby financial success—that surpassed even Wilson.

In fact, on June 10, 2012, the barefaced reality of Tyler Perry's accomplishments was televised during the broadcast of the sixty-sixth annual

Tony Awards show. On that night, Perry (who was not nominated) took the stage in front of hundreds of established theatre industry folk and millions of at-home spectators to present the award for best revival of a play to *Death of A Salesman* producer Scott Rubin. Perry's day of recognition by "legitimate" theatre makers had come. Of course, never being one to miss an opportunity, prior to announcing the nominees, Perry used his opening lines to assert his own worthiness by reminding those assembled that the very same Beacon Theatre in which they were gathered for the awards show had hosted numerous of his own sold-out productions that had catered to millions of spectators. In this moment, Perry's message was clear: he has paid his dues. However, even more resounding than Perry's bravado was the unuttered yet unavoidable message that was being sent by the Broadway League and the American Theatre Wing by allowing Perry to present this award: he is one of *us*. Without a nomination or an award under his belt and, one can assume, just by virtue of his popularity and economic portfolio, Perry's theatre had managed to cross over without actually crossing over! What did this mean for African American theatre?

On its own, the 2011–12 Broadway season was an impressive year for African American performers and African American-based content on the Great White Way. It was no surprise then that the Tony Awards rewarded the caliber of work put forth by numerous African American artists by granting them nominations. Included among the list of celebrated African American actors that night were Philip Boykin, David Alan Grier, James Earl Jones, Norm Lewis, Audra MacDonald, Da'Vine Joy Randolph, and Condola Rashad (daughter of actress Phylicia Rashad). Of this list, MacDonald took home the prize for best performance by a leading actress in a play for her role as Bess in the musical/opera *Porgy and Bess*. *Porgy and Bess*, originally created by Jewish American brothers George and Ira Gershwin and first produced in 1935, also won the award for best revival of a musical. It should also be noted that the acclaimed African American playwright Suzan-Lori Parks served as the book adapter for this 2011 adaptation. Although not Black-authored, *Clybourne Park* (2010), written by white American playwright Bruce Norris, was also a big winner of the night, securing the award for best play. *Clybourne Park*'s significance lies in the fact that the play uses some of the characters, issues, and settings from Lorraine Hansberry's 1959 play *A Raisin in the Sun* as source material for a revamped plotline of competing discriminations set in 1959 and 2009. Reimagining the life of some of Hansberry's original characters, Norris expands Hansberry's original interest in race and class discrimination to include a consideration of prejudice writ large: racism, classism, sexism, homophobia, and bigotry. Also notable is the fact that white American actor Jeremy Shamos, who played two characters in Norris's version, received a nomination for best performance by a featured actor in a play, partially due to his performance as Karl Lindner, the unforgettable character from Hansberry's play who tried to discourage the Younger family from moving into his white Chicago neighborhood. In total, *Porgy and Bess* and *Clybourne Park* received fourteen nominations. Other African American-related productions to receive nominations that night included Lydia Diamond's *Stick Fly* (2008) and the musical adaptation of the iconic film *Ghost* (Jerry Zucker, 1990), entitled *Ghost the Musical* (2011).

With this kind of talent, innovation, and prestige on deck, what is the significance of Perry's transition from a producer, director, writer, and performer of insular Black gospel musicals that operated under the radar of Broadway and mainstream America, into his most recent position as the accepted representative of contemporary African American culture and Black entertainment? Could another "representative" of African American Theatre have handed Scott Rubin his award? Had the "popular" in theatre overwhelmed the "legitimate," so much so that the former could no longer be ignored?

Black Popular Culture: Insert [Theatre] Here

My reading of Perry's moment is less about the rise of the artist himself but is instead a reading of the rise of Black theatrical popular culture. To be more specific, what millions of televised viewers saw on that night at the Tonys was an unprecedented elevation of Black popular theatre that had come to existence within the DuBoisian parameters of for us, near us, by us, and about us,[27] yet had caused such increasing tremors in the halls of legitimate theatre and culture that it could no longer be ignored.

Granted, by 2012 Broadway theatre had long since become a mediatized cultural product. Although there are varying degrees and exceptions to this phenomenon, in general, the media had become the sustenance that commercial theatre largely relied on. Take, for example, the rise of celebrity casting on Broadway that was exemplified in the 2004–2005 New York theatre season. In unprecedented numbers, this season marked the beginning of a trend that Broadway has not turned away from: the casting of countless stars, popularly known for their television and film roles, within Broadway, Off-Broadway, and Off-Off-Broadway productions. In an article published on September 12, 2004, entitled "Woody, Whoopi, Miller, Mamet and Elvis," *New York Times* journalists Bruce Weber and Carol Coburn provided a snapshot of the forthcoming New York theatre season from the months of September through April that included cast, production, and play synopsis information. According to their list, media celebrities were taking part in a theatre production every single month of that year's season. In the month of September, for example, Frances Fisher, Matthew Modine, and Mary Louise Parker were all starring in leading roles. In October, Mario Cantone, the comedic actor who at the time was easily recognized for his recurring role in *Sex and the City* (HBO, 1998–2004) opened his own one-man show called *Laugh Whore*, and Matthew Broderick—coincidentally the husband of *Sex and the City*'s lead actress, Sarah Jessica Parker—starred in the Off-Broadway revival of Larry Shue's 1984 play *The Foreigner*. The following months saw many more of these *timely* and *relevant* celebrity appearances, such as Edie Falco of *The Sopranos* (HBO, 1999–2007), starring in Marsha Norman's original 1983 play *'Night Mother*, as well as Phylicia Rashad of *The Cosby Show* (NBC, 1984–92), starring alongside Lisa Gay Hamilton of *The Practice* (ABC, 1997–2004), in the Broadway debut of August Wilson's *Gem of the Ocean* (2003). To further the examples, in this same season, Billy Crystal performed in his own one-man show entitled *700 Sundays*, Jessica Lange played the role of Amanda Wingfield in Tennessee Williams's 1944 play *The Glass Menagerie*, and Christina Applegate held the lead role in the Broadway revival of the 1966 musical *Sweet Charity*.[28]

In fact, by March 2005, the phenomenon of having media stars headline theatre productions had become such a staple that even the *Wall Street Journal* had taken notice. In an article entitled "Broadway's New Deal: To Woo Celebrities, Theaters Offer Profit Slices, Time Outs; Pleasing Denzel and Delta," journalist Robert J. Hughes discussed the increasing ways in which celebrity stars were receiving lucrative packages from producers as enticements to star in Broadway productions. From the objectives of the producers, these celebrity packages, while costly, would almost guarantee increased ticket sales. Listed amongst the celebrity names I have already mentioned, this same season saw Kathleen Turner starring in Edward Albee's 1962 play *Who's Afraid of Virginia Woolf?*, Denzel Washington playing the title role in William Shakespeare's *Julius Caesar*, and Delta Burke, formerly of the television sitcom *Designing Women* (CBS, 1986–93), starring in the Broadway revival of Robert Hughes's 1987 play *Steel Magnolias*. Burke starred alongside actress Frances Sternhagen, who would be recognizable to *Sex and the City* fans, at the time, for her role as Bunny MacDougal, the mother of Charlotte York's (Kristin Davis) first husband, Trey MacDougal (Kyle MacLachlan).

These celebrity actors were only a few of many who signed on to productions with very hefty Broadway packages. According to Hughes, Broadway had adapted to its audience's identification with media celebrities to such an extent that these lucrative packages had gone from rare occurrences in the past for special stars (for example, Katharine Hepburn and Nicole Kidman were known to have received compensatory packages for their Broadway performances in 1969 and 1998, respectively) to "standard operating procedure" for almost every media actor.[29] Also worthy of mentioning, many New York City theatre producers and financial backers were crediting the 2003–2004 production of Hansberry's previously mentioned play *A Raisin in the Sun*, directed by the African American director Kenny Leon, with making the high-profile packages a Broadway staple. Leon's production cast the hip-hop celebrity producer Sean Combs as Walter Lee Younger, the prominent male character in the play. Combs reportedly received an undisclosed amount of the profits and, even with his cut, the show proved to be extremely profitable for all involved. Following the impressive financial success of Leon's *A Raisin in the Sun*, investors were more willing to cater to the whims of celebrities even if it meant cutting in on their own potential money just to broker the deal.[30] With regards to this, Hughes offered the following rationale:

> Theater producers' willingness to pay more to snare big names partly reflects the changing nature of the Broadway audience. This year, at least

half of ticket buyers will be from outside of the New York metropolitan area, up 21% from five years ago, according to the League of American Theatres and Producers. Because out-of-towners are less likely to know a local stage star, producers say, it's more important than ever to book movie and TV actors. This spring season, there will be at least 20 such celebrities, more than double the number of last spring.[31]

To be sure, from this season onwards, contemporary Broadway producers had begun to correlate celebrity appearances with packed theatre houses. As producer Robert Fox was quoted as saying, celebrity participation "makes people sit up and think about attending."[32]

I have recounted this more recent history to suggest that through his own self-fashioning as a self-made actor, writer, director, and producer—and as a result of his loyal fan base that supports him across theatre, film, and television platforms—Tyler Perry had made Broadway, the purveyor of legitimate American theatre, stand up and take notice. Keeping the historical traces that I have discussed in this chapter in mind, on June 10, 2012, popular African American theatre, as developed and produced by Tyler Perry, became the game-changer that directed yet another shift in American theatre and cultural entertainment. There in Harlem, on the Beacon Theatre stage, the deathly rupture that had caused America's entertainment divide between low and high cultured offerings during the mid-nineteenth-century Astor Place riot had come to a mend. The literary experimentation in form and aesthetics that had been valued in dramatic writing since the 1920s now had a Black musical theatre contender that could outsell the former's product in spite of artistic innovation, and stand on equal footing with the financial profits made by the popular, yet legitimized and largely white, musical theatre. Moreover, although damaging and dominant stereotypes find themselves to be ever present in Tyler Perry's theatrical, filmic, and television offerings, on that night in June, the fear of widening the circulation routes for these images paled in comparison to the financially motivated efforts to harness lucrative Black entertainment that catered to all-Black audiences à la the early twentieth-century efforts of Keith and Albee's TOBA-segregated Black vaudeville circuits.

Even more significant, and a point that cannot be overstated, as a historic moment, this welcoming of Tyler Perry into the fold meant that there was also at least some validation being given to his particular brand of theatre and his choice of audience. Performatively and presentationally different from the white-produced and -controlled minstrel images of the late nineteenth and early twentieth centuries that often depicted African Americans as dim-witted, buffoonish, and vulgar, among other negative characteristics,[33] Perry's contemporary African American images can be easily blamed for perpetuating some similar, yet contemporarily different, alleged African American traits. Undeniably, his productions have the propensity to circulate and/or reinforce notions that dangerously reduce African Americans to a non-exhaustive list of negatives that include: loud-talking, childlike, adulterous, greedy, abusive, violent, rude, delinquent, and sexually promiscuous. As Mel Watkins astutely points out in his biography of the early twentieth-century African American actor Lincoln Perry, better known as Stepin Fechit, whose comedic performances continue to be negatively critiqued: "Today's Black performers have vast options and still opt for routines or projects that are mired in either salacious or degrading stereotypes."[34] Without a doubt, Tyler Perry's products are guilty of Watkins's accusations and, as cultural scholar and critic Nelson George reminds us, in the twenty-first century, "[c]omedy and stereotypes go hand in hand."[35] However, complicating the matter is the fact that Perry's negative stereotypes are not limited to his comedic characters like Madea or Mr. Brown.

For example, the established format of Perry's gospel musical dramas create a theatrical narrative in which the comedic characters are often the secondary focus of the major plotline. Even within his "Madea"-titled plays, the large and feisty grandmother appears on stage only during opportune moments: she delivers her comedic lines, expresses her laughable take on life and religion, interacts with and pokes fun of the audience, and then leaves the scene. In all cases, the main and unfolding dramas within Perry's productions occur between non-comedic characters that are stereotyped in ways that are different than their comedic counterparts. In *Diary of A Mad Black Woman* (2001), for example, the play's main conflict is between the greedy, abusive, and wealthy husband Charles, Jr., and his wife, Helen. Helen suffers from such low self-esteem that in one non-comedic scene the audience sees her get down on all fours and bark like a dog obediently, after being ordered to do so by her husband. In his 2008 play, *The Marriage Counselor*, in which neither Madea or Mr. Brown are characters, we see an educated materialistic wife have an adulterous affair with an ex-boyfriend because he is a professional basketball player and able to buy things her hard-working, simple, and pious husband cannot afford. She soon finds out that her lover mentally and physically abuses women after she becomes his latest victim. As Patricia Hill Collins would say, problematic and controlling images such as Perry's are part and parcel of the "racist and sexist ideologies [that have] permeate[d] the social structure to such a degree that they become hegemonic, namely, seen as natural, normal, and inevitable."[36] Boldly stated, regardless of comedic intent, Perry's theatre falls victim to the subordination of not only the African American image writ large, but chiefly the continued oppression of African American women through such damaging representations.

It should be unsurprising then, that with the advent of Perry's films, many African American critics have made reference to the class-based and negative portrayals of African Americans presented therein. Some then use this reading to make assumptions about the kind and quality of people who attend Perry's work and how the viewing pleasure of this group is derived. For example, in the same 2009 article—"How Do You Solve A Problem Like Madea?"—from which I took the above Nelson George quote, critical studies scholar Todd Boyd opines: "Tyler Perry is simply reflecting the thinking of a lot of uneducated, working-class African Americans." On the other hand, in an extended quote, George attributes Perry's success to his being able to speak to "the most ignored group in Hollywood," African American women, and then explains:

> You could see these films as parables or fables. There's a Black prince figure who shows up for Black women who've been frustrated, unhappy, or abused ... Tyler Perry speaks to a constituency that is not cool ... There's nothing cutting edge about the people who like Tyler Perry. So for a lot of people, it's like, "What is this thing that's representing Black people all over the world? I don't like it. It doesn't represent me."[37]

Statements like Boyd's and George's are similar to the assessment African American theatre practitioners have publicly voiced about Perry's theatrical spectators.

In 2006, the BET (Black Entertainment Television) network dedicated an entire show to the controversy enveloping Perry's theatre, as part of its now-canceled weekly news show *The Chop Up* (BET, 2006–2007).

Entitled "The New Minstrel Show," the episode took television audiences to the site of the 2005 National Black Theater Festival (NBT), held in Winston-Salem, North Carolina. There, the show's producers collected comments from a multitude of Black theatre artists, educators, and entrepreneurs with regards to the popularity of Perry's plays. Highlighted on the episode were the comments received from late NBT founder, producer, and artistic director Larry Leon Hamlin, actor Malcolm-Jamal Warner (made famous by his role as Bill Cosby's son Theo on *The Cosby Show*), and performance artist Daniel Beaty. Taken from these interviews, the following excerpted quotes represent their views on Perry's theatre and his spectators:

LARRY LEON HAMLIN: There are people who like that and that's fine, but then there are other people who really just like quality theatre of excellence and that's what we offer ... If we look at the profile of those people that attend those productions, I think it's very easily understood. It's the intellect.

MALCOLM-JAMAL WARNER: I would really hate for it to come to the point where Tyler Perry type plays become the new Black theatre standard.

DANIEL BEATY: There are definitely things in it, you know, that are kind of lowbrow.[38]

Later in the show, Perry is seen giving this response to an unspecified comment:

I think traditional Black theatre is suffering because of comments like that one. What makes the people that go to your shows better than the people who go to mine? I don't understand that ... It's insulting on so many levels to, not just me, but to the millions of Black, the hard-working folk, that want to go out and laugh and have a good time. It's insulting to them as well. So until they start to acknowledge those people and welcome them, then there will be this problem.[39]

From George to Boyd to Hamlin to Warner and then to Beaty, the above quotes exemplify the disdain for Perry's work by practitioners and critics of African American performance and cultural production who consider Perry's work to be substandard. Yet, no matter the points of contention, Perry's defense of his work continues to rest in the never-before-seen theatre audience numbers and box-office film receipts that mark his successful ability to please "millions" of fans. These fans who—like many of the early Black vaudevillian performers, performances, and spectators—were seen as popular yet unfit, at least until the night of June 10, 2012, perhaps, when the strength of their buying power stood front, centered, and embodied by Perry.

Indeed, the strength of contemporary "Chitlin Circuit" theatre is that it has continued to thrive despite its imperfections and marginalization due to the demands of its audiences and the attuned supply of its practitioners. Through the unprecedented and unexpected success of the contemporary "Chitlin Circuit," the marginalized experiences and interests of an ignored segment of America's Black citizens have emerged and broken through the barriers of recognition. Although a substantial amount of attention has been paid to the formation, content, and circulation of Black popular culture within local, national, and global frameworks, these considerations most often focus on how it is expressed primarily through the mediums of film, television, music, visual arts, and print.[40] Glaringly, Black and/or African American theatre are rarely invited a seat at the table of these discussions.[41]

Yet, as I stated in the beginning of this chapter, the contemporary "Chitlin Circuit" theatre, as produced by Perry and his peers, stands alone as a Black theatrical form that has managed to secure a prominent position in mainstream America, despite the fact that it is created and maintained by African American popular culture interests. Like numerous media and cultural studies scholars, such as Herbert J. Gans, Lawrence W. Levine, and Peter Stallybrass and Allon White, have respectively asserted: the content, appeal, and longevity of popular culture forms should be recognized as inherently political exactly because of the ways in which they produce pleasure for citizens whose interests lie outside of the dominant cultural order.[42] Moreover, African American studies scholar Richard Iton reminds us that the "political legitimacy" of the popular lies in the fact that it is able to "render the invisible visible," the "unheard audible," "the invisible audible," and the "unheard visible."[43] Unsurprisingly, then, the circuit's popularity should be recognized as having far-reaching implications well beyond the terrains of theatre.

While the ramifications of Perry's participation in this symbolic and historic event that lauded a remarkable season of Black Broadway achievement have yet to be seen, I contend that this night should be remembered as a historical marker as well as a historical triumph. As the events of June 10, 2012, unfolded, American theatre was once again contending with a changing aesthetic world. Stuart Hall reminds us that the "role of the 'popular' in popular culture is to fix the authenticity of popular forms, rooting them in the experiences of popular communities from which they draw their strength, allowing us to see them as expressive of a particular subordinate social life that resists its being constantly made over as low and outside."[44] On that night, Black and popular African American theatre was granted recognition by the "legitimate" American theatre world. And of even greater import, in spite of the grievances that will continue to be applied to their tastes and preferences, the entertainment interests of a marginalized segment of African Americans moved from the margins to center stage. Tyler Perry, perhaps the most unlikely representative of African American theatre, stood in as the bridge across this long-standing theatrical divide.

Notes

1. Larry Stempel, *Showtime: A History of The Broadway Musical Theater* (New York: W. W. Norton & Company, 2010), 28–31.

2. Ibid., 33.

3. Ibid.

4. For more history on the segregated Black routes of early twentieth-century American vaudeville theatre, see Henry Louis Gates, Jr., "Dept. of Disputation," *New Yorker*, February 3, 1997, 44–55; Errol Hill and James Hatch, *A History of African American Theatre* (New York: Cambridge University Press, 2003).

5. On any given night, performers presented an array of small shows in no particular order. These shows were unrelated in form, content, style, and performance quality. For more information, see Robert W. Snyder, "The Vaudeville Circuit: A Prehistory of the Mass Audience," in *Audiencemaking: How the Media Create the Audience*, ed. James S. Ettema and D. Charles Whitney (Thousand Oaks, CA: Sage, 1994), 215–31; Robert Butsch, *The Making of American Audiences: From Stage to Television, 1750–1990* (New York: Cambridge University Press, 2001).

6. Amiri Baraka, "Soul Food," in *Home: Social Essays* (New York: William Morrow & Co., 1996), 102.

7. Snyder, "The Vaudeville Circuit," 222.

8. Ibid., 228.

9. According to Butsch, Variety Theatre was most popular during the early to mid-nineteenth century. On any given night, Variety Theatre performers would perform an array of small shows—in no particular order—that were all unrelated in form, content, style, and performance quality. The venues that house Variety shows ranged from saloons and music halls to middle- and upper-class society theatres. See Butsch, *The Making of American Audiences*, 95.

10. Butsch also discusses the existence of theatre houses during this time that catered to middle- and upper-class clientele who were interested in seeing melodrama. Plays such as *Richard III*, *Uncle Tom's Cabin*, and *Macbeth* were also popular productions on these stages. Museums also created museum theatres during this time, which also became popular venues for these melodramatic productions, often catering to largely middle and upper class female audiences. See Butsch, *The Making of American Audiences*, 69, 72, 81.

11. David Krasner, *A Beautiful Pageant: African American Theatre, Drama, and Performance in the Harlem Renaissance, 1910–1927* (New York: Palgrave MacMillan, 2002), 272.

12. Ibid., 273.

13. Hill and Hatch, *A History of African American Theatre*, 206.

14. Krasner, *A Beautiful Pageant*, 274–75.

15. Ibid., 275.

16. David Savran, "Toward a Historiography of the Popular," *Theatre Survey* 45.2 (2004): 212.

17. For more information on the history of Black musical theatre within an American context, see Warren Burdine, "Let the Theatre Say 'Amen,'" *Black American Literature Forum* 25.1 (1991): 73–82; Warren Burdine, "The Gospel Musical and its Place in the Black American Theatre," in *A Sourcebook of African American Performance: Plays: People, Movements*, ed. Annmarie Bean (New York: Routledge, 1999), 190–203.

18. Savran, "Toward a Historiography of the Popular," 214.

19. The 1986–87 season also marked a notable moment in Black theatre for New York's Off-Broadway circuit as the Negro Ensemble Company marked its twentieth season with a production of Leslie Lee's *The War Party*, while the Public Theater produced George C. Wolfe's *The Colored Museum*. See Mel Gussow, "Season Preview: Theater; Neil Simon, Arthur Miller, and a David Hare Musical," *New York Times*, September 7, 1986, sec. 2.

20. Jerard Gerard, "Broadway is offering Black Theatergoers more reasons to go," *New York Times*, March 29, 1988, sec. C: C13.

21. Ibid.

22. Ibid.

23. Ibid.

24. Jerard Gerard, "Despite Praise, 'Turner' May Be Forced to Close," *New York Times*, April 21, 1988, sec. C.

25. Ibid.

26. "Five Broadway Shows to Close," *New York Times*, June 24, 1988, sec. C.

27. W. E. B. Du Bois, "Krigwa Players Little Negro Theatre," *Crisis* 32.3 (1926): 134.

28. Bruce Weber and Carol Coburn, "Woody, Whoopi, Miller, Mamet and Elvis," *New York Times*, September 12, 2004, sec. 2, col. 2.

29. Robert J. Hughes, "Broadway's New Deal: To Woo Celebrities, Theaters Offer Profit Slices, Time Outs: Pleasing Denzel and Delta," *Wall Street Journal*, March 11, 2005, W1.

30. Ibid.

31. Ibid.

32. Ibid.

33. There are numerous books that discuss the performances and damaging representations contained within turn-of-the-century American minstrelsy. Notable sources include Eric Lott, *Love and Theft: Blackface Minstrelsy and the American Working-Class* (New York: Oxford University Press, 1993); Annmarie Bean, "Blackface Minstrelsy and Double Inversion, Circa 1890," in *African American Performance and Theater History*, eds. Harry J. Elam, Jr., and David Krasner (New York: Oxford University Press, 2001), 171–90.

34. Mel Watkins, *Stepin Fechit: The Life and Times of Lincoln Perry* (Westminster: Knopf, 2005), 289.

35. Benjamin Svetkey, Margeaux Watson, and Alynda Wheat, "How Do You Solve a Problem Like Madea?" *Entertainment Weekly*, March 20, 2009, 27.

36. Patricia Hill Collins, *Black Feminist Thought* (New York: Routledge, 2000), 5.

37. Svetkey, Watson, and Wheat, "How Do You Solve a Problem Like Madea?" 23.

38. *The Chop Up: The New Minstrel Show*, Black Entertainment Television, August 20, 2006.

39. Ibid.

40. As examples, see Harry J. Elam, Jr., and Kennell Jackson, eds., *Black Cultural Traffic: Crossroads in Global Performance and Popular Culture* (Ann Arbor: University of Michigan Press, 2005); Gina Dent, ed., *Black Popular Culture: A Project by Michele Wallace* (New York: The New Press, 1998).

41. I should note that a rare exception to this occurrence appears in the *Black Cultural Traffic* publication. See Catherine Cole, "When is African Theater 'Black'?" in *Black Cultural Traffic: Crossroads in Global Performance and Popular Culture*, eds. Harry J. Elam, Jr., and Kennell Jackson (Ann Arbor: University of Michigan Press, 2005), 43–58.

42. Herbert J. Gans, *Popular Culture and High Culture: An Analysis and Evaluation of Taste* (New York: Basic Books, 1999); Lawrence W. Levine, *Black Culture and Black Consciousness: Afro-American Folk Thought from Slavery to Freedom* (New York: Oxford University Press, 1978); Peter Stallybrass and Allon White, *The Politics and Poetics of Transgression* (Ithaca: Cornell University Press, 1986).

43. Richard Iton, *In Search of the Black Fantastic: Politics and Popular Culture in the Post-Civil Rights Era* (New York: Oxford University Press, 2008), 19.

44. Stuart Hall, "What is this 'Black' in Black Popular Culture?" in *Black Popular Culture: A Project by Michele Wallace*, ed. Gina Dent (New York: The New Press, 1988), 26.

CHAPTER THREE

Tyler Perry, T.D. Jakes, and the Birth of Gospel Cinema
—Keith Corson

The box-office success of Tyler Perry's first foray into film, *Diary of a Mad Black Woman* (Darren Grant, 2005), was understood on two levels upon its release. For the mainstream media, it was a complete surprise, with *Diary of a Mad Black Woman* debuting as the top-grossing domestic film in its opening weekend despite having a small budget, limited formal advertising, and playing on only half of the screens allotted for most wide national releases. Adding to the surprise was the fact that the film lacked a bankable star, with Tyler Perry being an unknown quantity to mainstream America in 2005. For the core audience that had supported Perry's stage productions, however, the success of his first feature film must have seemed inevitable. On the strength of his name alone, Perry had been able to stage wildly successful touring plays and, by 2002, he successfully expanded into the home video market by self-distributing filmed versions of his theatre productions.

It was only logical that Perry would not only transition to making full-fledged narrative films but also that he would find success. The continued success of Perry's films confound critics and defy the growing globalized focus of the film industry as well as Hollywood's preference for multiethnic casting, using African Americans as part of a (largely white) ensemble rather than making films set within predominantly Black communities. Since the late 1990s, feature films primarily geared toward African American spectators have largely been pushed to the margins of low-budget, direct-to-DVD releases, which makes the ascendance of Perry all the more noteworthy when placed in the broader context of the contemporary film industry. Perry joins televangelist T.D. Jakes in reshaping popular Black-focused cinema; both produce films primarily imbued with Christian morality that are geared toward

African American women. One-time collaborators and would-be competitors, Perry and Jakes function as two sides of the same coin, with the former being a secular entertainer infusing his films with religious messages, and the latter using secular tropes to help make his sermons more palatable. Regardless of their differing approaches, Perry and Jakes have played crucial roles in the development of the "gospel cinema" movement. The term "gospel," of course, is complex and has many different usages. The gospel, or the sharing of the "good news" of Christ, is a term that often moves beyond simple reference to the New Testament (i.e., the gospel of Matthew, Mark, Luke, or John) to denote style, particularly in terms of music. As such, the term carries with it a cultural designation based on the legacy of gospel music, which is tied to African American religious tradition. My use of the term builds off this cultural connotation, mobilizing gospel cinema not only as a textual extension of gospel theatre and gospel music, but also as a designation of space and social practice such as the "Full Gospel" church and its participatory services.

In terms of theatrical distribution, the films of Perry, Jakes, and a handful of followers have become the primary model for a financially viable Black-focused cinema. This movement, which I label "gospel cinema," is informed both by the structure and sensibilities of the Black church, providing a social experience aimed primarily at a Black female audience. Much like gospel music, the film movement is rooted in Christian values and communities, often with blurred lines between religiosity and entertainment.[1] However, gospel cinema can be defined apart from its religious elements and understood instead through its audience and aesthetic orientation, with filmgoing meant to be an interactive and communal experience with room for participation built into the narrative. This chapter will place the rise of gospel cinema within the context of African American film history, finding points of connection with previous cycles of Black-focused production while considering the unique nature of gospel cinema in terms of its aesthetics, politics, business strategy, and target audience. The central question, then, is whether gospel cinema provides a model for the future or if it is simply the current iteration of the short-lived production cycles that have defined Black-focused film.

Beginning with the handful of Black-cast musicals that were released with the coming of sound in the late 1920s, Hollywood's interest in creating features populated primarily by African American performers has been intermittent. The ebb and flow of Hollywood production cycles of Black-focused film and the willful neglect of Black spectators has defined African American cinema. This has been countered by independent voices that include race film producers from the 1910s to the 1950s, the LA Rebellion in the 1970s, Spike Lee in the 1980s and beyond, and a growing number of direct-to-video productions over the past two decades. The few concentrated upsurges in the production of Black-focused film—namely, Blaxploitation in the 1970s, and "hood" and "buppie" films in the 1990s—have been exceptions to Hollywood's preferred methods of imagining blackness on screen. Stars like Sidney Poitier, Richard Pryor, Eddie Murphy, Whoopi Goldberg, Denzel Washington, and Will Smith have fit the bill for prominent Black performers who largely exist in narrative worlds otherwise bereft of a Black community, functioning as stand-ins for the Black experience both on screen and in the marketplace.

More typically, Hollywood has utilized its own brand of tokenism to create the façade of diversity. Tyler Perry's small role in the summer blockbuster *Star Trek* (J. J. Abrams, 2009) can be viewed, on the surface at least, as yet another iteration of Hollywood's shift toward multiethnic casting. Whether seen as an extension of a liberal consciousness that hopes to convey a sense of racial and cultural multiplicity or a more cynical financial consideration of studios and producers hoping to attract the widest possible audience, the diversifying of ensemble casts in Hollywood's biggest budgeted productions has been a hallmark of the post-civil rights era, evidenced in films including *The Towering Inferno* (John Guillermin, 1974), *The Empire Strikes Back* (Irvin Kershner, 1980), *Independence Day* (Roland Emmerich, 1996), and *The Avengers* (Joss Whedon, 2012). The oddity of seeing Perry outside of the comfortable confines of his own production is particularly striking because, unlike so many African American film stars, his screen persona is rooted in diegetic worlds where blackness is the norm and not the exception.

With this history in mind, what can we make of Tyler Perry? Is he an independent voice working outside of the system? Is he part of a broader cycle of Black-focused film? Or is he another example of a standalone star meant to single-handedly represent the Black experience for Hollywood? Paradoxically, Perry represents all three. Discussions of Perry's career have been largely fixated on his personal biography, issues of representation, and questions about his sexual identity, with each point of engagement dictated by one's taste for his work. His admirers look at Perry's work as a point of inspiration, with his rags-to-riches story being a real-life embodiment of a Horatio Alger myth and his films a natural extension of his own personal and spiritual transformation. His harshest detractors—most famously Spike Lee—find Perry's work to be retrograde and riddled with broad stereotypes, rehashing the rhetoric of positive and negative representation that is largely tone-deaf to the complexities and layered meanings of performance traditions. The middle ground includes those who are not completely dismissive of Perry yet fall outside of his base of support, tending to look toward his sexuality as a way of explaining his films and plays and questioning the motives for his cross-dressing performances as Madea, camp aesthetic, and the choice of "women's pictures" as his milieu. The latter is perhaps the most nuanced yet problematic approach, asking serious questions and critically engaging his texts while also putting Perry in the unfortunate position of having to explain his personal life in order to justify his creative decisions.[2] What all of these approaches lack is a way of placing his work within the context of a broader social, cultural, and economic landscape that explores why he has found success and what his continued impact may be in the coming years. By looking at Perry through the framework of a broader movement, specifically gospel cinema, I engage with the shifting modalities and practices of African American cinema.

For the terminology of this film movement, I am drawing on gospel theatre—the stage movement that began in the early 1990s and in which Tyler Perry became a key figure. Playing along the lines of the "Chitlin' Circuit" (a term popularly modernized to "urban circuit"), gospel theatre has operated outside of the norms of traditional Broadway-based theatre, staging productions through limited runs in cities like Atlanta, Houston, and Washington, DC. Playwrights such as Shelly Garrett and David E. Talbert helped pave the way for Perry, establishing the thematic hallmarks and built-in regional audiences that came to define gospel theatre and, later, gospel cinema.[3] The rise of gospel theatre both reflected and contradicted theatrical trends. On one hand, it was a logical stand-in for the demise of Black theatre companies that had developed in the late 1960s and early 1970s (the New Lafayette Theatre, the

Negro Ensemble Company, etc.), with their disappearance and limited opportunities for Black playwrights on or off Broadway in the 1980s obscured by the successes of August Wilson and Charles Fuller. On the other hand, the arrival of Black female writers such as Anna Deavere Smith, Suzan-Lori Parks, and Robbie McCauley made the logic of a women's theatre movement located outside of the artistic establishment somewhat curious, if not problematic. But the appeal of gospel theatre has not simply been located in Black women's desire for texts that speak directly to their experiences. Instead, it is reflective of geographic, aesthetic, and cultural differences rather than common misconceptions of a singular, monolithic "Black community."

Regardless of the shifting gender dynamics of New York-based theatre, the fact remains that regional theatre has been able to remain popular and financially solvent, while the critically lauded work of Parks, Smith, and McCauley have been commercially marginalized, with each writer dependent on grant funding and working outside of the theatre to make their living.[4] What gospel theatre offers is a less intellectualized product that speaks toward female experiences through a decidedly Christian, yet largely depoliticized, lens. Here is a movement that is keenly aware of its audience and is crafted to suit their needs, creating a synthesis between author and audience in terms of expectations and desires. From the standpoint of being a lasting cultural institution, its ability to thrive without the approval of established theatre critics and tastemakers offers an independence that is financial, aesthetic, and ideological. Of course, this idea of making a "critic proof" movement has been central to the success of Tyler Perry and gospel cinema.

Perry entered the landscape of gospel theatre in 1998 with his first play, *I Know I've Been Changed*, which opened in Atlanta before being booked across the urban circuit.[5] Reflecting the Christian self-help ethos that is now familiar in Perry's work, *I Know I've Been Changed* set the foundation for the narrative formula of female protagonists finding redemption and overcoming trauma. Perry's own trauma, including sexual abuse as a child, is reflected in his writing, although much of his experience is transferred to female characters. Instead of looking at Perry's preoccupation with female characters or his stylistic excesses as an indicator of his sexuality—an approach informed by film directors like George Cukor and Vincente Minnelli—Perry's female focus is largely a byproduct of concurrent trends in self-help and spirituality. Perry credits the role of his personal faith in Christ alongside the influence of Oprah Winfrey and daytime television's promotion of self-help authors.[6] In turn, the rise of Black televangelists and the megachurches of pastors like Creflo Dollar and T.D. Jakes has brought about a fusion of Christianity and secular, self-help rhetoric, with Tyler Perry's work both reflecting and promoting this shifting theology.

Following the success of *I Know I've Been Changed*, Perry worked with T.D. Jakes to help translate the preacher's series of spiritual and personal empowerment workshops, *Woman Thou Art Loosed*, into a stage play. Perry has been credited as the director for the stage production, with Jakes as the presumable author of the novel on which the play is based.[7] However, with his large body of writing and other creative forays, Jakes is presumed to rely on ghostwriters for most of his efforts, cultivating his brand and building bridges to and from his megachurch, suburban Dallas's Potter House.[8] Jakes uses his books, plays, and movies to help promote his church, while at the same time he can rely on his congregants in Dallas and those watching him on television to support each endeavor. Whether or not Perry played a greater role in the creation of the novel or stage play for *Woman Thou Art Loosed* is an open question, but the formal and thematic similarities with Perry's oeuvre seem to suggest that his contributions outweighed simply directing the touring stage production. In fact, Perry's own official biography refers to the process vaguely as a "collaboration" with Jakes, eschewing a clear sense of authorship.[9]

Over the next few years, Jakes used the success of *Woman Thou Art Loosed* to expand the reach of his church and develop a multimedia platform for his teachings. Perry, on the other hand, returned to his own original plays and introduced the character of Madea in his 2000 production of *I Can Do Bad All by Myself*. Perry's success, spurred by the popularity of his Madea character, began to outpace the limitations of the urban circuit. Capitalizing on the growing interest and demand to see his plays, Perry began releasing rudimentary filmed versions of his stage plays directly to home video. These "canned theatre" productions may have lacked the interactivity and vitality of a live show, as well as the production values and pacing of traditional narrative filmmaking, but the growing demand for anything Perry was releasing, especially if it featured his Madea character, helped sell DVDs and, in turn, functioned as a form of promotion for his touring stage plays. All of these factors worked together to expand his audience reach. Perry began to receive sporadic national attention, including appearances on *The Oprah Winfrey Show* (ABC, 1986–2011), but his celebrity remained relegated to his core audience that supported the urban theatre circuit and the limited number of customers who consume direct-to-video products. The leap to feature filmmaking was Perry's next step. However, T.D. Jakes adapted his stage play before Perry had a chance to be the first to find out if the style and tropes of gospel theatre could be successfully translated into a feature film.

From Stage to Screen

While Perry was busy laying the foundation for turning his Madea character into a media empire, T.D. Jakes was producing a feature film adaption of his stage play *Woman Thou Art Loosed* (Michael Schultz, 2004). The narrative reflects the Potter House's mission. Part secular self-help, part evangelical soul saving, Jakes's ministry pays special attention to the plight of women. Giving voice to issues such as spousal abuse, the trials of single parenthood, and patriarchal control, Jakes preaches that through accepting Christ a woman can find herself "loosed" from all of her burdens, free to find happiness and fulfillment. Jakes, one in a long line of prosperity preachers (dating back in popular consciousness to Oral Roberts), takes a different approach to redemption. Rather than heavenly rewards being rooted in the afterlife, his preaching puts forth the concept that a good Christian can expect a return on their investment of faith in this life.[10] Within the span of ten years, Jakes had worked his way up from being a country preacher in West Virginia ministering to a few dozen congregants to a nationally recognized preacher, overseeing a megachurch and a multimillion-dollar faith-based corporation and appearing on the cover of *Time* magazine in 2001 with the headline: "Is this man the next Billy Graham?"[11] Jakes has expanded his preaching into the realm of television, self-help books, music, and theatre, not to mention the lucrative retreats, revivals, and conventions on which his ministry business was founded. *Woman Thou Art Loosed* was designed to expand Jakes's reach into the multiplex.

Directed by Michael Schultz, a prolific Black director, the film adheres to many of the themes and sensibilities of gospel theatre, focusing on realistic performance and a reserved tone that has not been replicated by Perry. It can be accurately stated that the story belongs to Jakes (or Perry and any other un-credited collaborators) while the mood and tone belong to Schultz, a veteran film director with a stage background in the sort of high-art theatre that Perry and Jakes eschew.[12] On the surface, Schultz was an odd choice to realize the arrival of gospel cinema. Directing Richard Pryor in *Car Wash* (1976) and *Which Way Is Up?* (1977), Schultz had created two of the most loathsome screen versions of money-hungry preachers, modeled on the infamous Black prosperity preacher Rev Ike. Now, with Jakes, Schultz was essentially a co-conspirator in putting forth a prosperity doctrine that has often been cited as disingenuous and exploitative of his congregants (who, not coincidentally, are referred to as "customers" on the Potter's House website).[13] Yet Schultz, who was ambivalent about Jakes's sincerity and financial motivation, found a way to combine his own sensibilities within the framework of the ministerial narrative by focusing on the female protagonist rather than the dogmatic monologues of Jakes (who plays himself in the film).[14] Jakes had been targeting female congregants for years. With *Woman Thou Art Loosed*, he provided a venue in which serious issues concerning Black women, a group historically underrepresented in film, would be given voice on screen.

This negotiation between the faith-based Jakes and the more secular Schultz may have played a role in how *Woman Thou Art Loosed* functioned textually; but as far as establishing itself within the framework of exhibition and promotion, the film was primarily considered as a religious entity, one of the first mainstream Christian features targeted toward African Americans.[15] Previous films like *The Preacher's Wife* (Penny Marshall, 1996) and *The Fighting Temptations* (Jonathan Lynn, 2003) use the church more as an incidental setting than an extension of a defined doctrine. By the time it was released in 2004, however, the Christian feature film was fast becoming a major niche market, supported by Protestant strongholds throughout the south and the Midwest. Films like *The Omega Code* (Robert Marcarelli, 1999) and *Left Behind* (Vic Sarin, 2001) had succeeded via independent distribution, modest budgets, and an audience that was primarily cultivated through word of mouth and in-church promotion rather than traditional advertising.[16] While the Christian market had previously been reached through low-budget mail-order video releases and TV movies produced for Christian networks, the success of *The Omega Code* showed that Christian-themed films could reach an audience on par with secular releases. Earning $370 million domestically, it was the runaway success of *The Passion of the Christ* (Mel Gibson, 2004) that prioritized the Christian marketplace in Hollywood.[17]

Following the success of *The Passion of the Christ*, a number of studios began to take on Christian films and even start film divisions, such as Fox Faith, specializing in reaching an evangelical consumer base. Following a broader cultural segmentation, evangelicals became more forthright in creating a self-contained social and media environment that muted dissenting opinion. Christian films, in turn, have been promoted as an autonomous substitute to mainstream cinema. Films like the Mormon-focused *States of Grace* (Richard Dutcher, 2005) have used modest budgets in hopes of cornering their limited market, while others have used a nondenominational approach to reach a broader Christian audience. Alex Kendrick, the most successful director of evangelical-leaning films, has had a run of hits including *Facing the Giants* (2006), *Fireproof* (2008), and *Courageous* (2011), benefitting from ministers urging their congregations to support his films at the box office during Sunday sermons. Receiving similar endorsements from the pulpit, Tyler Perry's films have far exceeded Kendrick's in terms of visibility and box-office gross.

Of course, there are key structural and ideological differences between evangelical films, Gibson's standalone success with *The Passion of the Christ*, and the gospel cinema movement I am exploring. On the one hand, the evangelical films are an extension of the political rhetoric of the religious right, with a predetermined audience accustomed to a self-contained media experience directly catering to their viewpoint, be it through the Christian Broadcasting Network (CBN) or Contemporary Christian radio formats. On the other hand, *The Passion of the Christ* was embraced by evangelicals, Catholics, and other denominations for its religious message, but the film was just as notable for being Gibson's first directorial effort since *Braveheart* (1995) won an Academy Award for Best Picture. Nevertheless, both Gibson's success and the continued presence of evangelical films played a key role in convincing studios to not only finance projects with religious themes but also look toward neglected audiences in the "Bible Belt." Gospel cinema, I contend, lacks the political infrastructure of white Christian films and the crossover ambition of studio forays into faith-based cinema. Instead, it relies on independent financing, grassroots promotion, brand loyalty, and Black audiences.

On screen, the ideological and liturgical divisions between Black and white Christians are manifest in their cinematic offerings. Rather than attempting to speak to and for everyone, gospel cinema is consciously crafted around the expectations and social practices of its primarily Black female audience. White Christian films provided a model for theatrical success through religious and not racial (read Black) and social identification. For gospel cinema, the faith-based model of evangelical filmmaking has informed modes of promotion and distribution, but filmmakers like Perry and Jakes have placed moments of religious didacticism within a largely secular framework. Instead of taking a confrontational or morally absolutist approach, gospel cinema promotes Christian ideology in small doses, focusing on recreating the social space of the "Black Church" rather than espousing scriptural lessons. *Woman Thou Art Loosed* is the initial iteration of the movement and not the prototype, largely because gospel cinema is defined by its audience as much as any formal or narrative conventions.

Released by art-house distributor Magnolia Pictures, *Woman Thou Art Loosed* found modest success at the box office in limited release, grossing $6.8 million while maxing out at 521 screens (wide releases typically play on 3,000 or more screens).[18] For a small release, the box-office performance was solid if not remarkable, but *Woman Thou Art Loosed* did not indicate that it was the beginning of the next major trend in African American cinema. The film struggled to identify and categorize itself within a specific genre. Was it a religious film? Was it a melodrama? Was it both? The prominent use of T.D. Jakes's name seemed to suggest so, but aside from those familiar with Jakes and the vaguely spiritual tone of its title there were few other outward markers of it being a Christian film (at least in terms of promotion). Was it an African American art-house release? Distributed by Magnolia, who operate a prominent art-house theatre chain, the film also made the rounds of film festivals, winning Best American Film at the Santa Barbara Film Festival. At the same time, the producers of the film crafted it as popular entertainment, even if it lacked star power or the level of distribution associated with mainstream releases. To critics and industry observers in 2004, *Woman Thou Art Loosed* read like a curious attempt rather than a sign of things to come, which helped color the response to *Diary of a Mad Black Woman* when it was released just a few months later and promptly became the number one film in the country. With both films being about women and starring Kimberly Elise, there is little on the surface to differentiate the two productions for most critics. The biggest difference between *Woman Thou Art Loosed* and *Diary of a Mad Woman*—one that critics underestimated through their lack of familiarity with the urban theatre circuit—was the power of Tyler Perry's name.

Tyler Perry's Appeal

Although his films stray more toward the secular than T.D. Jakes, it is impossible to separate the spiritual elements of Perry's films from any analysis of his work. From biblical references to setting key scenes within the confines of the neighborhood church, Perry's narratives are often dictated by overarching Christian ideals even when they are not being explicitly related to scripture. Even *Good Deeds* (Tyler Perry, 2012), which does not involve the prerequisite trip to church or any prolonged dialogue about the Bible, can be read as a fable of Christian charity. The neighborhood church is often prefigured as a central community space in Perry's films. Perry attempts to bridge class and geographic space through ideas of family and shared responsibility for everyone in the community, with Madea representing a neighborhood matriarch whose responsibilities often transfer to those with whom she shares no blood relation. Yet Madea also problematizes a solely faith-based reading of his films, especially since she is not a churchgoer and often exhibits transgressive values that are at odds with the values of the church. The actions and perspective of Madea notwithstanding, Perry's films posit the idea of a Black community in need of points of connection, with the church often filling that need. Moreover, as small neighborhood churches struggle to keep up with the commuter draw of suburban megachurches, the multiplex theatre can be viewed as an extension of the Black church. On the opening weekend of Perry films, his stories bring together a dispersed community for a shared experience that engenders a sense of belonging.

Perry's initial breakthrough in feature films with *Diary of a Mad Black Woman* is less remarkable than his continued success and ability to gain power in the film industry. Rather than a star-for-hire or a director constantly in search of financing and distribution, Perry is one of the few African American film artists to find success outside of Hollywood while remaining largely autonomous.[19] He chooses his own projects and has access to major distribution without being beholden to executives, focus groups, or many of the other studio machinations that frustrate directors. Perry's model of small budgets, little need for advertising, and steady profits has afforded him the luxury to not only choose what projects he directs, but also to decide when and how they should be released. Part of Perry's formula for success is dependent on the films themselves, which are unique in terms of tone and content. There have been attempts to borrow from his aesthetics and marketing strategies, but the success of Perry turning himself into a distinctive brand has brought with it a loyal following that has not consistently translated to other Black-focused features. At the same time, Perry as a producer (one of his many hyphenates) has been careful in how he situates his films within the broader spectrum of the film industry, cultivating a need for his films and functioning as a counterbalance to mainstream releases. Thus, Perry has found synergy between Black content and business strategy. Only recently, as he has attempted to deviate from this formula, has Perry struggled to maintain his Midas touch.

As much as Perry and the rise of gospel cinema has been associated with narrative style and ideology, it can also be understood through its engagement with Black audiences and the development of a new business model for Black producers. In a climate that is increasingly focused on big-budget features and a broad audience with global box-office appeal, Perry has managed to chart a new course that not only survives without foreign box office, but also shuns notions of what a profitable target audience looks like. While the two most prominent Black-focused production cycles—Blaxploitation in the 1970s and "hood" films in the 1990s—were primarily geared toward young men, and actors such as Sidney Poitier, Eddie Murphy, and Will Smith became crossover stars,

Perry's films star Black women, and his audience is primarily female, Black, and older than the 12-to-24 year-olds most often targeted by Hollywood. Exit surveys for *Diary of a Mad Black Woman* showed that 58 percent of the audiences for the film were Black women over thirty-five, a demographic that has remained consistent for his films through 2012.[20] Internationally, Perry's films have followed the longstanding logic (or lack thereof) regarding Black-starring productions, bypassing foreign box office, with South Africa being the only country where Perry's films receive consistent theatrical distribution.[21] That Perry has a narrowly defined audience is not unique when placed within the broader media landscape, but unlike modestly distributed "indies," direct-to-video releases, and made-for-TV movies, he has found a way to remain solvent while competing directly against major studio theatrical releases.

Perry's films combine independent and studio practices, with modest budgets and low overhead coexisting with a frontloaded wide release strategy that is dependent on opening weekend box office. Perry has released all of his films through Lionsgate, a studio built on offbeat "indies" that were often too controversial for major studios and their art-house subdivisions.[22] Playing on 2,100 screens, the typical Perry film departs from Lionsgate's traditional method of limited releases, critical praise, and slow, steady box-office returns.[23] Using his growing brand, often with the possessive "Tyler Perry's" affixed to the front of the title, his films are insulated from pre-release bad reviews because they are not screened in advance for critics.[24] Instead of relying on traditional marketing and critical acclaim, Perry has cultivated a rapport with the Black press, Black radio, BET, and Oprah Winfrey (not to mention churches) that allows him to promote his films without Lionsgate having to make a substantial investment in formal advertising. Most importantly, Lionsgate has managed to navigate a busy release calendar and pinpoint favorable times to release a Perry film without having any of his audience siphoned off by a blockbuster release or competing Black-focused film, often releasing two Perry films annually in the slowest box-office seasons, between summer blockbusters and winter holiday and Oscar releases. Perry's success has come from blending his narrative formula with Lionsgate's business approach, with his then-least successful film *Daddy's Little Girls* (Tyler Perry, 2007) suffering from being released only one week after Eddie Murphy's *Norbit* (Brian

Robbins, 2007). Otherwise, Perry's films have been distanced from other Black-focused features, which is less of a problem as Black-starring production has dropped off, aside from gospel cinema. Increasingly, his films and would-be imitators have become the only iteration of Black-focused film to find theatrical distribution, leaving gospel cinema to compete with mainstream studio releases.

Taking the business strategy that Perry has perfected and others have emulated into account, gospel cinema can be understood primarily in terms of audience, with a growing number of films catering toward Black women. The root of gospel cinema is more than a simplistic notion of an underserved Black female audience willing to support films made with them in mind. Audience participation transforms Perry's films into gospel films. The decision to not provide advance screenings for critics speaks to the fact that Perry's films have a built-in audience that minimizes the impact of reviews. More importantly, his films operate outside of the narrative guidelines and cultural points of reference that inform the genre pictures, blockbusters, and art-house fare that populate the theatrical release calendar. As such, critics have struggled to contextualize the work of Perry, veering from derisiveness to curiosity when it came to assessing Perry's mix of emotional sincerity, folk humor, and camp sensibilities. The stop-and-start pacing, which makes individual scenes function more like brief episodes than as part of a streamlined narrative, is the most consistent criticism amongst film critics. The drastic shifts in tone, particularly from the flippant comedy of Madea to overwrought and painfully sincere melodrama, are too often read as examples of Perry being a novice filmmaker rather than examples of bringing a theatrical device and gospel mode to cinema.

The most common adjective used by critics to describe his films is the dismissive "sudsy," fixating on a penchant for melodrama by comparing it unfavorably to daytime soap operas. Critics have also struggled to make sense out of the Madea character, often drawing comparisons to the fat-suit cross-dressing of Martin Lawrence and Eddie Murphy, which in turn has transformed into critiques of stereotyped representation. More importantly, the inability or unwillingness of the critical establishment to understand films geared toward women, and their tendency to be dismissive (at best) or angry (at worst) about gospel cinema, speaks to a recurring devaluing of female perspectives. What Perry's films represent, and what gospel cinema has been founded upon, is a far more complex and nuanced negotiation between the female audience and cinema than critics recognize.

bell hooks's concept of the oppositional gaze, the ability of women (especially Black women) to read between the lines of film texts to unearth new meaning, provides a key insight into how Perry's films are consumed.[25] The surface narratives of one-dimensional dream men, emotional trauma, family dynamics, and spiritual salvation tell only part of the story, as Perry's audience creates their own meaning, most notably through the communal experience of seeing his films on the opening weekend in a full theatre. A perfect example can be found in *Madea Goes to Jail* (Tyler Perry, 2009), where Derek Luke's (as the character Joshua Hardaway) teary confessional about unknowingly playing a role in his friend being gang-raped in college was met with laughter by some audiences.[26] Whether Luke's overwrought and clumsy performance and Perry's dialogue are meant to elicit this response is debatable, but the scene shows that a gospel cinema audience, instead of functioning as passive spectators, transforms the text through active engagement.

Since they are denied advance screenings, the critics who have reviewed Perry's films have been forced to see his films with an audience, and engaging in the participatory nature of opening weekend screenings became a recurring theme in most reviews. However, most reviewers have taken a distanced approach, viewing Black female audiences through a perspective akin to cultural anthropology.[27] Critics often miss the transformative nature of these screenings and the essence of gospel cinema. In bypassing the limited releases of independent films and pushing for large opening weekend crowds, gospel cinema has been able to cultivate an interactive experience that mimics its stage antecedents. Defying the logic of presumed passive filmgoing, in which the audience is meant to sit in quiet contemplation, Perry has been able to translate the stage experience to the big screen by turning his films into events that require active (and vocal) participation. In this respect, gospel cinema is less an articulation of Christian ideology than it is a translation of stage and church traditions, creating an organic "call and response" that breaks down the sender and receiver model. Yet the values and often the physical space of the church remain an essential element in the films of Perry and his peers, making the notion of a gospel cinema dependent on both audience and ideology.

Capitalizing on Gospel Cinema

While Perry is gospel cinema's prime mover, he has been joined by a number of filmmakers looking to capitalize on the inroads he has made with Black female audiences. Hollywood is nothing if not prone to following trends, and the box-office success of Perry has spawned attempts at replicating his formula, making and marketing Black-focused women's pictures that are informed by Christian ideology. The question that remains is whether gospel cinema is a viable movement that has room for multiple voices, or is it yet another production cycle that will soon run its course? With as literal of a title as possible, *The Gospel* (Rob Hardy, 2005) was one of the first theatrical releases to follow *Woman Thou Art Loosed* and *Diary of a Mad Black Woman*. Shot on digital video and made for $4 million, *The Gospel* was picked up by the specialty distributor Screen Gems (a Sony subsidiary), which was attempting to build on the successes of Jakes and Perry, releasing the film on 969 screens in its opening weekend.[28] Grossing a respectable $15.7 million at the box office, the film looked to point toward a multiplicity of Black voices in film and the viability of gospel narratives concerned with not just female but also male characters. However, other attempts at using faith-based narratives did not fare so well. Veteran director Bill Duke's moralistic take on the down-low phenomenon, *Cover* (2008), took an independent distribution route, earning a paltry $79,436 in limited release.[29] Duke returned the following year to direct T.D. Jakes's production, *Not Easily Broken* (2009), based on the preacher's novel of the same name. The film outperformed Jakes's initial effort, *Woman Thou Art Loosed*, grossing $10 million while playing on 725 screens.[30] Five years removed from his initial foray into feature films, *Not Easily Broken* was far off the pace of his former collaborator Tyler Perry, but T.D. Jakes has since shown a more concerted investment in film that can be read either as an expansion of gospel cinema or a direct challenge to Perry's ubiquitous dominance.

Jakes moved away from using his own novels as source material and foregrounded more secular themes when he produced *Jumping the Broom* (Salim Akil, 2011). Borrowing from Perry's fixation on class division and the sense of shared community, not to mention casting Perry regular Tasha Smith, *Jumping the Broom* uses Christianity as a supporting narrative element rather than placing it at the center of the film. Jakes does appear as the preacher in the film's climactic wedding ceremony and there are evocations of the Bible throughout the film. However, the film's primary focus remains on the culture clash between rich and poor that has become a staple of Perry films. More importantly, *Jumping the Broom* mimicked the box-office success of Perry's films, grossing $37 million with only $6.6 million spent on production, replicating the model of saturation-booking geared toward a big opening weekend.

Additionally, although it failed to make a dent at the box office, the title of Jakes's next film, *Woman Thou Art Loosed: On the 7th Day* (Neema Barnette, 2012), suggests a return to more explicitly faith-based material, with the film functioning along the lines of the couples therapy rhetoric that Perry explores in *Why Did I Get Married?* (Tyler Perry, 2008). Finally, Jakes turn toward producing secular entertainment came full circle with *Sparkle* (Salim Akil, 2012), a remake of Sam O'Steen's 1976 film. While retaining the Curtis Mayfield songs and the dramatic arc of the original, there are significant changes from the O'Steen version, trading the 1958 New York setting for 1968 Detroit, bringing with it a drastically different political context, particularly relating to race and gender. Another significant change from the original text is the foregrounding of the community church, which serves not only as a musical training ground for Sparkle (Jordin Sparks) and her sisters, but also stands as a moral counterbalance to the pitfalls of fame, drugs, and sex. Here, Jakes infuses the musical drama with a nod to gospel cinema (particularly through popular and gospel music) without abandoning its largely secular aim.

The most notable entry into the landscape of gospel cinema came with *First Sunday* (David E. Talbert, 2008). A forerunner of Perry in the urban theatre circuit, David E. Talbert attempted to transition to cinema via independent production with *A Woman Like That* (David E. Talbert, 1997) before settling on low-budget direct-to-video films. *First Sunday* looked to transition Talbert into the mainstream, placing him as a peer of (or competitor to) Perry, much as they had been in theatre circuits in the late 1990s. The film was a success at the box office, grossing $37 million, yet the decision to cast recognizable stars like Ice Cube, Tracy Morgan, and Katt Williams displaced Talbert in the film's advertising, missing the opportunity to brand himself alongside Perry as a stage-to-screen progenitor. Talbert has since returned to the direct-to-DVD model with packaging that mimics Perry's films, attempting to turn his name into a brand like Perry's. Je'Caryous Johnson, another playwright from the urban circuit, has used the same direct-to-DVD model, placing his name and image prominently and uniformly on all of his releases. So far, Johnson has yet to make the leap to larger budgets, theatrical distribution, and greater financial risks. Johnson, like a growing number of independent filmmakers, is exploiting the gospel cinema trend and flooding the home video market with new titles explicitly geared toward the same women Perry and Jakes are hoping to lure into the multiplex on opening weekends. Just as the Blaxploitation cycle became dominated by low-budget independent features geared toward limited grindhouse and drive-in distribution, the growth of gospel cinema is taking place outside of first-run theatrical distribution, with direct-to-video as the modern equivalent of the exploitation film market. Televangelist Creflo Dollar has been rumored to be starting his own film division, while BET has optioned three faith-centered novels by ReShonda Tate Billingsley with the intention of turning them into made-for-TV films.[31]

While the scope of gospel cinema has grown exponentially in the past few years, the continued viability of a cinematic space that replicates the interactivity of stage plays is a point of uncertainty. Essentially, the theatrical release of gospel cinema remains primarily an extension of Perry's films. Yet Perry has shown signs of restlessness, veering from his successful formula to try his hand at art cinema with *For Colored Girls* (Tyler Perry, 2010) while attempting to refashion himself as an action star in *Alex Cross* (Rob Cohen, 2012). Perry has also tinkered with the formula for his Madea films, first releasing *Madea's Witness Protection* (Tyler Perry, 2012) as counter-programming in the summer blockbuster season while simultaneously courting a crossover audience by casting Eugene Levy as a co-star.[32] The power of Perry's brand has extended to television and publishing, and perhaps the hold he has on his loyal audience will allow him to find success in the busiest box-office months, opening up more space for other Black-focused films to find success in the lean spring and fall months that Perry has dominated. On the other hand, perhaps Perry's varied interests, or audience fatigue with his narrative formula, will spell the end of (or at least the tapering of) his successful run, especially as he has failed to connect with audiences outside of his core African American female demographic or make inroads overseas. The globalized blockbuster logic of Hollywood aside, Perry has given birth to one of the more vibrant and nuanced film movements in the history of African American cinema. Whether or not a low-budget, Black-focused model fits in with the thrust of the film industry, gospel cinema has served as a key articulation of a specific racial perspective in a supposedly post-racial era, one that aspires to reconsider the notion of a singular Black experience by recognizing regional, class, and ideological differences.

Notes

1. The blurred lines between the sacred and secular in gospel music, be it through performance or reception, can be seen in the work of Yolanda Adams, Kirk Franklin, the Winans family, Take 6, the Staple Singers, and Al Green.
2. For a clear example, see Wesley Morris, "Good Deeds," *Boston Globe*, February 25, 2012.
3. Rebecca Louie, "Prophet Margins," *Vibe*, April 2005, 136.
4. McCauley and Smith both work in academia, while Parks has written for film.
5. Zondra Hughes, "How Tyler Perry Rose from Homelessness to a $5 Million Mansion," *Ebony*, January 2004, 90–92.
6. Ibid.
7. The writing of stage play adaptation of *Woman Thou Art Loosed* is credited to Terry McFadden.
8. Shayne Lee, *T.D. Jakes: America's New Preacher* (New York: New York University, 2005), 148.
9. See Perry's official biography, http://www.tylerperry.com/biography/.
10. See Lee, *T.D. Jakes*.
11. *Time*, September 17, 2001.
12. Schultz directed the inaugural production for the Negro Ensemble Company, earned a Tony nomination when he transitioned to Broadway, and directed Derek Walcott's *Dream on Monkey Mountain* at the Mark Taper Forum after leaving New York to become a filmmaker.
13. See Lee, *T.D. Jakes*.
14. Personal interview with Michael Schultz, October 10, 2006, Santa Monica, California.
15. Of course, Spencer Williams had made films with explicit Christian narratives, including *The Blood of Jesus* (1941) and *Go Down, Death!* (1944), but these were not films released by Hollywood studios.
16. Rick Lyman, "A Sleeper Film Awakened by a Hungry Audience," *New York Times*, October 25, 1999.
17. See http://boxofficemojo.com/movies/?id=passionofthechrist.htm.
18. See http://boxofficemojo.com/movies/?id=womanthouartloosed.htm.

19. Stars like Sidney Poitier and Richard Pryor exercised control through their own production companies yet were nevertheless beholden to major studios for financing. Will Smith's Overbrook Entertainment is likely the closest to Tyler Perry Studios in terms of scale and autonomy.

20. See http://boxofficemojo.com/news/?id=1736&p=.htm and http://www.boxofficemojo.com/news/?id=2013&p=.htm.

21. Lionsgate distributed the first few Perry releases themselves in South Africa before selling the distribution rights to local companies for all of his following films.

22. Examples include *The Pillow Book* (Peter Greenaway, 1997), *Buffalo '66* (Vincent Gallo, 1998), *Gods and Monsters* (Bill Condon, 1998), *Affliction* (Paul Schrader, 1998), *Dogma* (Kevin Smith, 1999), *American Psycho* (Mary Harron, 2000), *Monster's Ball* (Marc Forster, 2001, *Secretary* (Steven Shainberg, 2002), *Cabin Fever* (2003, Eli Roth), and *Saw* (James Wan, 2004).

23. The smallest of Perry's releases was *Diary of a Mad Black Woman* (1,483) and the widest was *Alex Cross* (2,539), both of which he did not direct.

24. The lone exception being *For Colored Girls*.

25. bell hooks, "The Oppositional Gaze: Black Female Spectators," in *Black American Cinema*, ed. Manthia Diawara (New York: Routledge, 1993), 288–302.

26. As anecdotal as this evidence is, this was my experience when seeing the film on its opening weekend at the Magic Johnson Theater in Harlem.

27. Examples abound, but the clearest is A. O. Scott's "Serving a Buffet of Morality and Humor," *New York Times*, March 22, 2008.

28. See http://boxofficemojo.com/movies/?id=gospel.htm.

29. See http://boxofficemojo.com/movies/?id=cover08.htm.

30. See http://boxofficemojo.com/movies/?id=noteasilybroken.htm.

31. Cynthia Littleton, "BET Adds Spiritual Themes to Primetime," *Variety*, September 18, 2012.

32. Perry unsuccessfully tried his luck at counter-programming again with *A Madea Christmas* (Tyler Perry, 2013), relying on his core audience and the power of his brand to sell a film during one of the release calendar's most competitive seasons.

CHAPTER FOUR

Worship at the Altar of Perry: Spectatorship and the Aesthetics of Testimony

—Brandeise Monk-Payton

In a season-three episode of writer and cartoonist Aaron McGruder's animated television comedy *The Boondocks* (Cartoon Network, 2005–2014), fictional character Winston Jerome defiantly claims that he is the sole "representative of Jesus Christ in the film and television industry," urging Robert Freeman to join him in his quest to spread God's Word to the masses. The episode is a satirical commentary on African American media producer Tyler Perry's sheer dominance in the US entertainment industry; here, Jerome as Perry uses religion as a ruse to indoctrinate his actors, employees, and audience, ultimately in order to manufacture an empire that quite literally worships him.[1] While *The Boondocks* plays with and makes humorous these spiritual attachments to Perry, what would it mean to take seriously the salience of his forms of image-making for the churchgoing sect of the African American community? I argue that such a question necessitates a conceptualization of spectatorial practices that can account for the intensely intimate relationality produced between audience and screen image, which cultivates Perry's unique cinematic ministry. Indeed, it is the faith-based sociality that erupts from such a viewing experience of his films that seems to defy—or, at the least, displace—criticism at the level of his controversial ideological messages.

Perry's representational misfires along the categories of race, class, gender, and sexuality have been the subject of countless reviews of his work from critics, scholars, and even fellow filmmakers. In a 2009 interview with journalist Ed Gordon on syndicated talk show *Our World with Black Enterprise* (TV One, 2006–2014), Spike Lee frankly discusses what he deems the "troubling imagery" within Tyler Perry's cast of characters and their accompanying narratives on the film and television screen.[2] For Lee, Perry renders (hyper)visible debilitating caricatures of blackness made infamous as tools of oppression within the dominant media industry. The filmmaking divide between Lee and Perry has been much-publicized in recent years and finds its locus in the discourse of classifying what is traditionally deemed as "high" and "low" culture, which emphasizes the perceived artistic expertise of Lee's filmic endeavors in contrast to the undeniable popular reception of Perry's projects despite their questionable form and content. Thus, criticism of Perry seems to be symptomatic of a general anxiety surrounding the future trajectory of contemporary Black American cinema in Hollywood at the level of the ideological effects his aesthetic has on larger politics of representation that are central to the articulation and function of blackness in the media and popular culture.

However, what these assessments frequently don't reconcile is the emotional attachment involved in and produced by Perry's aesthetic—in other words, the distinctly affective spectatorial position that emerges while consuming his films. Reception in this context refers to the intimate encounter produced publicly through an engagement with the cinematic text.[3] In this sense, Perry's films both evoke and invoke the spiritual sensibility of the Black church. The Black church serves as a therapeutic venue for its members, utilizing heightened sentimentality for the bringing together of its constituents in a collective worship environment. Such an approach to filmmaking elucidates the purchasing power of a southern, Christian, African American community and validates them as an economically viable audience for particular faith-based messages.[4]

Perry's filmic messages operate under the auspices of a claim to morality emphasizing the logic of the testimony. What I term Perry's "testimonial aesthetic" allows for the cinematic text to construct a narrative of trauma or transgression that culminates in a spiritual experience of conversion. This moment is recounted publicly on the screen and is crucial to the mechanics of the film theatre-as-church in the dual process of image testifying and spectatorial witnessing. I suggest that Perry's successful media empire can be attributed to such a religious aesthetic that privileges his audience in the delivery of his films as testimony. Such pedagogical preaching through the cinema allows spectators to learn collaboratively and infuse the text with their own experiences normally rendered absent on screen. Here, the "troubling" nature of Perry's images that Lee and other critics put forth is radically reconfigured in the affective public space of worship.

Pathologizing Perry: The State of Contemporary Black Cinema

Tyler Perry made his debut as a screenwriter in 2005 with the cinematic version of his stage play *Diary of a Mad Black Woman* (Darren Grant, 2005) and has since rose to dominance within Black Hollywood as a producer, director, and writer of African American-oriented media content. From humble beginnings creating theatre pieces on the "Chitlin Circuit" to helming a lucrative entertainment empire, it is clear that Perry has rapidly become one of the most visibly successful African Americans within a film and television industry that is still pervasively exclusionary of minority voices. Yet Perry's dominance within Hollywood is not met without criticism and it is this status of critique that will be examined further in both popular and scholarly discourse on the filmmaker as it relates to the politics of representation. For Gayatri Spivak, representation is considered to have a dual yet mutually constitutive meaning in its reference to being both "proxy and portrait."[5] In this sense, to be a proxy is to be the figure that speaks for one's political constituency as an act of delegation. In addition to delegation, representation can also been seen as a depiction or portrait. Crucially, these two modes of representation reinforce each other. Thus, in order to become the voice for one's community, the community must be identified or rather, *framed*, in a certain manner as a category that necessitates representation.

The politics of representation is particularly pronounced when it involves the loaded practice of cultural production. Within minority communities, the "burden of representation" is evoked to highlight the role of iconicity that constructs an individual as the proxy of a community through his or her artistic pursuits. As Sharon Willis notes, Spike Lee's *Do the Right Thing* (1989) became a watershed moment in Black cinema precisely because Lee set a precedent for the potential commercial success of Black filmmakers; accordingly, his film was seen as a potential "window onto the world" of the African American experience in mainstream media's inaccurate reading of it as a realist text predicated on coherent and cohesive spectatorial identification.[6] Despite this overdetermination of the effects of his films on audiences, throughout the 1990s, Lee gained fame as the premier voice of African American cinema, making films that were lauded as challenging static representations of blackness in Hollywood. Referring to this critical attention as the "Spike Lee Discourse," Wahneema Lubiano importantly questions such celebratory musings of Lee, arguing that his position as a deified marker of Black authenticity displaced other filmic possibilities in the African American tradition, particularly those projects made by Black women.[7] While Lubiano argues for the increased awareness of the work of female filmmakers, it seems as though Lee's currency in producing projects that are considered successful contributions to Black American cinema by mainstream industry standards has waned—only to be replaced by yet another Black male filmmaker with Perry's arrival onto the scene, which disrupts Lee's reign of visibility as evidenced by Lee's continued public admonishment of Perry in recent years.[8]

Indeed, in an interview with CNN's Don Lemon to promote his film *Red Hook Summer* (Spike Lee, 2012), Lee addressed the current state of Black film, commenting, "I'm a student of cinema ... I know the damage that has been done through the imagery throughout the history of television and movies."[9] There are two observations to be made concerning such a remark that are pertinent to the controversy surrounding Perry. First, Lee points to a trajectory of image-making within Hollywood that has served to position Blacks and blackness as inferior, ultimately rupturing the African American psyche. Lee has attempted to shed light on these debilitating traditions that continue to pervade popular culture, most notably through his film *Bamboozled* (Spike Lee, 2000), a satirical examination of blackface minstrelsy in the contemporary moment. The filmmaker echoes the sentiments of cultural theorist bell hooks, who has previously noted the fundamental problem of representation in visual media, arguing that "we experience our collective crisis as African American people within the realm of the image."[10] Thus, for the Black subject, there should exist an awareness of how hegemonic image construction has crippled African American senses of identity and ways of being in the world, thereby serving to shackle instead of liberate Black consumers of mass media culture.

For Lee, that Perry does not seem to take into account such a fraught history of representation, let alone critique it, in his films is a point of contention. Second, Lee—consciously or not—situates himself within an esteemed lineage of Black filmmakers who have been formally educated in cinematic narrative, style, and technique.[11] As a Master of Fine Arts graduate of New York University, he in part seems to suggest that his pedigree affords him a valid space to critique other African American cinematic endeavors. Such an assumption subtly perpetuates hierarchies of taste by reconstituting dichotomies between the highbrow and the lowbrow as well as the elite and the popular. Particularly salient is the divide Lee attempts to highlight between the professional and the novice filmmaker, whereby Perry's perceived lack of access to a historical archive of Black images in the US is rendered a detriment to his cinematic knowledge and ultimately his practice, as he is deemed to produce those images that are seen as crude instead of refined like his counterparts in the independent film industry.

Such an emphasis on Perry's naivete in the realm of representation allows Lee to make another distinction, this time between the types of images that both filmmakers produce. While Lee conceives of his cinematic vision of African American identity as "prototype," effectively creating original models of blackness, it is contrasted with Perry's indulgence in the perpetuation of stereotype. Thus, figures in his film and television endeavors are seen as repetitive caricatures that are reminiscent of the "coonery and buffoonery"[12] of media texts such as the early television sitcom *The Amos 'n' Andy Show* (CBS, 1951–53). In this way, Perry is seen to be capitulating to the mainstream film industry's historical malignment of blackness instead of resisting it by showcasing alternative depictions of the African American experience that contest dominant Hollywood structures. Put differently, Perry seems to reinscribe what is termed Hollywood's "cinema of recuperation" from the late 1970s to the 1980s. The recuperative project of the film industry during this time period promoted cinematic conservatism as a strategy that allowed for what Ed Guerrero argues is the "resubordination of the black image."[13] While the cinema of recuperation is associated with a decline in Black-oriented films and Black representation in Hollywood, it can be related in part to the logic of Perry's success, or rather, the ease with which the mainstream film industry seems to accept his work as the singular most prominent and economically lucrative depiction of Black experience. Thus, Lee's dissent emerges from the concern that Perry's work is easily registered through the lens of a popular white imagination of blackness that is deemed palatable for mass consumption and perpetuates hegemonic image production. In this vein, the goal to recode racialized images at the movies in order to contest the containment of blackness associated with recuperation is completely foreclosed.

However, the critique of Perry that is predicated on the status of stereotype in his projects returns the issues concerning representational practice to an all too deceivingly simple demarcation of positive and negative imagery. As many scholars of Black media and popular culture have noted in the past, the binary of good and bad images cannot be the endpoint of the discourse on the politics of representation. Therefore, the charge of stereotype is inadequate to describe what Sasha Torres calls the tendency to flatten readings of textual objects so much so that complex responses to the stereotype in question are ultimately not seen as available interpretations. Indeed, such a stifled analytical reading does not consider the possibility of a more nuanced exploration of the function of stereotype, for example, centered on audience reception of such images and the potential "for the creative and unpredictable cultural work it does."[14] Certainly the portraits that Perry paints of the Black experience have been critiqued, particularly when concerning his depiction of gender and sexuality.[15] Yet the focus on delineating between positive and negative imagery is an act that Perry states is symptomatic of Black communities in particular. In a 2009 *60 Minutes* (CBS, 1968–present) interview, he reflects: "We don't have to worry about anybody else trying to destroy us and take shots because we do it to ourselves."[16] In the same interview, he suggests that the characters he creates, such as Madea, are "bait" for him to discuss larger themes concerning faith, family, friendship, and other topics that concern Black communities. In this way, Perry attempts to elide discussion on the question of representation by emptying his characters of signification (and thus individual accountability) in favor of the presentation of universal narratives, especially through the framework of the parable. This logic relies on viewer expectations to be entertained by specific familiar performances of blackness that have been cultivated and thus resonate with the experiences of a subset of the African American audience.

The question of audience is paramount to the success of Perry's brand in Hollywood. Therefore, the issue of representation and its invocation of the regressive rhetoric of the stereotype are transformed, and perhaps even rendered inconsequential, when in the realm of reception. Indeed, as Lionsgate Entertainment Co-chairman and Chief Executive Officer John Feltheimer notes in a 2011 press release: "Tyler Perry is one of the most powerful and unique entertainment brands in the world today, with a fan base that is virtually unrivalled in its loyalty and passion."[17] Here, Perry is believed to have a strong bond to his audience, an emotional attachment that affirms his relationship to a specific segment of the African American population. His catering to the demographic of Christian Black women from the south renders visible a community that has not been traditionally courted as a viable revenue stream in mainstream media. Thus, while Lee and others critique Perry at the level of representation, in response, the filmmaker importantly begins to shift the conversation to the lived experience of those people who buy tickets and sit in theatre seats to watch Perry's stage plays and his films. He notes on *60 Minutes*: "It's attitudes like [Lee's] that make Hollywood think that these people do not exist and that's why there's no material speaking to them, speaking to us."[18] In addition to articulating the necessity to provide a space for such an audience to see issues pertinent to their lives reflected on screen, Perry also presents himself as a member of the community that patronizes his productions. This sociocultural alignment of filmmaker and audience interestingly makes apparent the critique of a tradition of intellectual Black cinema (that could arguably include Lee in some respects) that was seen as divorced from African American communities. In a series of articles initially published in the *Black Film Review* in the late 1980s, leading scholars Clyde Taylor and David Nicholson, joined by filmmaker Zeinabu Irene Davis, debate the status and future of the Black independent film movement. Taylor indicts the perceived privileging of auteurism in Black filmmaking which not only serves to individualize, a practice that is antithetical to the ethos of collectivity, but relatedly in its commitment to strategies of formal cinematic excellence, distances itself from popular Black audiences. Davis refutes Taylor's criticism of the LA Rebellion school of filmmakers and writes of the desire for the audience to have a different relationship to the moving image based on a new cinematic language that such Black independent filmmakers can offer.[19] The tension in these debates in part seems to arise from how Black experiences and expressivity can be conveyed on screen and whether this fundamentally requires an opposition to Hollywood standards and a reconfiguration of audience expectation.

Indeed, that the images created by Perry have unparalleled success in their circulation commercially as products that are aligned with conventional industry standards and are seen as representative of African American experiences in totality is the primary point of conflict that allows critics such as Lee to construct the filmmaker as an abject figure within contemporary Black cinema. However, Tommy Lott states that the tendency of film criticism is to aesthetically judge without paying attention to questions of audience appeal. Such a de-emphasis on reception ultimately does a disservice to the discussion of cinema practice— in particular, for film that resides in a marginal space for a minority demographic. This produces a hierarchy of situating "the aesthetic values of the black artist above those of the black audience."[20] Put differently, what Gladstone L. Yearwood calls a "re-education of the viewer" that is necessary for the progressiveness of Black film is predicated on the assumption of a naïve audience that has to be saved from being helplessly interpellated by the standard codes and conventions of Hollywood film fare.[21] Thus, Perry's retort to Lee centers on affirming the already existing knowledge that Black audiences have of their own moviegoing practices:

> I am sick of him talking about me, I am sick of him saying, "This is a coon; this is a buffoon." I am sick of him talking about black people going to see movies. This is what he said: "You vote by what you see," as if black people don't know what they want to see.[22]

In addition to shifting the conversation to spectatorship, Perry simultaneously seems to critique the value judgments placed on certain cinematic texts particularly by those who are seen to be "quality" filmmakers who are cognizant of advanced or avant-garde form and style. In this way, a reconsideration of the aesthetic at the level of reception has the potential to be a fruitful way to recuperate Perry from those who indict him on the politics of representation and ideological critique. Here, attention must be paid to spectatorial agency and the capacity for a different relationship to the image predicated on the affective desire of the audience to engage in a particular mode of African American expressivity, sensibility, and relationality in common.

Witnessing at the Movies: Towards an Aesthetics of Testimony

The role of aesthetics has long permeated discussions concerning the articulation of the (im)possibilities within Black cinema. Clyde Taylor has refuted the traditional privileging of Western aesthetics, which is seen to affirm ideologies of the dominant white culture on issues of beauty that displaces art in the Afro-modern tradition. For him, a turn towards what he terms the "postesthetic" as "an effort to revivify and validate meanings dismissed or obscured in imperial knowledge" is necessary for Black cinema.[23] In this way, Taylor builds upon Sylvia Wynter's notion of a deciphering practice which "sets out to take the image/sound signifying practices of film (and television) as the objects of a new mode of inquiry"[24] that will validate and celebrate different modes of expressivity that engender meanings that are counter to Western conventions.

Yet, though much credence is to be given to issues concerning the aesthetic in relation to the question of form, it must be noted that aesthetic choices in film are in large part determined by political and economic imperatives that affect production and distribution. Many Black independent filmmakers such as Davis have spoken about this struggle, utilizing different stylistic strategies to combat a lack of resources and funding for their projects. Over the years, due to his work in theatre, Perry has established himself as a media mogul who has the financing to circumvent the industrial constraints of Hollywood that serve to hinder his cinematic counterparts. Geographically, the decision to locate his Tyler Perry Studios in Atlanta, Georgia, removes him from Hollywood as the dominant site of filmmaking and situates him in an environment that is not only southern in nature but, with its large African American demographic, frequently thought of as a Black cultural Mecca. In this way, his filmmaking can be considered to benefit from what Hamid

Naficy distinguishes as a "cinema of alterity" whereby "its mode of production may variously be characterized as independent, personal, artisanal, interstitial, third cinema, collective, ethnic, immigrant, or exilic."[25] Due to such an infrastructure, Perry's films can be said to occupy a relatively autonomous space in which a lucrative business deal with Lionsgate Entertainment allows the independent studio to co-produce and distribute his various projects while Perry still retains total creative control over his product. In a press release, he states:

> Together, Lionsgate and I have built the ideal filmmaker/studio relationship, and I'm thrilled that it will be continuing. We share an entrepreneurial spirit and have a great business rapport. But more importantly, Lionsgate has been incredibly affirming of my relationship with my audience—I've always had the artistic freedom to speak what I want, how I want, and when I want through my films.[26]

However, although Perry emphasizes his status as a liberated filmmaker utilizing a "guerilla style,"[27] unlike Naficy's conceptualization of this cinema of alterity, Perry's films do not contest dominant strategies of storytelling presented in mainstream cinema. They are not recognized as oppositional and do not employ techniques of rupture to produce innovative images on screen, a desire that one would like to ascribe to a popular filmmaker from a marginalized community. And, in fact, this refusal to resist convention is perhaps one of the fundamental tenants of the critique of Perry's media empire. A salient example of this critique is the outcry over his adaptation of Ntozake Shange's 1975 stage choreopoem, *For Colored Girls Who Have Considered Suicide When the Rainbow Is Enuf*. Due to Perry's subscription to established Hollywood filmmaking techniques, the film version with a shortened title, *For Colored Girls* (Tyler Perry, 2010), did not seem to artistically play with the medium or utilize the apparatus to reflect the contours of Black experiences, or in this case, an experimental Black feminist text. Yet what can be considered Perry's filmic resistance actually emerges from the audience that it seeks to court. In this way, a film's enunciation and legibility is not predicated on a mainstream or even elite audience, but announces itself quite rigorously as a product for a particular viewer situated in a specific context of experience. Perry's films address the African American

Christian community in an aesthetic mode that recognizes and affirms the worship practices of the Black church.

Per James Snead, Black film has the ability to recode spectatorial expectations within the actual syntax of Hollywood through the formal and stylistic qualities of editing and montage.[28] Therefore, while Perry might not change the "master narrative" of Hollywood that depicts both implicitly and explicitly the hegemony of whiteness in cinema, he does disrupt conventions and recode expectations at the level of spectatorship through a mobilization of viewer affect. Affect in this context is a reaction to a text that cultivates a sense of intimacy within a community. Scholar Jacqueline Stewart's examination of African American responses to early cinema in Chicago is instructive here in a reconsideration of Black film reception. For her, during the pre-classical cinema era, African Americans retained and mobilized their agency in the face of dominant discourses that sought to limit their navigation of modern culture through what she terms, "reconstructive spectatorship."[29] Such a viewing practice accounts for the communal and physical ways in which Blacks are situated as audience members in a theatre that is not predicated on an individualistic psychoanalytic theory of the cinema-as-apparatus, but rather reception in states of distraction and imaginative possibility.

Crucial to this argument is the sheer public-ness of moviegoing during early cinema with its emphasis on the scene of exhibition. Perry's rootedness in Black theatre positions the site of exhibition as a critical component of his success. While the liveness of the theatre contributes to the immediacy produced between the audience and the act on stage, the experience of watching Perry's films can be seen to continue in this tradition. This is in part because many of his film projects are adaptations of stage plays, which affords the viewer a sense of familiarity with the text. In addition, the theatrical and cinematic productions rely on stories that foreground the role of faith in the path to self-actualization and establish communal bonds through testimonial practices. Not dissimilar to the confession, testimony is a performative gesture that occurs in public in the service of a therapeutic exercising of one's personal struggles. This gesture is then recognized and affirmed by the congregation in the space of the church; such an encounter emphasizes theatricality, in the form of an excess of vocalization, and physicality by both those who testify and those who witness the testimonial, an important aspect of the dialogic experience of worship.

However, while testimony in the church is an encounter amidst and between subjects that alters both parties involved, what does this process mean in the context of cinema specifically? On one level, the images on screen produce a narrative, which represents a character's journey through trials and tribulations that is then consumed (i.e., encoded and decoded) by an audience. On another level, the voice behind the screen is explicitly Perry's, who usually serves as writer, producer, and director on his projects. Returning to *The Boondocks* critique mentioned earlier is instructive here as it comments on how Perry becomes legitimated as the premier Black filmmaker who is the vessel for God's Word. Such "official" testimony creates a different relationship that is in tension with the dialogic atmosphere that emerges within the church setting, elucidating the spectatorial act of understanding Perry's films as gospel—in other words, representative of the "truth" of blackness. Worship in this sense is seen as the viewer's praise of Perry's movies as entertainingly resonant expressions of African American experiences. Through film, Perry preaches sermons to an increasingly devoted audience that anticipates his projects and brings Black folk to movie houses in droves.

While such spectatorial devotion is a concern for those who believe that Perry actually delivers the *wrong* messages to his fanbase, it is important to consider what else this viewing practice may offer to audiences, which can reveal an important differential logic of cinematic address underpinning his films. As mentioned previously, Perry gained loyal patronage on the Chitlin Circuit. bell hooks writes of the Chitlin Circuit as a Black vernacular network that emphasizes collective care and communion, stating that "a very distinctive black culture was created in the agrarian South, by the experience of rural living, poverty, racial segregation, and resistance struggle, a culture we can cherish and learn from. It offers ways of knowing, habits of being, that can help sustain us as a people."[30] hooks thinks of the circuit as aiding in the daily practice of self-preservation for Black communities in the midst of white supremacist patriarchy. Here, it is a strategy of survival through the cultivation of solidarity. While, for hooks, there is a political component to such a collective environment, it also manifests itself as an aesthetic, one in which Perry seems to adopt through the frame of the church. The film-as-sermon explores faith as a viable form of alternative meaning-making and counter-knowledge for African American audiences that helps to sustain the identity and culture of one's community. In this way, it may be difficult for a non-Black audience to access such a sensibility; the opportunity to participate in such worship exists but cannot be fully realized in terms of spectatorial address. The sentimentality and spectacularity of testimony expressed on screen through Perry's narratives contains a spiritual inflection that is transmitted to the audience-as-congregation through an emotional bond. Indeed, Sara Ahmed provocatively argues that emotions do not reside in individuals but rather "work to bind subjects together."[31] Rather than expressed as private feelings, emotions circulate between people as a relational activity. In this way, Perry creates a Black cinematic language through a spectatorship that is centered on the acts of testifying and witnessing provided by a shared religious experience.

Good Deeds' Ministry of Melodrama

Due to the metaphysical nature of spirituality, African American cinematic endeavors that acknowledge the primacy of faith might be seen to operate on a different regime of social action from how Black film has been generally defined in the past. Indeed, the statement made by Lott in which "Black filmmaking practices must continue to be fundamentally concerned with issues that presently define the political struggle of black people"[32] contrasts in large part with a filmmaker, such as Perry, who emphasizes the ethical instead of the material political concerns within the African American community. Indeed, Perry's interests revolve around the status of both the breaking and upholding of morals. Characters deal with trials and tribulations that can ultimately only be assuaged through redemption by a religious higher power. In this way, elements of the Black church and Christianity more generally figure prominently in Perry's screen ministry across all of his film narratives.

In contrast to the hugely popular *Madea* movie series, which centers on Perry's drag performance of the no-nonsense southern matriarch Madea and a working-class Black ethos, Perry's other forays into film tend to explore the intricacies of the Black middle-class experience.

His twelfth production, *Good Deeds* (Tyler Perry, 2012) is the story of title character Wesley Deeds III (Tyler Perry), the CEO of his deceased father's computer software company in San Francisco.[33] Deeds seems to have the perfect life on the surface: a successful business, a beautiful fiancé Natalie (Gabrielle Union), and a luxurious lifestyle. However, his life lacks any degree of spontaneity. As he states in voiceover at the beginning of the film, he is a "fifth-generation Ivy League graduate," born into privilege and groomed for greatness. Since he was a child, everything in his life has been dictated to him according to the aspirations of his wealthy parents and, as a result, he has never lived the life that he desires. In the midst of keeping up with appearances despite being unfulfilled and lacking a true sense of self, Deeds meets and falls in love with single mother Lindsay (Thandie Newton), a janitor who works at the Deeds Corporation. Poor and homeless, Lindsay teaches Deeds how to find and embrace his own identity independent of expectations imposed on him externally due to his family pedigree.

Such an emphasis on pedagogy within the narrative is a thread that runs throughout Perry's films. Indeed, the strengthening of one's morals is predicated on these lessons presented on screen. The framework of the parable is crucial to Perry's cinematic preaching as it connects him to his churchgoing audience. Religious rhetoric is noticeably absent from *Good Deeds* yet it still informs much of the narrative. The only direct reference to the Bible in the film comes from Deeds's mother, Wilimena (Phylicia Rashad), who admonishes Wesley's younger brother, Walter (Brian White), commenting, "It takes the patience of Job to deal with him." However, the entire relationship between Wesley, the good and upstanding son, and Walter, the misogynistic alcoholic, seems to be a retelling of the parable of the Prodigal Son. The film also invokes the parable of the Good Samaritan in its positioning of Deeds as an individual who helps strangers in need. Thus, Perry is able to infuse his narratives with spiritual messages rooted in the New Testament of the Bible for entertainment.

Such lessons are frequently articulated through the filmic mode of melodrama and, in particular, the conflicts that occur within the Black community over class status. Perry puts on display the excesses of Black success, which serve to transform such depictions of affluence into abjection. The melodramatic crux of these faith-based films becomes the revealing of concealed deep-rooted issues usually associated with familial relationships. Underneath the sophistication and sleekness of the lives of these upwardly mobile African Americans are characters with faults, secrets, and a high level of relational trauma. When such issues are brought to the surface, they are expressed in a moment of elevated emotionality. In *Good Deeds*, this occurs during a scene in which the Deeds Corporation celebrates the closing of a lucrative deal. A party to congratulate the company is disrupted when Lindsay enters the office to talk to Wesley and inadvertently comes into contact with his fiancé, mother, and brother. Wesley's family looks on disapprovingly at the woman, with Wilimena telling Lindsay in a not-so-subtle manner that her son has a "penchant for projects." The scene explodes into melodrama with the juxtaposition of the perceived respectability of the wealthy and the disreputability of the less fortunate; when Wilimena slaps Walter for a drunken tirade that embarrasses the family, it culminates in a fight between the two brothers. Perry's filmmaking style renders such a public display of interpersonal drama as spectacle, complete with the heightened tension afforded by a dramatic musical score, close-ups, basic dialogue, and the sheer theatricality of the performances. The scene ends with the primary characters stuck in an elevator together; in a reversal of expected roles, it is Lindsay who emerges as the most respectable character, soothing Wesley from the drama associated with his bourgeois existence.

Deeds continues to disrupt the carefully orchestrated social script that he is supposed to follow by involving himself with Lindsay. Lindsay's life is full of struggle; evicted from her apartment, she and her daughter are homeless and living in their van. Deeds is increasingly intrigued by her tough exterior and frank attitude as she challenges him to expose and be comfortable with his true self and to "live in the real world." In the film, the "real world" includes knowing how much a gallon of milk costs in addition to listening to music by rapper Tupac Shakur. Through Lindsay, Deeds ostensibly gets in touch with many facets of African American culture that he has never experienced in a whitewashed world of wealth. He transforms from what Lindsay refers to as a "disconnected, cold, stiff, uptight" man into someone who embraces unpredictability and lives without accordance to a master plan. In his increasing unscriptedness, he becomes an individual who breaks established codes in order to find his own identity independent of what has been prescribed to him. At the end of the film, his sudden move to Africa with Lindsay and her daughter is an attempt at affirming a commitment to (re)connect himself with a motherland that has been displaced by his upper middle class American Dream status. By framing the story with Deeds's voice and through his perspective, it operates as a testimonial about his life-changing journey. This element of character testimony is intertwined with Perry's position as star; as the only non-Madea film he has made in which he plays not a peripheral but central role, the testifying that occurs has a different and more personalized inflection that allows for the spectatorial worship of Perry so intrinsic to his filmmaking style.[34]

In large part, for Perry's films to be effective at the level of viewer witnessing of individual testimony, they have to rely heavily on classic Hollywood narrative conventions in order to suture audiences into the cinematic worship experience. Utilizing formulaic storytelling strategies from romance and drama genres, there is very little room for Perry to rupture traditional formal and stylistic qualities that would allow for cinematic resistance to dominant Western aesthetics. Terri Simone Francis speaks of the difficulty for general African American audiences of embracing non-mainstream vernacular aesthetics, ultimately positioning Black film in a challenging space that is "caught between industrial circumstances and its ideals."[35] She advocates for a Black filmmaking practice that reflects on and ultimately resists classic film conventions through the expression of a "blues cosmology." The blues are a central aesthetic and cultural component that musically testifies to the plight of Black folk, vocalizing stories of struggle in a way that does not attempt to solve or overcome suffering. In other words, its commitment to the "unresolved and circular" contests Hollywood's desire for cohesive narrative closure. Because the blues finds its strength in improvisation—in contrast to mainstream cinema, which thrives on instrumentalization for its success—such a blues cosmology harbors the potential for liberation for Black filmmaking.[36]

However, I suggest that Perry does not utilize the blues but rather emphasizes gospel as his primary mode of cinematic communication. While the blues, though secular, is associated with spirituals, Lawrence Levine states that gospel differs from spirituals in that "the gospel ethos was largely one of pure faith."[37] In relation to Perry's films, gospel does not refer specifically to its musical underpinnings but instead gestures towards its primary biblical definition as the teachings of Christ. With the filmic lessons that Perry provides through the development of on-screen parables, the spectator is constructed as a student. In order for the parable to resonate with audiences and be effective in its teachings, it requires the universality and simplicity offered by classical narrative similar to that which would be produced in mainstream cinema. For *Good Deeds*, Wesley Deeds's decision to travel to Africa with Lindsay and her daughter is naturalized as the logical conclusion to his filmic testimony, completing his transformation as an individual from selfish to selfless in a profound leap of faith. Such a gospel ethos contributes to the affective spectatorial position that emphasizes how the audience bears witness to Perry's own testimonial release as a filmmaker that is mediated through his fictional screen imagery. The worship experience cultivated in the atmosphere of the theatre-as-church allows for the circulation of this collective catharsis between film producer and consumer.

Conclusion

In the early 1980s, Yearwood states that "within a theory of a black cinema aesthetic, the audience ultimately confirms or denies the efficacy of black cinema."[38] Even at this beginning moment in African American cinema scholarship, there exists a preoccupation with spectatorship as an important key to understanding the potential of Black film. There is definite resistance to and disavowal of sustained scholarly engagement with Tyler Perry predicated on his status as a dismissed object within the fields of film and media studies. An updating of Black cinema scholarship is necessary to account for his influence in the industry and within the Black public sphere. Indeed, in the current era of Black filmmaking, Perry has captured the attention and spirit of a segment of the Black audience, single-handedly cultivating a strong fan following for his films.

Perry frankly comments, "I'm not an artist . . . I set the camera up and tell my story." Despite his lack of formal training, he has created a niche audience-as-congregation by affecting them at the level of cinematic address through faith-based films that inspire and uplift through his filmmaking as testimonial practice. Taylor once noted the failure of the Black independent film movement, commenting that "in a medium that was built to handle it, the Black filmmakers have seldom looked for the vitality, style, and pageantry of Black life, the culture's appreciation of spectacle, performance, and virtuosity."[39] While he meant it as an observation of a lack of infusing film with the unique expressivity of Black culture at the level of production and narrative, one could argue that Perry achieves such a goal through exhibition and spectatorship. Like his stage plays, Perry's films have a theatrical quality that cultivates a relationship between the audience and the screen. Indeed, what the filmmaker offers for the viewer is an emphasis on a certain type of faith in the images and their resonance with the life experiences of the viewer.

An emphasis on worship as a cinematic framework complicates an expressed desire for African American film to be explicitly political and operate as a contestation of the dominant ideology of blackness that Hollywood has traditionally provided. In this sense, reactions to Perry's films critique him due to his perceived capitulation to not only Western aesthetics but also stereotypical images of blackness, creating no room for resistance in the realm of image-making. The anxiety surrounding the notion that Perry's representations have become *representative* of African American communities within mainstream media is a topic that still requires examination. However, merely deeming Perry's images as stereotypes devalues their productive function in creating a collective audience that emphasizes an ethos of Black communities predicated on a shared spirituality. What's more, perhaps it is precisely his adherence to dominant filmmaking that may allow him to resist through a reconfiguration of spectatorship. Thus, while he does not rupture the hegemony of mainstream cinematic practices in form and style, his films operate on a different aesthetic register that is affective in nature. Intimacy here is constructed by the moral sensibility associated with the testimony apparent within the Black church. Emotion is felt not individually but is circulated by the practice of worship within the space of the theatre-as-church and the screen-as-pulpit.

Audience reverence of Perry is not without its faults, and critical attention must be paid to the equally pressing concern that his spreading of the gospel as a "good deed" fuels the capitalist marketplace and the representational problematics that make it difficult for alternative

African American filmmaking practices to intervene. In other words, his desire to inspire and uplift may also be doing other kinds of work that pathologizes and demonizes in its streamlining of images for Black audiences. As such, the popular rhetoric of "no good deed goes unpunished" is apt here, for it reflects the misfires of his philosophy and rightly politicizes his morality play.[40] However, in this essay, I have gestured towards a reading of the intersection between Black cinema aesthetics and spectatorship and attempted to account for some of the primary logics undergirding Perry's success. In his tactic of cinematic ministering, he makes available another type of filmic literacy, rendering visible a form of spectatorial worship associated with the faith-based practices of testifying and witnessing within African American communities who believe in God—and by extension, Perry himself.

Notes

1. "Pause," *The Boondocks*, directed by Sung-hoon Kim and Seung Eun Kim (June 20, 2010; Sony Pictures Television, 2010), DVD. The controversial episode suggests that Perry's Christian framework actually serves as a way for him to satisfy his desire to cross-dress and sleep with men. Indeed, Perry's sexuality has been the fodder of much debate since his emergence as a celebrity in mainstream US media.

2. *Our World* with Black Enterprise, hosted by Ed Gordon (May 18, 2009; Black Enterprise, Inc.).

3. The study of audiences has been a largely fraught component of media and cultural studies largely predicated on different methodological concerns, and it becomes an increasingly important critical project particularly for marginalized subjects. In this essay, my reading of the audience in terms of intimacy does not take on a phenomenological lens, via Vivian Sobchack, or seek to account for Perry's films within the realm of the "body genre," per Linda Williams. Nor do I assess the audience ethnographically, per Jacqueline Bobo's seminal qualitative study of Black women as cultural readers. I am interested in intimacy and public culture through theories of affect offered by Sara Ahmed, Lauren Berlant, and Teresa Brennan, particularly as it relates to the Black Christian worship environment and experience being a transmitted encounter between subjects that is at once social, discursive, physical, and metaphysical. Vivian Sobchack, *The Address of the Eye: A Phenomenology of Film Experience* (Princeton: Princeton University Press, 1991); Linda Williams, "Film Bodies: Gender, Genre, and Excess," *Film Quarterly* 44, no. 4 (Summer 1991): 2–13; Jacqueline Bobo, *Black Women as Cultural Readers* (New York: Columbia University Press, 1995); Sara Ahmed, "Affective Economies," *Social Text* 22, no. 2 (Summer 2004): 117–39; Lauren Berlant, *The Female Complaint: The Unfinished Business of Sentimentality in American Culture* (Durham:

Duke University Press, 2008); Teresa Brennan, *The Transmission of Affect* (Ithaca: Cornell University Press, 2004).

4. For more on the labor of moviegoing within capitalism and the temporal as well as affective investment involved in the perpetuation of Gramscian hegemony through the cinematic, see Marcia Landy, *Film, Politics, and Gramsci* (Minneapolis: University of Minnesota Press, 1994).

5. Gayatri Chakravorty Spivak, *The Post-Colonial Critic: Interviews, Strategies, Dialogues*, ed. Sarah Harasym (New York: Routledge, 1990), 108.

6. Sharon Willis, "A Theater of Interruptions," in *Film Analysis: A Norton Reader*, eds. Jeffrey Geiger and R. L. Rutsky (New York: W. W. Norton & Company, 2005), 777–79.

7. Wahneema Lubiano, "But Compared to What? Reading Realism, Representation, and Essentialism in *School Daze*, *Do the Right Thing*, and the Spike Lee Discourse," in *Representing Black Men*, eds. Marcellus Blount and George P. Cunningham (New York: Routledge, 1996).

8. Lee's critiques of Perry have greatly subsided since his initial outcry in 2009. In an interview with Oprah Winfrey on *Oprah's Next Chapter* (OWN, 2013), he relays to Winfrey that he and Perry are "mad cool now." He refutes that their previous tension is due to what Perry states as differing socioeconomic status and regional upbringing. Instead, he reiterates that it is an issue of form: "My criticism of him was just the imagery. To me, it was just taste. He has a way to see stuff, I see it different. He's doing a great thing. We're cool. We got no drama, no friction, and one day we might work together."

9. Spike Lee, interview by Don Lemon, CNN, August 19, 2012.

10. bell hooks, *Black Looks: Race and Representation* (Boston: South End Press, 1992), 6.

11. Here, I am speaking not only of the Los Angeles Rebellion School of Filmmakers emerging from UCLA, but also a figure like writer/director John Singleton, who received his bachelor's degree from the University of Southern California's School of Cinematic Arts.

12. Lee, interview by Don Lemon; *Our World* with Black Enterprise.

13. Ed Guerrero, *Framing Blackness: The African American Image in Film* (Philadelphia, Temple University Press, 1993), 114.

14. Sasha Torres, *Black, White, and In Color: Television and Black Civil Rights* (Princeton: Princeton University Press, 2003), 1.

15. Robert J. Patterson, "'Woman Thou Art Bound': Critical Spectatorship, Black Masculine Gazes, and Gender Problems in Tyler Perry's Movies," *Black Camera* 3, no. 1 (2011). In the essay, Patterson utilizes Black feminist and queer of color critique to reveal the debilitating patriarchal and heterosexist underpinnings of Perry's screen images.

16. *60 Minutes*, hosted by Byron Pitts (2009; CBS News Productions).

17. "Lionsgate Extends Partnership With Tyler Perry With New Multiyear Deal," Lionsgate press release, March 31, 2011.

18. *60 Minutes*.

19. Zeinabu Irene Davis, "The Future of Black Film: The Debate Continues," in *Cinemas of the Black Diaspora: Diversity, Dependence, Oppositionality*, ed. by Michael T. Martin (Detroit: Wayne State University Press, 1995), 450.

20. Tommy Lott, "A No-Theory Theory of Contemporary Black Cinema," *Black American Literature Forum* 25, no. 2 (Summer 1991): 228.

21. Gladstone L. Yearwood, "Towards a Theory of a Black Cinema Aesthetic," in *Black Cinema Aesthetics: Issues in Independent Black Filmmaking*, ed. Gladstone L. Yearwood (Athens: Center for Afro-American Studies, 1982), 81.

22. "Tyler Perry: Spike Lee Can Go Straight to Hell!" *Hollywood Reporter*, April 19, 2011. Press conference in anticipation for *Madea's Big Happy Family*.

23. Clyde Taylor, "We Don't Need Another Hero: Anti-Theses on Aesthetics," in *Blackframes: Critical Perspectives on Black Independent Cinema*, eds. Mbye Cham and Claire Andrade-Watkins (Cambridge: MIT Press, 1988), 84.

24. Sylvia Wynter, "Rethinking 'Aesthetics': Notes Towards a Deciphering Practice," in *Exiles: Essays on Caribbean Cinema*, ed. Mbye Cham (Trenton: Africa World Press, 1992), 261.

25. Hamid Naficy, "Between Rocks and Hard Places: The Interstitial Mode of Production in Exilic Cinema," in *Home, Exile, Homeland: Film, Media, and the Politics of Place*, ed. Hamid Naficy (New York: Routledge, 1998), 128–29.

26. "Lionsgate Extends Partnership With Tyler Perry With New Multiyear Deal."

27. "Tyler Perry," *Visionaries: Inside the Creative Mind*, directed by Michael Bonfiglio (August 28, 2011; Radical Media, 2011). In this documentary series, which premiered on the Oprah Winfrey Network (OWN), cameras follow Perry as he discusses the intricacies of his success.

28. James Snead, "Recoding Blackness: The Visual Rhetoric of Black Independent Film," in *Circular for The New American Filmmakers Series 23* (New York: Whitney Museum of American Art, 1985), 1–2.

29. Jacqueline Stewart, *Migrating to the Movies: Cinema and Black Urban Modernity* (Berkeley: University of California Press, 2005), 94.

30. bell hooks, *Yearning: Race, Gender, and Cultural Politics* (Boston: South End Press, 1990), 38.

31. Sara Ahmed, "Affective Economies," *Social Text* 22, no. 2 (Summer 2004): 119.

32. Lott, 232.

33. *Good Deeds*, directed by Tyler Perry (2012; Atlanta, GA: Tyler Perry Studios/Lionsgate, 2012), DVD.

34. This personalized testimony exists not only in Perry's cinematic endeavors but also in his circulation on digital media platforms. Specifically, his website presents his musings as both promotional and interactive opportunity for his product and fans, respectively. For more on this idea, see Robin R. Means Coleman and Timeka N. Williams, "The Future of the Past: Religion and Womanhood in the Films of Tyler Perry, Eloyce Gist, and Spencer Williams Jr.," in *Interpreting Tyler Perry: Perspectives on Race, Class, Gender, and Sexuality*, eds. Jamel Santa Cruze Bell and Ronald L. Jackson II (New York: Routledge, 2014), 160.

35. Terri Simone Francis, "Flickers of the Spirit: "Black Independent Film," Reflexive Reception, and a Blues Cinema Sublime," *Black Camera* 1, no. 2 (Summer 2010): 21.

36. Ibid.

37. Lawrence W. Levine, *Black Culture and Black Consciousness* (New York: Oxford University Press, 2007), 176.

38. Yearwood, 81.

39. Clyde Taylor, "The Paradox of Black Independent Cinema," in *Cinemas of the Black Diaspora: Diversity, Dependence, Oppositionality*, ed. Michael T. Martin (Detroit: Wayne State University Press, 1995), 438.

40. Most recently, Perry's *Temptation: Confessions of a Marriage Counselor* (2013) has received harsh popular media criticism for its shaming treatment of those infected with HIV/AIDS and damning policing of Black women's sexuality.

CHAPTER FIVE

"All My Life I Had to Fight": Domestic Trauma and Cinephilia in Tyler Perry's Archive of Feelings

—Ben Raphael Sher

Tyler Perry is likely the first mainstream filmmaker to repeatedly make connections between his own experiences of domestic trauma (particularly, in Perry's case, physical and sexual abuse) and cinephilia.[1] I define cinephilia as a passionate love for film that creates within the spectator a desire to make films, or certain films, his or her own. This passion may include: watching a film over and over again, garnering each nuance from the information presented in the screen space (from indexical details in a film's *mise-en-scène* to its fictional characters); the tendency to seek out behind-the-scenes, historical, and contextual information about a film; the collection of films and film memorabilia; and/or the desire to produce film, art, photography, criticism, or literature related to cinephilic perception. Cinephilia can take place in a movie theatre where a 35mm print is being projected, and it can also take place at home in front of a television screen.

While current academic understandings of cinephilia may be seen as emerging from a particular body of scholarship, the term resonates well with what Tyler Perry and other artists do as public figures and in their work. Indeed, Perry's cinephilia insists that we expand upon and complicate current cinephilia scholarship. In particular, the repeated connections that Perry makes between cinephilia and domestic trauma stretch the boundaries and possibilities of cinephilia. They also illuminate, in a very prominent forum, some of the complex ways in which people use media in order to process trauma and its aftereffects.

Tyler Perry's cinephilia, like all of his work, is marked by rich and sometimes troubling contradictions. In particular, Perry uniquely illuminates the pain that can be a fundamental component of cinephilic pleasure. Sedgwick writes: "A disturbingly large amount of theory seems explicitly to undertake the proliferation of only one affect, or maybe two, of whatever kind—whether ecstasy, sublimity, self-shattering, *jouissance*, suspicion, abjection, knowingness, horror, grim satisfaction, or righteous indignation."[2] Perhaps because cinephilia is, by definition, a type of fondness or love, scholarship about it has tended to take for granted its positive affects: ecstasy, *jouissance*, knowingness.[3] By placing cinephilia in constant conversation with domestic trauma, Perry draws attention to the many complicated affects with which it can be intertwined, which certainly include the self-shattering, suspicion, abjection, horror, righteous indignation, and potential lack of knowingness that often come attached with trauma and trauma survival.

Perry's films are known for bringing multiple influences into often uneasy, unusual, and, for many, uncomfortable conjunction with each other, including film, television sitcoms, soap operas, camp, Black vaudeville and theatre, popular music, art, Christian traditions and performative styles, poetry, opera, and therapeutic and self-help rhetoric. Just as Perry infuses his work with multiple artistic and cultural influences, he emphatically asserts that his films and plays are tightly intertwined with his own life experiences. Samantha N. Sheppard describes how, through Perry's discourse about his films, he blurs the line between his fictional stories and his life story. She writes:

> Perry uses his films as a discursive space to invest—not just financially but ideologically—in the narrative of himself as someone of value. One could argue that Perry uses Black women's stories of abuse—in basically all his films—as a way for him to work through his own personal traumas and relay his own experiences of suffering. According to Perry, "a lot of the stories that I tell, it's just about people getting healed and moving on. That's just my own experiences that I've put into film and television and everywhere else." Making such deposits in his work, Perry's productions are "biomythographies." A genre created by Audre Lorde, biomythography is a mixture of personal biography and fiction to "create a representational space where homes, identities, and names have mythic qualities." Perry's films and characters, which all come from the "foundations" of his life and the lives of those around him, function to create a cinematic

biomythography, where Madea, Uncle Joe, Brian, Terry, Ben, and Wesley—all characters Perry has played in his films—are different versions or "new spellings" of his name.[4]

Taken together, Perry's work and his public persona also compose an archive of feelings. In *An Archive of Feelings: Trauma, Sexuality, and Lesbian Public Cultures*, Ann Cvetkovich argues that the consumption and production of creative work can create archives in which artists and consumers deposit their feelings. She describes a wide range of "archives of feelings" that include Dorothy Allison's novel *Bastard Out of Carolina* (1992), which, like Perry's work, blends fiction and memoir to recount the story of a girl's physical and sexual abuse, and spawned an enormous and vocal cult following. Cvetkovich argues that sometimes fiction is a necessary way for an artist to communicate traumatic and post-traumatic feelings and experiences, which rarely exist in the memory as objective narratives. Cvetkovich also discusses several documentaries by Jean Carlomusto, who uses clips from mainstream American films to represent the unspeakable feelings wrought by traumas that have taken place in her own family, and in the queer community.[5]

Tyler Perry's films are quite comparable with the works described by Cvetkovich in their blending of the fictional, the autobiographical, and media appropriation in order to convey difficult, traumatic emotions and affects. In Perry's films and public persona, as in Cvetkovich's archives of feelings, "the memory of trauma is embedded not just in narrative but in material artifacts, which can range from photographs to objects whose relation to trauma might seem arbitrary but for the fact that they are invested with emotional, and even sentimental, value."[6,7] Similarly, like the works described by Cvetkovich, Perry's archive of feelings creates public cultures; the people who gather en masse to watch, interact with, celebrate, and often find therapy in his work, partly through recognition of the films and genres that he references and re-appropriates. By considering Tyler Perry's body of work as an archive of feelings devoted to the processing of domestic trauma and its affects, we might develop greater understanding of the seeming incongruity that marks his mash-ups of fiction, life experiences, genres, and media references that he has invested with emotional, even sentimental, value. Thinking about Perry's body of work as an archive of feelings allows us to chart his cinephilia by considering his constructed public persona and the media that he appropriates and champions, in addition to the films and plays that he's written and directed.

Perry's very public enactment of Black, male cinephilia both confirms and expands upon the theories of scholars who have written about Black spectators' relationships with mainstream media. Manthia Diawara's groundbreaking "Black Spectatorship: Problems of Identification and Resistance" problematizes seminal psychoanalytic theories of spectatorship by pointing out that the authors of these theories take for granted that the ideal, hypothetical, and largely passive spectator that they imagined to be white.[8,9] Largely drawing upon his own experiences as a spectator, Diawara argues that many Black audience members resist identifying with the offensively represented Black characters in mainstream films. bell hooks points out that Diawara makes generalizations about all Black spectators that may or may not be accurate. In particular, hooks emphasizes that the experiences of Black female spectators are left out of Diawara's argument.[10] Throughout her work, hooks explores the relationship of Black women to media, finding that it often entails a complex combination of identification *and* resistance, absorption *and* distance, pleasure *and* criticism. Perry provides an unusually rich portrait of this kind of fraught, sometimes contradictory spectatorship, arguably problematizing what kinds of spectatorship can be associated with "maleness" or "femaleness."

Jacqueline Bobo, Anna Everett, Jacqueline Najuma Stewart, and Jane Gaines have all demonstrated that examining and historicizing the experiences of as many actual (as opposed to theoretical) spectators as possible reveals that the spectatorship of different members in one identity group will be marked by similarities, but will also differ from person to person because of various factors that should be taken into account. Everett restores the voices of Black film critics from the first half of the twentieth century to cultural consciousness, and finds that the history of Black spectatorship is more complicated than many have suggested. For example, her book counters "the myth of a monolithic response by African Americans to *Birth of a Nation*," showing that responses to the film were varied, complex, and sometimes marked by dissidence.[11]

Stewart's, Gaines's, and Bobo's close analyses of specific case studies illuminate nuances of individual spectators' experiences that authors who do the important work of analyzing a whole collective group could not uncover. Stewart historicizes representations of Black spectators of early cinema in the historical novels *Native Son* (Richard Wright, 1940) and *The Bluest Eye* (Toni Morrison, 1970). She suggests that they present highly plausible portraits of the ways in which movie theatres served as spaces where spectators could get pleasurably lost in the fantasy of mainstream cinema, while also being oppressed by the rigid inequalities of the white patriarchy that such films perpetuated. For example, in *The Bluest Eye*, Pauline Breedlove's efforts to escape from her tortured, impoverished life and imagine herself as Jean Harlow are decimated when her tooth comes out in a candy from the concession stand. At the same time, segregated movie theatres somewhat ironically give the male protagonists of *Native Son* the opportunity to resist racist social structures, by allowing them to look at and respond to a white starlet as an object of desire.[12] Stewart turns to fiction to repair the absence of such experiences from the historical record, since similar ones were undoubtedly a part of "real" American history. In Gaines's close analysis of James Baldwin's childhood cross-identification with Bette Davis and Joan Crawford, she offers the somewhat counterintuitive insight that "rather than seeing [this cross-identification] as retrograde, we need to see the ingenious eclecticism of black queer identity formation as able to find itself through whiteness, to go deeply into whiteness and take out the best parts."[13] Bobo's study of *The Color Purple*, which focuses on women's varying responses to Steven Spielberg's 1985 film, argues that many women are aware of the film's sometimes problematic underlying ideology, but still take subversive pleasure in its radically feminist qualities. Gaines articulates what all of these authors have demonstrated through their work: "A black attitude or reading is by no means uniform or predictable even while the black eye may be consistently jaundiced in the most productive of ways."[14]

These authors make clear the importance of viewing individual case studies of spectatorship as thick texts, in order to understand how spectatorship is imbricated in broader webs of sociopolitical, psychological, and emotional phenomena. They create rich portraits of how the traumas that Black people experience while living in a racist, patriarchal culture (Miss Pauline's oppressive poverty and desire to achieve the "white standard of beauty"; the absence of people of color in the films that Baldwin loved, and his father's hatred of his "frog eyes") can inform an individual's media spectatorship.[15] However, these scholars' approaches to Black media spectatorship have rarely (if ever) been used to analyze contemporary cinephilia. Perry forcefully problematizes the ever-increasing amount of scholarship about cinephilia that overlooks issues of identity by demonstrating that cinephilia and the experiences that make up a person's identity are often inseparable. In particular, he shows how domestic traumas such as sexual and physical abuse may inform and complicate a person's media spectatorship, and his cinephilia, as much as gender or race.[16]

Stewart asks, "What kinds of 'evidence' can we mobilize to understand what happens in the minds of viewers as they watch films? How widely can we extrapolate from the experiences of particular viewers—as constructed in fictional accounts, as reported in the press, interviews, or oral histories, or even based on our own personal observations of audience behavior?"[17] Tyler Perry's archive of feelings, in which trauma and cinephilia play dominant, fundamental roles, offers a truly extraordinary arsenal of diverse evidence to mobilize.

The Roles of Trauma and Cinephilia in Tyler Perry's Public Persona

As he tells it, two major transitions in Tyler Perry's life and career were the result of variations on what Paul Willemen describes as cinephilic "moments of revelation": his decision to write plays about abuse survival after watching an episode of *The Oprah Winfrey Show* (ABC, 1986–2011), and his decision to publicly recount his full trauma narrative after watching *Precious, Based on the Novel "Push" by Sapphire* (Lee Daniels, 2009). In an interview with Terry Gross on the NPR series *Fresh Air*, Perry said:

> I was about 18 or 19 years old and I was watching the *Oprah* show, and she said it was cathartic to write things down. And I, at that time didn't know what cathartic meant, I had to go find a dictionary to look things up. Once I did I started writing a lot of my own experiences down, and there wasn't a whole lot of privacy in my house, so what I did was I used different characters' names in these experiences because I didn't want people to know that I had gone through them. A friend of mine found them and said man this is a really good play. And then I thought well maybe it is a play.[18]

In one of the first major theoretical accounts of cinephilia, Willemen influentially describes cinephilia's tendency to inspire creative production as one of its most fundamental elements. He defines cinephilic perception as the propensity to experience "moments of revelation": "moments which, when encountered in a film, spark something which then produces the energy and the desire to write, to find formulations to convey something about the intensity of that spark."[19]

Perry's cinephilic moment resonates with Willemen's analysis. However, it also encourages us to expand our perception of the term. What I describe as Perry's cinephilic moment of revelation watching *The Oprah Winfrey Show* differs from Willemen's definition in several ways. Willemen's article, like many writings on cinephilia, insists that cinephilia takes place during a theatrical screening of a fiction film. Indeed, he argues that cinephilia cannot take place in relation to most television—namely, non-dramatic series such as game shows, gardening programs, news programs, and talk shows.[20] Perry's work and public persona suggest, repeatedly, that a person may also have a cinephilic response to fiction and nonfiction television. A spectator's engagement with television is, after all, an engagement with moving image media that shares many formal and narrative properties with film. Furthermore, a spectator's engagement with television (or a film on video) creates a different form of intimacy than an engagement with a film in its theatrical release. Often, the television is viewed in the home, physically and emotionally situated in relation to any family or other social dynamics that exist there.[21] For Perry, his therapeutic relationship with Oprah Winfrey's television persona counteracted the oppressive and abusive family dynamics in his home.

Perry's first documented cinephilic moment of revelation also counteracts Willemen's suggestion that such moments in a film "can only be seen as designating, for [cinephiles], something in excess of the representation."[22] Willemen excludes an engagement with a film's representations from his definition of cinephilic perception. He defines representation as "what is being shown" by a film's makers.[23] It is what they intend for the spectator to perceive and understand about the diegetic world that they create. In other words, representations constitute the filmmakers' constructions of narrative, thematic, and ideological meaning. According to Willemen, cinephilia takes place in response to something *in excess* of this diegetic world and its intended meanings. For example, a cinephile might have a moment of revelation in response to the beauty of the wind in the trees behind the actors playing out the narrative of *Jules and Jim* (François Truffaut, 1962).

Contradicting this insistence that cinephilia must take place in response to something in excess of a text's intended meanings and representations, Perry's intense cathection to *The Oprah Winfrey Show* and, in particular, the moment in which Winfrey stated that it is cathartic to write about your traumas, takes place in direct relation to Winfrey's (and her show's producers) construction of narrative, thematic, and ideological meaning. Perry responded, with an unusual intensity that I define as cinephilic, to the diegetic world that Winfrey intended to create, rather than something in excess of it. However, even though Winfrey inspired Perry to write by overtly describing the cathartic possibilities of writing, Perry's moment of revelation also took place in response to something in excess of her direct advice. It was equally inspired by Winfrey's image, her way of being, her relationship with her audience, her reputation in the public sphere, and, likely, her outspokenness about her own experiences of child abuse and rape. He tells Terry Gross:

> I tell you that's what's so amazing about seeing her and having her come along in my life when she did. This woman on television who looks like she could be a relative of mine, and she speaks well and she's respected and people really love her. That gave me a lot of hope in watching her.[24]

Throughout Perry's work, he responds to mainstream films' and television shows' representations, including characters, dialogue, costumes, and set design. Describing his cinephilia on the DVD audio commentary of the play *Madea's Class Reunion*, Perry says:

> I'm a huge fan of movies, I just love movies, and everything I do there's just some moment that comes up where I remember a great scene or a great character ... I see a lot of movies but I only remember the great characters. When I go into one of those moments and I start thinking of all of those scenes, they start coming into my brain one by one.[25]

Perry's second highly publicized cinephilic moment of revelation took place in 2009, during a viewing of *Precious*, a film about a girl who deals with horrific sexual and physical abuse. Perry's overwhelming physical, emotional, and mental experience of watching the film again inspired Perry to write. On his website, he recounted a detailed trauma narrative of physical and sexual abuse. In the same open letter, he also announced his decision to executive produce the film. He wrote:

> If life begins at 40, then I owe the little boy that I was my life. Case in point, not long ago, I was brought a film to watch to see what I thought of it ... I sat at home watching this movie not knowing what to expect. After the movie was over, I sat there for a long time just thinking about what I had just witnessed ... It hit me so hard, I sat there in tears realizing that somehow, by the grace of God, I made it through. My tears were tears of joy, being thankful that I made it.[26]

Perry's statement that the film "hit me so hard" suggests a physical and emotional response similar to Christian Keathley's theory of cinephilia, which draws upon Roland Barthes's concepts of "the third meaning," "the punctum," and "*jouissance*" in order to explain ways in which cinephilic perception functions on physical, emotional, and intellectual levels. Barthes describes the third meaning as an undercurrent of a film that often contradicts the film's temporality, shots, and sequences. It reveals something to the spectator that is counter-logical to the film's narrative, and yet true.[27] In his letter, Perry writes: "I watched all the things that Precious, a 16-year-old girl in the film, went through. I watched her mother be unusually cruel to her and I realized at that moment that a large part of my childhood had just played out before my eyes."[28] He seems to respond to something in *Precious* that runs somewhat counter to its form and narrative, even as it intertwines with them: the film's symbolic resonance with his own memories, experiences, and feelings. Perry, a male who was beaten by his father and sexually abused by neighbors, describes watching a girl being beaten and sexually abused by her mother and sees "a large part of my childhood ... played out before my eyes."[29]

Barthes describes the *punctum* as a detail in a photograph that attracts the spectator to it, that reaches out beyond and perhaps contradicts the photo's *studium* (its most overt, culturally determined "meaning," akin to Willemen's definition of representation). Barthes specifies that the *punctum*, more than just something inherent in the text, is the result of an exchange between the text and the spectator. As such, the *punctum* is individuated. Different spectators are touched by different *punctum* when looking at a photograph, and some are not touched by it at all. Barthes describes the *punctum* as what the spectator "adds to the photograph and *what is nonetheless already there*."[30] Keathley argues that the *punctum* reaches out from the film's *studium* (its constructed meanings) and pricks the cinephile. The concept of the *punctum* resonates strongly with Perry's described experience of watching the film. However, Perry's cinephilia problematizes Keathley's theory, which, like that of Willemen, forcefully excludes an engagement with representation from cinephilic perception. Keathley explains that:

> In the context of Barthes' overall critical project, the third meaning and the *punctum* can be understood as eruptions of figuration in a text otherwise dominated by representation. In *The Pleasures of the Text*, Barthes contrasted representation to figuration, arguing that while the former is an organization of cultural and ideological meanings, resulting in *plaisir* (pleasure), the latter is beyond such generalizable meaning, marked by *jouissance* (bliss)—the individual's fetishistic, bodily experience of pleasure ... Placing figuration on the side of fetishism, and setting representation against it, Barthes wrote, "That is what representation is: when nothing emerges, when nothing leaps out of the screen."[31]

It seems clear that Perry was "poked" (or, to use his word, "hit") largely by the film's representations: Precious's experiences of abuse and growth, etc.[32] Similarly, while Perry's physical and emotional reaction to the film—that is, his "tears of joy"—sounds somewhat similar to *jouissance* (an individual's fetishistic bodily experience of pleasure), the joy is inseparable from his deeply painful experiences, memories, and affects. His tears of joy remind him that he made it out of terrible circumstances. Perry's work demonstrates that the bliss associated with *jouissance* need not be separated from pain, and that the pleasure associated with cinephilia can be rooted in affects such as abjection, horror, sadness, and loss.[33]

Perry's "writing" in response to *Precious* did not end with his website announcement. Shortly thereafter, he recounted his narrative of abuse on a high-profile episode of *The Oprah Winfrey Show*. He helped conceptualize and was featured on a two-part episode of *Oprah* titled "200 Men," one of the most highly publicized and widely seen discussions of sexual abuse against men in media history.[34] Finally, Perry's abuse confessions became part of the publicity for *Precious* and *For Colored Girls* (Tyler Perry, 2010), Perry's controversial film version of Ntozange Stewart's choreopoem *For Colored Girls Who Have Considered Suicide When the Rainbow Is Enuf* (1974). The film draws upon traditional Hollywood genres and narrative tropes in recounting multiple tales of women's trauma.

In the discourse surrounding his work, Perry has discussed his cinephilia, and how it has helped him to process traumas and find professional success. His work also relies on the cinephilia of his audience members (in particular, their engagement with mainstream American films and TV shows that represent African Americans). In Perry's plays and films, and their advertising, Perry and his staff repeatedly count on the audience's knowledge of and affection for popular culture. In an article about Lionsgate's marketing of Perry's film debut, *Diary of a Mad Black Woman* (Darren Grant, 2005), Tim Palen, LGF's executive VP of worldwide theatrical marketing, said: "We launched the campaign early with the 'Orchid' poster, which was sort of *Lady Sings the Blues*. It could touch Tyler's core audience, the older African-American women, and let them know it's a very special movie and we take it seriously."[35] The posters for the film *Madea's Big Happy Family* (Tyler Perry, 2007) recreated iconic Hollywood movie posters and television advertisements, with Madea cast as their star, including *The Godfather* (retitled *The Godmother*), *The King's Speech* (*The Queen's Speech*), *True Grit* (*True Grits*), *Jersey Shore* (*Georgia Shore*), *Black Swan* (*The Real Black Swan*), and *The Brady Bunch*. Perry's advertisers attempted to attract audiences by implying that his films engage with iconic popular culture, either seriously or parodically.

These advertising techniques are at least partially inspired by ample evidence that Perry's audiences love his pop-culture references, as is in evidence on the DVD recording of his play *Madea's Class Reunion* (2003). Whenever he re-enacts scenes from various films and television shows, his audience goes wild. He gives few clues identifying his references. The audience clearly recognizes them immediately after seeing just a few gestures or hearing a single line of dialogue.

Perry encourages his audience members to have intense physical, emotional, and intellectual—that is, cinephilic—experiences, similar to those that he had watching *The Oprah Winfrey Show* and *Precious*. Sheppard argues that Perry

> turns his audience into a congregation, shifting the way in which the movie theater is experienced to accompany the stylistic desires of a spiritual audience that engages in "call and response." Given his preacher-entertainer aesthetic, Perry's films prosthelytize and testify, allowing audiences to "talk back" to the screen and their representations.[36]

In so doing, Perry illuminates the somewhat blurred line between cinephilia, therapy, and the cathartic experiences that one may have at a religious service. Perry's work suggests that a cinephilic engagement with a film may constitute a therapeutic and/or religious engagement as well. All of these events share fundamental similarities: they take place in a room in which people face each other while an interactive exchange takes place between performers and spectators, and in which "audiences" and "creator/performers" both participate in spectatorship and production. In each forum, the performers and the spectators often have intense emotional, physical, verbal, and intellectual experiences that are somewhat unique to those particular environments. These events or venues encourage people to experience revelations, which help them to see something (often, their lives) differently, and in new ways. Perry himself has made these connections—between highly cathected spectatorship, therapy, and church—in interviews. He states:

> My hope is that when people see the plays or the film that they will see themselves. If I can put a mirror in front of you and you can say, "Wow, I do that"—even if you don't admit it to anyone out loud—you admit it to yourself and say, "That's something that I need to work on." If I can offer some sort of suggestion as to how to change it or show you an example of a better way to do it—I got an e-mail from a woman who said, "My sister was being abused by this man and you did in two hours what we couldn't do in twelve years." She finally left him ... My hope is that it is just a mirror. I don't want it to be preachy; I don't want it to be church. I just want it to be a mirror that the audience can say, "Is this something I need to work on? Is this something I can change?"[37]

Perry notably compares the role of his plays and films to that of a therapist (who constructively mirrors a client's experiences back to her in a way that can help her evaluate them), while distancing the works from what he describes as the "preaching" of religious leaders. This statement somewhat contradicts the religious content of his plays and films.

I find Perry's suggestions that his films, Christianity, and the right romantic partner can easily help a person solve deep emotional traumas problematic, as I am somewhat dubious that a person can fully process such traumas without help from a professional therapist. However, I respect Perry's assertion (opportunistic though it may be) that his films are intended to help those who can't afford therapy, or might be ambivalent about it. He has stated that

> these are people who can't afford therapy for the most part, who've never had it, who don't understand why they are in the situation, and here I am with this very simple but complex mirror in front of them and they're able to say, "Wow, that's me. What if I did that?"[38]

We need not take Perry's word that his films have had the therapeutic, cinephilic effects that he seems to intend. On the episode of *The Oprah Winfrey Show* on which Perry confessed his trauma history, Winfrey featured an interview with a woman who profoundly loves Perry's films and plays. She states that she healed from the traumas of childhood rape, abuse, and ensuing eating disorders with help from Perry's work:

> My grandmother introduced me to Tyler Perry and his plays and I have seen every single movie and I have seen every single play. He made me feel like I had a voice for the first time because certain subjects in the Black community, rape, molestation, homosexuality, those topics are just taboo and they're just not discussed. It's my form of therapy.[39]

Winfrey handpicked this audience representative, undoubtedly with Perry's approval. However, I don't think that her experience is unique. I have had cinephilic, therapeutic moments of revelation watching Perry's films, even as I find them troubling, and I've spoken with others who have as well.

Tyler Perry's Cinephilic Production

In his article "Cinephilia, or the Uses of Disenchantment," Thomas Elsaesser describes a new type of cinephile that has emerged in the era of television and home video. He points out that he associates three new types of cinephilic practice with these filmmakers: "re-mastering, re-purposing, and re-framing."[40] These cinephiles appropriate beloved films by, for example, making art that re-edits or pays homage to scenes from them. Tyler Perry fits well into this group of cinephile producers: his films re-master, re-purpose, and re-frame familiar film clips in new, unexpected ways.

Elsaesser argues that these cinephiles are often concerned with issues of identity: "They [re-master] in the sense of seizing the initiative, of re-appropriating the means of someone else's presumed mastery over your emotions, over your libidinal economy, by turning the images around, making them mean something for you and your community or group."[41] Perry recontextualizes scenes from movies that represent people who fit his demographic and those of his audiences: predominantly African Americans, women, and abuse survivors. However, unlike many other producers who might fall under Elsaesser's new category of cinephile, Perry's appropriations are often contradictory and disturbing, rather than progressive, in their underlying ideologies.[42] They reclaim sometimes problematic representations of identity, yet often recontextualize them in oppressive new ways. In the play *Madea's Class Reunion* (2003), the film *Madea's Family Reunion* (2006), and Perry's introduction to the 2006 Black Movie Awards (which he hosted), Perry demonstrates his engagement with some of his favored objects by repeatedly re-enacting sequences from the same media texts, all of which deal centrally with domestic trauma: *Lady Sings the Blues* (Sidney J. Furie, 1973), *The Color Purple* (Steven Spielberg, 1985), *What's Love Got to Do with It* (Brian Gibson, 1993), and Norman Lear's sitcom *Good Times* (CBS, 1974–79). Perry has described his high level of cathection to the media that he re-enacts. For example, on the audio commentary to *Madea's Class Reunion*, he says, "I love *The Color Purple*, so there are all these *Color Purple* references."[43] His alternately loving and parodic recreations of these texts make the complexity of his cathection clear.

Madea's Class Reunion re-appropriates the format of the film *Grand Hotel* (Edmund Goulding, 1932). Several of Perry's stock characters, and a slew of new characters with the problems that typify Perry's work (infidelity, abusive relationships, prostitution, drug addiction), gather at a hotel where Madea's fiftieth class reunion takes place. In addition to playing Madea, Perry plays Dr. Willie Leroy Jones, a bellhop/bartender suffering from "dissociative identity disorder" (meaning, according to Perry's script, that he has "27 people living inside his head"). Because of his negligence as an employee, Dr. Jones finds himself at odds with the hotel's villainous, home-wrecking manager, Ann. When Ann finally fires Dr. Jones and refuses to give him his check (offering to mail it), he tells her that he'll ask for his check one more time before one of his personalities "beat[s] the hell out of you." After she picks up the phone to call security, Jones grabs her arm, tells her that she better "hang up that phone or I'll bust you in the face," and then drags her to a bench. He threatens her with hulking body language while reciting a slew of movie references, revealing that iconic film characters are among his head's twenty-seven occupants. To the audience's wild applause, he unleashes a montage of re-enactments and parodies.

After Dr. Jones drags Ann to the bench, he re-enacts Sofia's monologue from *The Color Purple*, originally delivered by Oprah Winfrey: "All my life I had to fight. I had to fight my brother, I had to fight my uncle ... I loves Harpo, God knows I do, Miss Celie." Tellingly omitting Sofia's proclamation that she'd kill her husband before letting him hit her, Perry follows the monologue with an incongruous series of lines from *Forrest Gump*, a parody of a poem by Maya Angelou, and a re-enactment of a notorious sequence from the *Good Times* episode "The Evans Get Involved," in which Penny's mother burns her with an iron. Dr. Jones takes on the role of Penny's mother, Ann the role of Penny, and a wine bottle the role of the iron. When Dr. Jones "burns" Ann after asking where she's been, she cries, "I was with J.J.!"—and the audience roars with laughter. Perry immediately transitions to a re-enactment of the sequence in which Shug and Celie kiss in *The Color Purple*, although the sensual kisses become ominous as Dr. Jones kisses Ann's fearful-looking face. After kissing her, he says, "Shug like a bee and me just like honey," sings a line from "Miss Celie's Blues," and then tells Ann to run, before jumping up, grabbing her arm, and re-enacting the scene in *What's Love*

Got to Do with It in which Ike Turner forces an exhausted and sick Tina to go out on stage. Dr. Jones inhabits the role of Ike while Ann, looking abject, appears in the role of Tina. Perry, impersonating Lawrence Fishburne, yells: "Anna Mae, where the hell you going? You gonna leave me like all the other suckers did? You trying to run out on me? This is Ike and Tina, you understand that, this is Ike and Tina! You better get out on that stage!" Ann performs Tina's dance fearfully while the audience laughs. Dr. Jones finally takes the cash register and leaves. Ann, her toughness obliterated, looks on.

Perry creates a similar dynamic in the film *Madea's Family Reunion*, in which the local court forces Madea to adopt Nikki (Keke Palmer), a troubled teenager. When Nikki arrives home from school late, Madea ominously wields a hot iron while the aforementioned sequence from *Good Times* plays on a TV screen behind them. As the sequence ends, Madea hits Nikki with a belt. When Nikki tells Madea that the kids on the school bus make fun of her, Madea gets on the bus to set them straight. A bully talks back to Madea and, again, Perry re-enacts Sofia's monologue—this time including the line "I'll kill him dead before I let him hit me!"—before shaking the boy violently.

When Tyler Perry re-enacts the scenes from these films, he appears to experience *jouissance*, a blissfully, "fetishistic, bodily experience of pleasure." I believe that it is at least partly the *jouissance* that Perry conveys—and the loving specificity with which he imitates and oddly re-edits film scenes—that inspires such giddy pleasure in the audience. At the same time, the interplay that takes place between the audience and Perry suggests that he relies on their cinephilia of Black popular culture as well.

In her work on *The Color Purple*, Bobo writes that Black female audiences can use their knowledge of Black film and literary history, and their representational politics, in order to respond to what she describes as an ideologically problematic film. They can reject the film, or, to use Elsaesser's descriptive language about cinephilia, they can "re-mix, re-master, and re-appropriate it." Bobo writes that the Black spectator who loves *The Color Purple* "constructs something useful from the work by negotiating her/his response, and/or gives a subversive reading of the work."[44] Bobo suggests that the "construction of something useful" from *The Color Purple* entails the construction of something *positive* from *The Color Purple*. Perry's cinephilic engagement with the film undoubtedly gives a subversive reading of the work. However, his resulting reconstruction of the film's parts is even more ideologically problematic than the original film.

Describing Perry's re-enactment of *The Color Purple* in the film version of *Madea's Family Reunion*, Sheppard argues that it

> functions as a way to pay respects to the profound influence of Alice Walker's womanist text. However, similar to Jacqueline Bobo's critique of Steven Spielberg's adaptation, as Madea, Perry's comedic invocation of the text "[displaces] black women as the center of the story and [reinserts] traditional demeaning images of them." Borrowing Walker's work as cultural cache, Perry's negotiation of reference and reverence produces the feminist and patriarchal tension in his films' representations.[45]

I both agree with Sheppard's reading and propose another, somewhat contradictory interpretation. When taken in the context created by Perry's public persona, his recurring re-enactment of Sofia's monologue (in male *and* female drag) suggests his profound identification with this moment and with Oprah Winfrey, which seems to lead to his pleasure in re-enacting it. By extracting Sofia's "all my life I had to fight" speech, which resembles his descriptions of his own life, Perry suggests a way in which he might have re-appropriated the sequence in processing his own traumas.[46] Perry extracts one of Sofia's most powerful moments of defiant strength from the film, a moment in which she states that she acknowledges the existence of an abusive patriarchy and refuses to become its victim. As such, he (and, for that matter, Madea) separates this powerful moment from *The Color Purple*'s narrative, in which Sofia is ultimately beaten, humiliated, and imprisoned for decades because of this power. One can imagine that resistant Black female audiences might have responded to the scene in similar ways, by taking inspiration from Sofia's power while putting aside its ultimate containment at the hands of white men.

At the same time, a "positive reading" of Perry's re-mastering of the film is problematized by the fact that Dr. Jones, Madea, and, on another level, Perry, channel Sofia's feminist power in order to inflict emotional and physical violence on children and an upwardly mobile professional woman. Similarly, in *Class Reunion*, Perry's re-mastering of Celie and

Shug's kissing scene changes it from a touching, sensual exchange that corrects abuse in the original film to a moment of perpetration. Perry exacerbates this transition by juxtaposing the sequence with violent scenes from *Good Times* and *What's Love Got to Do with It*, in which Perry changes in an instant from survivors Celie and Sofia to perpetrators, Penny's mother and Ike Turner.

In the *New Yorker*, Hilton Als points out that "Perry's (and Madea's) negative take on ambitious or successful Black women comes up again and again, leading one to ask whether it isn't ultimately a bit of self-flagellation—penance for his own enormous ambitions and success, which he sometimes tries to mask with Christian fervor."[47] In *Class Reunion*, the somewhat contradictory possibility of Perry's anti-feminism as self-flagellation is crystallized as Perry "schizophrenically" takes on the roles of men and women, victims and perpetrators, in his condemnation of an ambitious Black woman in a role of authority. I find it impossible to reconcile these comical sequences with Perry's sincere outspokenness against abuse in interviews. Perhaps he does as well. Describing the aforementioned montage of film references on his audio commentary for *Madea's Class Reunion*, Perry states:

> A lot of the stuff, the comedic moments, for me they happen in the moment and, sometimes they just pop into my head and I'll just say it ... Yeah, when I go into one of those moments and I start thinking about all of those scenes they come in my brain one by one. It was pretty strange for me to recall [the scene from *Good Times*] at that moment.[48]

These sequences exemplify the contradictory, un-reconcilable, and possibly semi-conscious post-traumatic affects that intertwine throughout Perry's cinephilia, and his archive of feelings.

Perry's tendency to take on multiple contradictory roles in his enactment of cinephilic *jouissance* becomes even more pronounced in his introduction to the 2006 *Black Movie Awards*, titled "Great Moments in Black Cinema." In this sequence, Perry painstakingly recreates the *mise-en-scène*, dialogue, and performances of *What's Love Got to Do with It*, *Waiting to Exhale*, *Lady Sings the Blues*, and *The Color Purple*. Perry, in male drag, plays all of the films' leading-man roles, while Perry, as Madea, plays their leading women. He portrays Ike *and* Tina Turner,

Sofia *and* Celie, Louis Kay *and* Billie Holiday, and Gloria Matthews (the character originally played by Loretta Devine in *Waiting to Exhale*) *and* Marvin King (Gregory Hines). In Perry's cinephilic re-enactments, the paradoxical combination of diva worship and identification, parody, feminism, anti-feminism, empowerment, victimhood, and perpetration that seems to manifest itself in all of his work becomes literalized to a bizarre extent. Perry pays adoring tribute to filmic female survivors of abuse, embodies them, and makes fun of them. He situates himself as the abuser of women, the rescuer of women, and the victimized women themselves. He plays both feminist and oppressive patriarch. In these moments, the films that have influenced Tyler Perry, his own films and plays, and his discourse about his personal life—all of which seem to have helped him to process his personal traumas—become superimposed on one another. Their highly contradictory affects and ideologies become inseparable.

Perry's canon of "Great Moments in Black Cinema" is composed almost entirely of films about Black female abuse survivors. His cinephilic recreations raise questions about Perry's (and, indeed, our broader culture's) relationship to media representations of abuse. Why, for example, were similarly seminal films about Black male abuse survivors like *Sweet Sweetback's Badasssss Song* (Melvin Van Peebles, 1971) and *Antwone Fisher* (Denzel Washington, 2002) excluded from the list of "great moments"? The most obvious answer seems to be that those movies (particularly the latter) leave no room for the beloved Madea. However, the question raises a more troubling issue that runs through Perry's work. In spite of Perry's outspokenness about abuse against males, and his admitted admiration for *Antwone Fisher*, he only conveys (and connects) his trauma and his cinephilia in his work by representing the abuse of women.[49] This, perhaps, draws attention to his knowledge about the kinds of on-screen abuse that consumers in the industrial marketplace, and American culture as a whole, can tolerate. It also suggests the difficulties that a person can have connecting with his identity as a male abuse survivor in a culture that, for decades, has only allowed the visibility of abuse and victimization of women.[50]

There are reasons—social, cultural, and industrial—why the vast majority of movies and popular culture about abuse survivors focus on women, one of the most prominent being the centuries-long invisibility of abuse against boys and men. A vicious circle creates this invisibility. Scholars contend that male survivors have remained invisible partly because cultural norms define victim-hood as a more acceptable role for women, a notion that permeates mainstream film and media.[51] Perry's cinephilia points to the problem that, until very recently, abused boys seeking to understand their emotional experiences by looking to mainstream media would likely only find them in depictions of abused women. This cultural tendency has both promoted and glamorized the abuse of women, and maintained the invisibility, stigmatization, and collective lack of comprehension of abused men and boys. Tyler Perry has taken great steps—likely more than any other celebrity—to make abuse against boys and men visible and comprehensible through his public persona. Yet, in the worlds of his films and plays, such abuse remains all but nonexistent.[52]

As I write this conclusion, *Tyler Perry's Temptation: Confessions of a Marriage Counselor* (2013), which draws upon the narratives and style of Douglas Sirk melodramas and the Diana Ross star vehicle *Mahogany* (Berry Gordy, 1975), is playing at local multiplexes. The film has generated controversy for presenting physically debilitating domestic abuse and HIV as a woman's deserved punishments for committing adultery and valuing her career over that of her husband. This development convinces me that Perry's work is losing its productive contradictions, and moving towards consistently perpetuating the cultural problems created by and reflected in the incongruous gender disparity in popular representations of abuse.

In closing, I wonder how our cultural terrain would change if Perry moved in the other direction. Could Perry make the first mainstream feature film to illuminate and analyze these cultural problems, instead of perpetuating them? What would such a film look like? Might it recount the story of an abused boy who can only understand his experiences of abuse by watching the women around him (including those in movies and on television)? How would Perry situate its women characters in relation to its men and boys? How would critics and Perry's core audiences receive a fictional film that challenges notions of "acceptable" abuse survival as much as Perry does in his public persona? Would fictional representation prove more threatening to audiences than public confession? If so, why? Finally, how would Perry's admirably public journey towards processing his traumatic experiences be affected if he integrated them more directly in his fictional worlds? I hope that, in the future, Perry may use his talents, influence, and hard-won wisdom to work towards answering some of these questions.

Notes

1. This chapter is part of a chapter of my dissertation, *Fraught Pleasures: Domestic Trauma and Cinephilia in American Culture*. The chapter also discusses the work of less mainstream film artists who have made this connection in their work, including Odette Springer, Johanna Demetrakas, Jonathan Caouette, and Lee Daniels.

2. Eve Kosofsky Sedgwick, *Touching Feeling: Affect, Pedagogy, Performativity* (Durham: Duke University Press, 2003), 146.

3. See Thomas Elsaesser, "Cinephilia or the Uses of Disenchantment," in *Cinephilia: Movies, Love, and Memory*, eds. Marijke de Valck and Malte Hagener (Amsterdam: Amsterdam University Press, 2005), 27–45; Christian Keathley, *Cinephilia and History, or the Wind in the Trees* (Bloomington: Indiana University Press, 2006); Paul Willemen, "Through the Glass Darkly: Cinephilia Reconsidered," in *Looks and Frictions: Essays in Cultural Studies and Film Theory* (Bloomington: Indiana University, 1994), 223–59.

4. Samantha N. Sheppard, "She Ain't Heavy: She's Madea: The Tyler Perry Discourse and the Politics of Contemporary Black Cultural Production," in *Black Cinema Aesthetics Revisited*, eds. Michael Gillespie and Akil Houston, forthcoming. Many thanks to Sheppard for letting me read the manuscript of her forthcoming book chapter before publication.

5. Ann Cvetkovich, *An Archive of Feelings: Trauma, Sexuality, and Lesbian Public Cultures* (Durham: Duke University Press, 2003).

6. Ibid., 8.

7. Sheppard points to continuities between Perry's work and race films from the 1920s and 1930s (such as those directed by Oscar Micheaux). Although it is necessary to chart, in detail, the intentional or unintentional influence of these films on Perry's work, I mostly focus on Perry's engagement with Hollywood films from after 1950, since these are the films which he directly appropriates, and it seems to me that they are the ones with which he is most engaged.

8. Manthia Diawara, "Black Spectatorship: Problems of Identification and Resistance," in *Black American Cinema*, ed. Manthia Diawara (New York: Routledge, 1993), 211.

9. For early psychoanalytic theories of spectatorship, see Christian Metz, *The Imaginary Signifier: Psychoanalysis and the Cinema* (Bloomington: Indiana University Press, 1975); Laura Mulvey, "Visual Pleasure and Narrative Cinema," in *Film Theory and Criticism*, eds. Leo Braudy and Marshall Cohen (New York: Oxford University Press, 2004), 837–49.

10. hooks, "The Oppositional Gaze: Black Female Spectators," in *Reel to Real: Race, Sex, and Class at the Movies* (New York: Routledge, 1996), 210.

11. Anna Everett, *Returning the Gaze: A Genealogy of Black Film Criticism, 1909–1949* (Durham: Duke University Press, 2001), 8.

12. Jacqueline Najuma Stewart, *Migrating to the Movies: Cinema and Black Urban Modernity* (Berkeley: University of California Press, 2005), 101–107.

13. Jane M. Gaines, *Fire & Desire: Mixed-Race Movies in the Silent Era* (Chicago: University of Chicago Press, 2001), 38.

14. Ibid.

15. Ibid., 30.

16. So far as I am aware, Cvetkovich is the only other scholar who has pursued the connection between domestic trauma and what I would describe as cinephilia. However, she does not use the word "cinephilia" or discuss scholarship about cinephilia when analyzing media spectatorship in *An Archive of Feelings: Trauma, Sexuality, and Lesbian Public Cultures*.

17. Stewart, 95.

18. Tyler Perry, interview by Terry Gross, *Fresh Air*, NPR, October 15, 2012.

19. Paul Willemen, "Through the Glass Darkly: Cinephilia Reconsidered," in *Looks and Frictions: Essays in Cultural Studies and Film Theory* (Bloomington: Indiana University Press, 1994), 235.

20. Ibid., 230.

21. For an influential discussion of the ways in which television becomes intertwined with family dynamics and domestic space, see David Morley, *Television, Audiences, and Cultural Studies* (New York: Routledge, 1992). There is a growing body of work on cinephilia that takes place in relation to home video and new media. See Nandini Bhattacharya, "A 'Basement' Cinephilia: Indian Diaspora Women watch Bollywood," *South Asian Popular Culture* 2, no. 2 (October 2004): 161–83; Lucas Hilderbrand, "Cinematic Promiscuity: Cinephilia After Videophilia," *Framework: The Journal of Cinema and Media* 50, nos. 1–2 (Spring/Fall 2009): 214; Barbara Klinger, *Beyond the Multiplex: Cinema, New Technologies, and the Home* (Berkeley: University of California Press, 2006); Jonathan Rosenbaum, *Goodbye Cinema, Hello Cinephilia: Film Culture in Transition* (Chicago: University of Chicago Press, 2010); Scott Balcerzak and Jason Sperb, eds., *Cinephilia in the Age of Digital Reproduction: Film, Pleasure, and Digital Culture Vol. 1* (London: Wallflower, 2009); Scott Balcerzak and Jason Sperb, eds. *Cinephilia in the Age of Digital Reproduction: Film, Pleasure, and Digital Culture, Vol. 2* (London: Wallflower, 2012). None of these authors have discussed the possibility of cinephilia that takes place in relation to nonfiction television.

22. Willemen, 240.

23. Ibid., 237.

24. Perry, interview by Terry Gross.

25. Tyler Perry, "Commentary," *Madea's Class Reunion*, directed by Tyler Perry (Los Angeles, CA: Lionsgate Home Entertainment, 2005), DVD.

26. Tyler Perry, "We're all PRECIOUS in His sight," TylerPerry.com, Tyler Perry Studios, October 3, 2009, accessed February 8, 2012, http://www.tylerperry.com/messages/were-all-precious-his-sight/.

27. Roland Barthes, *Image Music Text*, trans. Stephen Heath (New York: Hill and Wang, 1978), 63.

28. Perry, "We're all PRECIOUS in His sight."

29. Ibid.

30. Christian Keathley, *Cinephilia and History, or the Wind in the Trees* (Bloomington: Indiana University Press, 2006), 34.

31. Ibid., 34.

32. Kathleen McHugh questions the widely made assumption that Barthes's *Camera Lucida*, and his concept of *punctum*, exclude representation in "The Aesthetics of Wounding: Trauma, Self-Representation, and the Critical Voice," in *Aesthetics in a Multicultural Age*, eds. Emory Elliot et al. (Oxford: Oxford University Press, 2002), 241–55.

33. *Precious* also makes a connection between domestic trauma and cinephilia, demonstrating that the latter can include negative affects. In the film, Precious repeatedly dissociates into blissful cinephilic fantasies at the moments when her abuse reaches its most unbearable severity. During one abuse sequence, she fantasizes that she is the star at the premiere of a film with a poster that replicates that of *Flashdance* (Adrian Lyne, 1983), with Precious in Jennifer Beals's pose. In another sequence, she fantasizes that she and her mother are starring in *Two Women* (Vittorio de Sica, 1960), de Sica's film about a woman who tries, and fails, to protect her daughter from being raped. Perry has said that Precious's tendency to disassociate into a fantasy world was one of the film's elements that most reminded him of his experiences, although he dissociated into happier moments in his own life, rather than films.

34. For Perry's account of his involvement with the conception of the "200 Men" episode, see Tyler Perry, foreword to Dr. Howard Fradken, *Joining Forces: Empowering Male Survivors to Thrive* (New York: Hay House, 2012), xv–xix.

35. Michael Archer, "Strategies on a shoestring: Tailor-made campaigns for a trio of Lionsgate Pix Hit the B.O. Bullseye," *Variety: Independent Distribution*, September 7 2005, X-2.

36. Sheppard, forthcoming.

37. Edie Riggins, "Diary of an Artist: Tyler Perry Shares His Gift," *Venice*, February 2005, n.p. Note: Accessed in the clipping file for Tyler Perry at the Margaret Herrick Library, Beverly Hills, CA.

38. Perry, interview by Terry Gross.

39. *The Oprah Winfrey Show*, syndicated, KABC Los Angeles, October 20, 2010, accessed February 8, 2013 at the UCLA Library Broadcast Newsscape database, newscape.library.ucla.edu.

40. Thomas Elsaesser, "Cinephilia or the Uses of Disenchantment," in *Cinephilia: Movies, Love, and Memory*, eds. Marijke de Valck and Malte Hagener (Amsterdam: Amsterdam University Press, 2005), 36.

41. Ibid.

42. Such producers include Marlon Riggs, Joan Braderman, Todd Haynes, and the makers of slash YouTube videos.

43. Perry, "Commentary," *Madea's Class Reunion*.

44. Ibid., 103.

45. Sheppard, forthcoming.

46. For an example of such a description, see Perry, "We're all PRECIOUS in His sight."

47. Hilton Als, "Mama's Gun: The World of Tyler Perry," *New Yorker*, April 10, 2010, 68–72.

48. Perry, "Commentary," *Madea's Class Reunion*.

49. Perry discusses *Antwone Fisher* in the featurette "Oprah and Tyler: A Project of Passion," directed by Cliff and Lisa Stephenson, *Precious Based on the Novel "Push" by Sapphire*, directed by Lee Daniels (Los Angeles: Lionsgate Home Entertainment, 2010), Blu-ray.

50. For a discussion of this issue in relation to *Precious* and *For Colored Girls*, see Jennifer Williams, "For Colored Boys Who Have Survived Sexual Abuse, Is *For Colored Girls* Enuf?" *Ms. Magazine Blog*, *Ms. Magazine Online*, November 15, 2010, accessed February 8, 2013, http://msmagazine.com/blog/2010/11/15/for-colored-boys-who-have-survived-sexual-abuse/.

51. See James Cassese, *Gay Men and Childhood Sexual Trauma: Integrating the Shattered Self* (N.p.: Harrington Park Press, 2000), 6–8; Richard B. Gartner, PhD, *Beyond Betrayal: Taking Charge of Your Life After Boyhood Abuse* (Hoboken, NJ: Wiley, 2005), 21–41.

52. In my research, I have found some small but notable exceptions to this rule. In Perry's first play, *I Know I've Been Changed* (1999), a man sexually molests his son, a secondary character. This play has not been published or released on video. It is, so far as I can tell, currently inaccessible. The summary of the play on Perry's website does not mention the character. The film *I Can Do Bad All by Myself* (2009) includes a passing mention that Byron, a side character with minimal dialogue, was put in the microwave by his drug-addicted mother when he was a baby. Madea frequently slaps around or threatens boys, but Perry presents these instances comically, without framing as abuse. On the infrequent occasions that abuse against men is present in Perry's work, he relegates it to the sidelines.

CHAPTER SIX

"Who I Am Is Conflicting with This Dress I Got On": Madea's Intimate Public and the Possibilities and Limitations of False Disguise

—Rachel Jessica Daniel

Since *Diary of a Mad Black Woman* (Darren Grant, 2005), Tyler Perry's fans and primary audience has had plenty to say about Mabel "Madea" Simmons, the character who has, by far, become most central to Perry's unprecedented success. This character—a cluster of contractions—is a sixty-eight-year-old ex-convict, stripper, and matriarch who Perry performs in drag. As one critic describes of Madea:

> There is always a note of complaint in her voice, but who can blame her. As the sometimes beleaguered go-to person for any number of younger relatives who find themselves in bad marriages, broke, or incapable of managing their children, the take-charge Madea busts ass while brandishing her handgun, fighting to impose emotional order in her world.[1]

Madea has no doubt remained a polarizing figure and many believe that Perry relies heavily upon long-standing stereotypes of Black women in his portrayal of her. However, for others, Madea, which is short for the endearment "Ma Dear," triggers a sense of nostalgia, familiarity, and even longing.

In a short biographical film, *The Birth of Madea*, Black actors spoke fondly about how Tyler Perry's Madea reminds them of their grandmothers, aunts, and mothers.[2] Likewise, the fan base around Madea routinely uses social media to actively express their adoration of the character. Fans use various online tools and platforms to document and share the character's culturally cherished dialect and popular phrases, including words like "heller," "hallelujer," or "the Lort" to signal their connection to one another, to Madea, and to Tyler Perry. For example, there is a Tumblr blog called "Say Something Else Smart to Me," which thoroughly lists and documents quotes from Madea and cites the film or play from which each quote stems. There is also an active Facebook fan page called "Madea's Quotes" which supporters use to post user-generated memes of Madea and statements from her films and plays. This active fan community also writes and adds their own statements that they believe the character would say if given the opportunity. Among the most widely circulated Madea memes is one that responds to Kim Kardashian's "Break the Internet" photo shoot in *Paper Magazine*. This particular meme shows Madea cocking her gun, and the words, "If I see Kim Kardashian's greasy ass come down my timeline one mo time.[3]" As the avatars and profiles of the people who participate in these online conversations about Madea demonstrate, Madea's community of fans and supporters is indeed primarily Black and female but the group that supports Perry's now-iconic character is also far from monolithic.

By the time Madea made her debut on film in 2005, she was already a beloved character who starred in many of Tyler Perry's plays and had a fan base that was already highly receptive to her particular brand of tough love. In order to more fully explore the terms of Madea's appeal, this chapter examines some of the implications of Tyler Perry's creation of an intimate public around his signature character. In the first part of the chapter, I thoroughly explore Madea's popularity among Black women and also demonstrate how the character successfully functions at the center of Perry's media output. In these sections, I explore the many complicated and often contradictory layers of appeal that Perry's performances of Madea encourage. In the second half of the chapter, I explore some of the ideological and political limitations of this character by investigating Perry's use of drag as a "false disguise" to perform Madea. My exploration crests around the investigation of specific social and cultural values that motivates Perry's unique construction of his famous character. By the end of the chapter, I posit whether or not the fans or Tyler Perry demonstrate a willingness to abandon the character who routinely yells back, "Oh hell no!" at attempts by others to silence her voice on stage and screen.

Receiving and Defending Madea

To better understand Madea's appeal to Black female spectators, it helps to return to the moment when the character made her first film appearance in *Diary of a Mad Black Woman*. The film's narrative focuses on Helen (Kimberly Elise), a woman who is abruptly and cruelly kicked out of her home by her husband, Charles (Steve Harris), who replaces her with his mistress. Madea (Tyler Perry), Helen's aunt, provides shelter and protection from Charles, as well as comic relief for the dramatic film. In different scenes, with a chainsaw, gun, and an old car, Madea terrorizes Charles, his mistress, and destroys their mansion. Despite these antics, or perhaps because of them, Helen feels safe enough with Madea to recount the abuse she suffered, and she eventually forgives Charles and finds new love. The story is one of pain and suffering but also of redemption, Christian forgiveness, and personal healing.

This establishing film, which was originally a popular Perry play, was immediately well-received by Perry's fans who had already discovered him in the theatre and through mass-circulated DVD copies of his stage performances. For this audience, Perry in drag and Madea's over-the-top antics translated well to the "new" medium of film; while the call and response aspect of live theatre was gone from the material's reception as a film, fans found ways to claim the image and storyline as just as suitable for the movie theatre. Madea's on-screen introduction was, however, an unfamiliar and unwelcome addition to mainstream media culture for many film critics. Specifically because of Madea and Perry's use of drag to perform her, renowned film critic Roger Ebert gave *Diary of a Mad Black Woman* a one-star review. According to Ebert, "this touching story is invaded by the Grandma from Hell, who takes a chainsaw to the plot . . . the Grandma is not merely wrong for the movie, but fatal to it—a writing and casting disaster."[4]

In the wake of such harsh reception from mainstream film reviewers, Perry's fans, many of whom had supported him as a playwright, defended *Diary of a Mad Black Woman* and informed critics like Ebert that they were simply out of touch with—and unappreciative of—the rich and complicated cultural history of Black church plays. When *Diary of a Mad Black Woman* became a film, Perry was most widely known as a playwright on what scholars like Henry Louis Gates have referred to as the "Chitlin Circuit."[5] These works are basically melodramas that include "abundant comic relief and a handful of gospel songs interspersed."[6] These plays not only function as common-sense reference points within Black secular and churchgoing communities, but they also continue to gross millions of dollars and uniquely attract almost exclusively Black audiences. With this cultural history in mind, then, Perry's fans argued to Ebert that, as a white cultural gatekeeper, Madea was never intended for *his* consumption or enjoyment. Instead, she was a figure that could best be understood by Black cultural insiders.

What ensued was a dialectic exchange between Ebert and Perry's fans. Ebert published his response to them in "Who *Is* That Mad Black Woman?" As he explained to his readers: "Last Friday I published a negative one-star review of *Diary of a Mad Black Woman*, and since then I have received more e-mails than about any review I have ever written ... [a]nd they were not all the same message, generated by some web site or its followers. Each manifestly came from an individual reader who felt moved to write."[7] Clearly impressed with Perry's fans' allegiance to his image of the seemingly problematic Black matriarch, Ebert explained that

> many of the messages say versions of the same thing: White critics don't get it. We don't know who Tyler Perry is, we have never heard of the millions of dollars his plays have grossed all over America, in theaters, churches, school halls and on DVD, and—most of all—we don't know that characters like his Madea are based on strong Black women the writers are all familiar with.[8]

Although Ebert did not retract his initial critique, his public addendum indicated some of the power of Tyler Perry's fan base, whose arguments further legitimated Madea and offered a pointed sympathetic understanding of Black melodramas as performing cultural work that may not be imminently apparent to viewers outside a given community.

As the first of many financially successful films in which Madea is central, *Diary of a Mad Black Woman* made $21 million during opening weekend alone.[9] To give Madea's box-office power some additional context, as of this writing all of Perry's Madea films—including *Madea's Family Reunion* (Tyler Perry, 2006), *Madea Goes to Jail* (Tyler Perry, 2009), *I Can Do Bad All by Myself* (Tyler Perry, 2009), *Madea's Big Happy Family*

(Tyler Perry, 2011), *Madea's Witness Protection* (Tyler Perry, 2012), and *A Madea Christmas* (Tyler Perry, 2013)—have grossed an average of $69.3 million per film. This average is substantial when we consider that other films targeting a niche Black audience, like Kevin Hart's romantic comedy *About Last Night* (Steve Pink, 2014), grossed less—$49 million in the case of that film—and the Oscar-winning *12 Years a Slave* (Steve McQueen, 2013) brought in a comparable $56 million domestically.[10] These figures indicate that not only did Tyler Perry's audience support Madea during the initial moments when he introduced the character, but his audience has also continued to reliably support his Madea-related projects. In fact, *Entertainment Weekly* rated Madea as number twenty-eight in the greatest 100 characters of the last twenty years.[11] This is all to say that Tyler Perry's media successes exist in large part because of Madea's niche appeal; his empire has been built around her contradictions and eccentricities.

If Madea has remained a popular and desired part of Perry's media involvement, what does this fact tell us about the character's appeal to Black women? While it is tempting to dismiss the character, as Ebert tried to do, as a flawed cluster of poorly performed stereotypes—as not fitting in with mainstream tastes and preferences for "good" film and art—how might doing so also dismiss and overlook the many complicated ways in which reception works for his audience? That is, does dismissing and failing to fully understand Madea also implicitly signal a dismissal and failure to understand his primary audience of Black women? What, specifically, do his fans appreciate about the character even when she is behaving problematically? While I do not attempt to answer all of these questions here, as such questions would require extensive ethnographic and reception-based research to even attempt to make certain claims, I do think there is room to theorize some of the ways the character of Madea might represent social and moral ambiguity and how she might also signify a particular and competing set of ideas and ideologies to Perry's intended and exclusive Black audience.

Madea and Perry's Intimate Public

Although many critics continue to blame Perry for his stereotypical portrayal of Black womanhood, the ticket sales and Perry's revenue indicate that Madea is, ultimately, a reflection of the audience's various and competing desires. In this regard, it might be more productive to consider what these performances suggest about the audience who most actively consumes the imminently recognizable "mad Black woman." For instance, contrary to the popular assertion that Madea is a distorted image of Black femininity, Madea is actually neither male nor female. As far as the character's views are concerned, the character is also not any simple construction of types; instead, her many performances reveal a gravitation toward both the sacred and profane, both feminist and anti-feminist ideologies, both pro-church and anti-church rhetoric, and middle-class and working-class sensibilities. Perry's character remains popular because she has the ability to speak to the various needs of those in the audience. For women spectators who want to hear what a man thinks, there are times when Madea switches to Perry's undisguised baritone voice. For those who buy tickets to see the mirage of a "Strong Black Woman," Madea shows up performing this too, and audiences can catch the impression of a matriarch who is unquestionably in charge of her extended household. For those who value an image of a traditional caretaker figure, Madea is also there cooking and cleaning as a force in the kitchen to keep the men in her home happy and well-fed.

Although members of other racial and cultural groups enjoy his work, Perry's Madea scripts often focus on Black women who are attempting to fix their relationships with God, women who have troubled family dynamics, and women who seek new romantic partners. The theme of triumph after tragedy in the domestic sphere and sexualized male characters who express a desire to marry and be faithful to Black women—all part of a typical Madea plot—attracts a Black female audience. In addition to these themes and plot devices, a major part of viewing and enjoying Madea films seems to be communal and collective viewing and participation. In this regard, Black women attend movie theatres to watch Perry's films together, buy tickets to his plays in bulk, circulate his taped stage plays to others, and vehemently defend and discuss Perry's work in different online forums. This mainly Black female audience that has believed from the beginning that Perry's contradictory character exists *for* them constitutes Madea's "intimate public." In no small measure, Perry has shrewdly identified this often-neglected Black female base as a foundational, reflexive audience. By specifically producing

Black "women's culture," Perry has been able to capitalize on what Lauren Berlant describes as a broader consumer market tradition. According to Berlant, women's culture has served as

> one of the many flourishing intimate publics in the United States. An intimate public operates when a market opens up to a bloc of consumers, claiming to circulate texts and things that express those people's particular core interests and desires. When this kind of "culture of circulation" takes hold, participants in the intimate public *feel* as though it expresses what is common among them, a subjective likeness that seems to emanate from their history and their ongoing attachments and actions. Their participation seems to confirm the sense that even before there was a market addressed to them, there existed a world of strangers who would be emotionally literate in each other's experience of power, intimacy, desire, and discontent, with all that entails . . .[12]

Berlant's point here about emotional literacy cannot be overstated. For example, although there have been narratives about and intended for Black women that have appeared in multiple forms on other platforms (like literature and theatre), the forming of this particular intimate public has helped make Black women's culture relevant to the film industry. This relevance is precisely because they have always felt that Perry's stories about working-class Black women were designed with them in mind.

One of the main attractions of these narratives has been Perry's willingness to explore Black women's relationships with difficult topics like abortion, sexual abuse, single motherhood, prison, and the foster care system. As an imagined and real community of like-minded strangers, Perry's fans can see in his narratives about hardship and healing the kind of emotional literacy that other cultural outlets fail to make relevant to Black women. While late-twentieth- and early twenty-first-century popular narratives about working-class communities have rarely circulated positive or have happy endings, Perry's plays and films offer an emotional currency—happy endings—to "regular," working-class Black men and women, women of size, children, and others who are otherwise ignored by mainstream media. As an intimate public, Perry's fans find in his narratives a language that expresses and reflects emotional—and not necessarily literal—commonalities, desires, wishes, and fantasies.

Christian discourse is a significant but also complicated part of the emotional economy that informs Perry's Madea films. To be sure, Perry's viewing public has remained invested in seeing his representations of Black communities that include romantic storylines and an overwhelmingly evangelical, Christian perspective since his early theatre performances. This thematic engagement with Christianity offers Perry's fans what Michael Warren has called "direct and active membership through language to place strangers on a shared footing."[13] As initially Perry's plays were actually performed in churches, for this particular sector of his demographic he invokes Black church culture to create a "shared footing" among strangers and, in doing so, invites the audience to relate to each other through their active participation in his plays. The way Perry uses and references church culture, however, is never straightforward, as oftentimes Madea exists as a cultural insider who is permitted to playfully ridicule the church. For example, in the taped stage play, *I Can Do Bad All by Myself* (2005), Madea has a phone conversation with Aunt Myrtle who wants to "pray" for Madea. Madea agrees, then puts the phone down and puts a cigarette to her mouth. Perry, as Madea, turns and says directly to the audience: "Watch me make her pray harder ... watch this." The character picks up the phone and yells "Hallelujah!" Madea then says, informing her now complicit audience in her antics, "she's speaking in tongues! Osama to you, baby, Osama Bin Laden." The audience roars at Madea's depiction of speaking in tongues precisely because she demonstrates and plays with her knowledge of the performative and hyperbolic aspects of Black church culture.

Another way in which Perry creates a shared footing around Madea's proximity to Black church culture is in the way Perry includes gospel music and other comedic moments and mini-sermons that are given by other characters, including Mr. Brown (David Mann), a dean at a church, and Cora (Tamela Mann), Madea's Christian daughter, in the typical Madea production. Both Mr. Brown and Cora are recurring characters in the plays and films, so Madea's interactions with them around this topic often build on previous associations and performances. The combination of gestures and specific language widely recognized by those familiar with Black evangelical church culture allows Perry's audience to participate as active members of Madea's intimate public whenever she jokes with the audience and breaks the fourth wall. Yet, because Madea is always functioning as a site of contradictions, she is as likely to reference aspects of "secular" Black popular culture, like contemporary rap songs or old-school R&B, as she is to mention gospel and church traditions. The play version of *Madea Goes to Jail* (2006) includes an example of this. In one scene, Madea begins to sing Betty Wright's secular hit "Clean Up Woman," which is a song about a woman who is all too willing to steal other women's husbands and boyfriends. As Madea sings the song on stage, the audience cheers, and Madea, in trying to catch them in a contradiction of tastes, says to the audience: "I thought y'all just came from church." The crowd, apparently loving the character's ability to point out their contradictions and complexity, enthusiastically cheers and jeers. In this brief exchange, Madea's chastisement reveals her understanding of the audience's own competing desires and cultural literacies. As Samantha N. Sheppard suggests, "through the character of Madea and her righteous ratchet behavior, Perry's films [and plays] are intended for both the saints and the sinners."[14] That is, many in the audience may indeed have gone to church and identify as Christian but this particular intimate public can also enjoy the performance of a secular song that might contradict their spiritual beliefs and values. Hence, Madea's conversation with the audience, and their excited response, which is signaled by their clapping, laughter, and affirmative cheers, is one moment of many that codifies how "call and response" and active participation inform the intimate public's "relationship" with Madea.

Madea's Multilayered Appeal

In addition to being at the center of Perry's complicated and influential intimate public, what other cultural logics and messages does Madea advance? Part of what Perry's audience seems to find most appealing about Madea is that she offers alternative options for spiritual and political engagement in the community. In most of the narratives that feature Madea—instead of waiting on the American justice system to correct and redress the instances of abuse, petty theft, alimony, or lack of suitable homes for Black children—the character steps in, offering practical solutions, and providing punishment and/or provisions for those who deserve or need them. For example, in the films *I Can*

Do Bad All by Myself (2009) and *Madea's Witness Protection Program* (2012), when Black children are caught stealing, Madea chooses not to report it to the police, instead allowing them work as a punishment. Under her watchful eye, the children become more confident, respectful of their elders, and harder workers. In the films *Diary of a Mad Black Woman* (2005) and *Madea's Family Reunion* (2006), Madea creates safe spaces for economically disadvantaged girls and women. Helen is an impoverished, divorced woman; Vanessa (Lisa Arrindell Anderson) is a single mother of two; and Lisa (Rochelle Aytes), her sister, is a victim of domestic abuse. Madea teaches women who are victimized by domestic violence how to protect themselves and seek revenge. Madea's home also becomes a catalyst for two generations of women to discuss the history of familial sexual abuse. In these films and others, Madea provides shelter, wisdom, and even protection from the lascivious gaze of her brother, Joe (Tyler Perry).

After using Madea to communicate a core set of values, Perry reinforced these themes and beliefs in other narratives that do not star his controversial character. In *Daddy's Little Girls* (Tyler Perry, 2007), for example, Monty (Idris Elba) faces the threat of losing his daughters to their mother and her boyfriend, Joseph (Gary Sturgis), both of whom are abusive drug dealers who terrorize the members of their community. Tired of a police force that lacks power, the community revolts against the drug dealers and supports Monty in his street fight with Joseph. Joseph eventually goes to prison because members of the community testify to his violence. They are silent about Monty's assault of Joseph, which indicates they have their own sense of justice. In this narrative, Perry positions an imperfect judicial system next to Black communities who are more than capable and willing to self-govern using a combination of prayer, faith, and community activism.

Perry also does important work by writing the love stories of Black women into the center of his script as opposed to allowing Black women to only play supporting roles in either the stories of Black men or white women. Perry's "Cinderella tales" for Black women fill a void in popular culture, which has oftentimes either portrayed highly sexualized or desexualized Black female characters. Perry's work also reminded Hollywood that Black women are also consumers. Since the success of *Diary of a Mad Black Woman*, films and taped stage plays that represent Black evangelical culture are easier to access through streaming services such as Netflix, or at major stores such as Wal-Mart. Additionally, there have been more films and television shows about Black women, including Perry's shows on Oprah Winfrey's network, OWN. Also, Madea created a space for prime-time characters such as Olivia Pope from ABC's *Scandal* (Shonda Rhimes, 2012–present), Mary Jane from BET's *Being Mary Jane* (Mara Brock Akil, 2014–present), and, most recently, Cookie from FOX's *Empire* (Lee Daniels, 2015–present).

Despite the fact that Perry has used Madea to help make visible an important Black female counterpublic and viewing audience, it has become commonplace to attack and dismiss his works wholesale. In a popular blog, "Very Smart Brothas," Damon Young argues that Perry is a "cultural antihero." He writes, "I can't help but think that the presence and popularity of Perry has both inspired Black filmmakers to be *better* and also reminded producers, moviegoers, and critics that Black movies deserve space in their collective consciousness."[15] I agree with Young; however, I would extend his argument to consider the role of Black audience members. The intimate public that supports Perry, the critics who vehemently dislike his work, and those who are on the fence about Perry's work are having frank conversations about the possibilities and limitations of racial representation in popular culture. Perry's Madea narratives have engendered public conversations about twenty-first-century performances of race, class, gender, and sexuality. If the twentieth-century Black political struggle was primarily focused on the right of African American citizens to first be free, then equal, the current Black political struggle continues to be organized around the problem and possibility of representation. By creating a character that appears to transgress boundaries of gender and other forms of identity, and by creating fictive Black communities that his audiences say *feel* authentic, Perry simultaneously offers his fans an escape from politically correct language and ways of being, while also offering critics content that is ripe for discussion and debate.

The Limitations of Drag and False Disguise

Now that I have identified some of the upswing, contradictions, and possibilities that Perry's intimate public sees and endorses in his depiction of Madea, I want to turn to a more extended examination of Perry's performance of the character in drag. The fact that Perry dresses up as a Black woman has infuriated his most vocal critics. One of the prevailing critiques of his work argues that his performance as Madea castrates Black men, and maliciously and opportunistically denigrates Black womanhood. According to this camp, Perry and other Black comedians—including Flip Wilson, Eddie Murphy, and Martin Lawrence—have only become successful because they dress up as women. In this regard, Perry's performance in drag is an offensive denial of Black masculinity, virility, and agency. From a feminist perspective, a Black man who dresses up and acts as a Black woman threatens to erase real Black women by not allowing them to be at the center of narratives that are about and are for Black women. Kate Davy, in discussing popular drag performances argues that ultimately, "while [female impersonation] certainly says something about women, is primarily about men, addressed to men, and for men."[16]

Although Davy is correct in asserting that drag is usually about men, Perry's performances are unique because his plays and films have always been addressed to women and are about women, as I have discussed. Perry also does not perform drag in a straightforward or convincing manner. That is, part of Perry's success depends on what Roger Baker refers to as a "false disguise." As theorized by Baker,

> false disguise happens when there is no attempt by the performer to pretend he is anything other than a man playing at being a woman: he may use an unequivocally male name . . . ; he may give the audience direct clues with self-referential asides . . . or . . . deliberately assume a masculine voice and attitude for a moment to remove any lingering doubts.[17]

This concept makes an important distinction between male drag performers who use makeup, hair, and props in such a way that a man appears to be a glamorous woman, and Black male comedians such as Eddie Murphy, Ricky Smiley, and Steve Harvey who dress up as women but retain physical reminders of their masculinity. In the way he uses drag to play Madea, Perry belongs to the latter group. He uses false disguise to ensure that his audience remains aware of the fact that Madea is simply an act, a comedic construction created just for them.

For example, in the taped stage play version of *Madea's Family Reunion* (2005), Madea, who is irritated with her uppity niece, comes to the door of the house half-naked. The audience can clearly see Perry's fake breasts flopping as she puts her hand on her hips while she yells. The cast yells back at Madea, and the dialogue is undecipherable because of the audience's loud laughter. During another moment, in the play *Madea Goes to Jail*, Madea breaks character as she gives the audience advice on how to tell if a man is cheating. She says, "I was getting ready to tell you but I can't. I wanted to but who I am is conflicting with this dress I got on ... Madea's strong, but she can't fight this playa." In both of these examples, Madea reveals that she is a man, Perry. By making visible her fake breasts and refusing to share what is presented as a "trade secret" of heterosexual masculinity, Perry continually reminds the audience that he is in false disguise.

When it comes to Madea's centrality in Perry's media empire, what kind of political or subversive import does his use of false disguise contain? In the spectrum of drag performances, there exists on one end drag performances that do political work by always signaling self-consciously the performativity of gender. As Judith Butler argues (and scholar Timothy Lyle helpfully summarizes), "drag acts have the political potential to point to the utterly constructed, fabricated nature of the social scripts regarding a natural, fixed gendered identity that is directly tied to a natural biological specific and a pre-existing ontology of sorts."[18] While drag can certainly perform this political work, most popular comedians who dress up as women are usually on the other end of the spectrum. They instead use drag to parody Black women, and the humor in these performances lies in the acceptance by the comedian and the audience that Black femininity can only be performed as ridiculousness instead of reminding the audience that gender is always performative in the first place. Lyle further explains that

> drag can emerge as an appropriation of the radically liberating practice by the dominant power structure. The practice of drag is thus "domesticated" and utilized as a tool to re-circulate conservative, normative logics and to sustain and even to perpetuate culturally sanctioned ideas about gender and its oppressive consequences for females (and those males who fall outside the gender binary).[19]

With Lyle's distinctions in mind, does Perry's use of false disguise reinforce "normative logics" or express to his audience the limits of gendered constructions and roles?

While there are certainly times when Perry's drag performance of Madea have the political potential to be transgressive and create discomfort, destabilization, and critical dialogue around our perceptions of proper gender roles within Black communities in general and in church culture specifically, Perry ultimately uses drag and false disguise to create a consumer fan base around relatively conservative views on identity. As one critic explains, in Madea's imagination there is no place "for anyone else who can't find social legitimacy, who doesn't fit into the parameters of what she deems proper behavior."[20] For instance, Madea espouses freely conservative rhetoric precisely because Perry never lets his audience forget that he is a man. In the play *I Can Do Bad All by Myself*, Vianne states, "After my divorce, all I want is a nice, loving sensitive man." To this, Madea responds, "Be careful what you ask for, you just might get it. Get you a nice, loving sensitive man, so sensitive he a tambourine player."[21] Madea suggests through her tone, motion, and allusion to the history of closeted Black gay men who are church musicians that she might end up with a gay man. This example—one of many instances in which Perry as Madea reminds the audience about strict gender roles in relation to sexuality—shows why the Black evangelical Christians of Perry's intimate public can in the end love Madea so much. By switching in and out of character, playing Madea as not quite female, Perry can offer his audience an uncompromised opportunity to enjoy a performer who supports a traditional interpretation of Christianity, rather than one who is politically invested in questioning gender roles. At the same time, however, by being more in his female character, Perry gives his audience the opportunity to enjoy the spectacle of drag, replete with all the contradictions and zaniness Madea offers.

By playing Madea as a man/woman and as a woman/man, Perry turns the character into a commanding ideological authority who can always use brute force and threaten those in her care whenever she deems necessary. It is impossible—particularly in the stage plays—to know when Madea will act as a woman or when she will shift to include Perry's masculinity. In many of these moments, as Peter Ackroyd reminds us, "the idea of a male mind and body underneath a female costume evokes memories and fears to which laughter is perhaps the best reaction."[22] Madea, in other words, is also a threatening presence—both literally and metaphorically. In addition to her size, and the fact that she is usually holding a gun—a phallic symbol of power—the audience's inability to truly "know" Madea's gender can evoke a complicated emotional response that gets conveyed as laughter. All of this works ironically as a comical device; the fact that Madea is played by a man offsets some of the tension her presence might otherwise leave unchecked.

Always navigating this precarious line, Perry attempts to restore a sense of order in his fictional Black universe through Madea, who repeatedly states that she is "from the old school." This "old-school" mentality in Perry's plays indicates a time in which it was culturally acceptable for Black people to spank their children. Madea's disciplinary methods are meant to strike fear in the hearts of children. Madea also scares the adults by pulling out several guns from her black bag when she is wronged. Her scare tactics also include discussions about how she poisoned her husband, or when she shot someone. During these scenes, Madea jumps up and down, back and forth, screaming, "Call the Po-Po!" Her breasts flap up and down repeatedly. The audience's response, which is a mixture of applause and laughter, suggest that Madea's violence, or the threat thereof, is hysterically funny.

In the plays and films, Madea always stops short of ever referring to herself as a feminist, but Perry nonetheless conflates tropes of strong Black womanhood around her. In the film, *Diary of a Mad Black Woman*, Madea, who is on house arrest, discovers a way to remove her ankle bracelet. In one of the promo shots for the film *Madea Goes to Jail* (2009), Madea is wearing an afro, all-black clothes and gloves, and has her hand raised in a Black Power fist. The image is reminiscent of historian and feminist activist Angela Davis during the Black Power movement. Like many Black feminists, Madea teaches women about self-love, self-worth, and the importance of knowing how to protect oneself from physical assaults. In the film version of *Diary of a Mad Black Woman*, Madea "calculates" what Helen ought to receive in the divorce. When Helen complains that she doesn't have the right to her husband's income, Madea gets her to consider "taking care of the house, cooking, and cleaning" as her own legitimate contributions to the functioning of the household. Madea even stresses that if Helen did not enjoy having sex with her husband she should also count that labor as a "major deduction." On Helen's behalf, Madea concludes: "Girl, that man owes you 64 billion, 283 million, 974 trillion, 5 thousand and 20 dollars and 82 cents. Now, you need to get your money." In this exchange, Madea, who understands the value of domestic work, is upset by the idea that Helen should receive nothing in a divorce. Domestic work is often called "women's work," and at times it is dismissed as unimportant because it is either unpaid or lowly paid labor. I read Madea's high assessment of Helen's work as a feminist critique of those who discount that labor. At the end of *Diary of a Mad Black Woman*, Helen relinquishes her rights to her half of the money, against Madea's advice, and finds happiness with Orlando (Shemar Moore), a blue-collar worker. Despite these associations however, Perry is able to have it both ways: as Madea, he can maintain some of his patriarchal privilege, but he can conflate and augment that with these tropes of strong Black womanhood.

In embodying both sites of "power"—Black paternity and maternity, the patriarch and the matriarch—Perry's performances as Madea typically support the supposition that Black women should marry men who are within or below their socioeconomic class to achieve happiness. This is a message that is repeated in other films by Perry, such as *Daddy's Little Girls*.[23] At no time does Madea insist on women's financial independence from men; she simply argues that women can and should make money off of the romantic relationships they have—either by killing their husbands and collecting insurance or taking it from a bank account. In this way, Perry's intimate public receives conflicting messages about gender roles: according to Madea, women are powerful and deserving of financial reward for domestic work; however, Perry's meta-narrative insists that Christian forgiveness trumps financial gain. Moreover, Madea's class-consciousness often punishes successful Black women. As on critic explains: "What's most offensive to Madea, in her universe of no-good men and the women who love them because they can't love themselves, are those women who try to catapult themselves above what she sees as their station in life."[24] In most of his films and plays, "good and authentic" women are responsible for domestic work and finding a good, Christian man to love and care for them. On the other hand, "exhibiting style, using passable diction, earning a good salary as a single woman: to Madea, these are all pollutants to the authentic black woman."[25] As a result, Madea's feminist appeal and Perry's narratives of empowerment are riddled with contradictions and class conflict.

False disguise, as I have discussed here, is always a masquerade that is highly performative. This fact does not prevent the performance style from having the potential to convey a set of problematic cultural truths. When Perry and other Black men dress up as Black women in a way that is supposed to reflect the power of Black women, it is easy for spectators to believe that all is well with these performances. On the surface, these drag performances cloak the problem of unequal gender dynamics, operating inside what Judith Butler calls the "the limits of discursive analysis of gender [that] presupposes and preempt the possibilities of imaginable and realizable gender configurations within culture."[26] Perry's drag functions, as Butler suggests, as a parody of gender identity that denaturalizes fixed meanings of femininity and masculinity and reveals certain ambivalences around such discursive configurations.[27] Thus, Madea's comedic performances paradoxically highlight the problems of "gender trouble"—oftentimes using a six foot four, 392-pound man in tights to underscore this fact.[28]

Death by Disguise: Madea's Imminent Demise?

Although Perry began his career with Madea, he has, in recent years, discussed the possibility of distancing himself from his most popular character. In 2009, Perry considered killing off Madea because of the physical difficulties of being in her costume. Ultimately, he reportedly decided against it; he did not want to disappoint his core fans, saying, "As long as they want to see her, she'll stay around. But, I'm telling you, if they ever stop coming, she's going to die a quick death."[29] Another incident, a prank, reveals that despite what he says, Perry remains committed to playing the character and also to protecting her image before his fans. For example, in a 2013 blog entry on the *Huffington Post*, comedian Orlando Jones announced that he would now take over the role of Madea, beginning with playing her in *A Madea Christmas*. The announcement turned out to be an April Fool joke, but the prank confused Madea's fans and infuriated Tyler Perry. When fans expressed disappointment and shock at the thought of Madea being replaced by another comedian, Perry texted humorlessly: "That was an April Fool's joke that HE did.

Not true. And not funny."³⁰ In light of his response to this joke, Perry's claim that he does not want to play Madea rings patently false. The fans have remained committed to seeing Perry's performance of false disguise on a regular, yearly basis, and Perry seems to take the tenets of his intimate public so seriously that, ironically, neither he nor they are willing to entertain jokes or parodies of her. The serious tone of Perry's statement demonstrates his desire to protect his brand and maintain the intimate connection that has fans have facilitated with the character.

Instead of "killing" Madea or allowing another actor to play her, Perry has found some ways to momentarily distance himself from his physical embodiment of the character. This certainly is no easy task. For example, NBC's famed sketch comedy show *Saturday Night Live* (1975–present) poked fun at Perry's inability to shake Madea. In a sketch for a fake buddy-film movie, "Tyler Perry's Alex Cross 2—Madea: Special Ops," guest star Jamie Foxx portrays Perry, who is playing both Alex Cross and Madea. Foxx's bifurcated character is visually split down the middle, with one-half dressed as Alex and the other-half dressed as Madea. This hilarious two-faced character schizophrenically speaks from both points of view, underscoring, as well as making light of, the ways in which Perry has utilized polyvalent voices in his own texts. In this regard, in 2006 Perry published *Don't Make a Black Woman Take Off Her Earrings: Madea's Uninhibited Commentaries on Love and Life*. The book became an almost instant *New York Times* bestseller. The book, which Perry wrote in its entirety, has a foreword and an epilogue written in his voice, but the body of the text is written in Madea's voice. By writing in her voice, Perry continues to fuse his identity with Madea's even when he is not wearing a fat suit. The frame for the book, with Perry alternating between his voice and his character's, also represents yet another way in which he is able to make use of false disguise to satisfy his audience's demand for more Madea content across different platforms.³¹

Despite these perhaps disingenuous attempts to distance himself from the character while also still capitalizing on her success and maintaining steady control of his brand, Perry continues to find ways to propagate Madea's function within his media empire in ways that extend and expand upon his initial intimate public. For instance, in January 2015, Perry released *Madea's Tough Love*, his first animated movie, on DVD. In the trailer, Madea appears to be convicted of wrecking a city block, and as a result she is sentenced to helping the children of the "Moms

Mabley Youth Center." The name of the center pays homage to Moms Mabley, one of the most successful comedians in American history. Mabley's ability to negotiate racial tensions through the use of humor indicates Perry's attempt to situate his work within the activist history and tradition of African American comedy and performance. Rated PG, the film is pitched for children, but adult fans on his Facebook page have expressed interest, with comments such as, "My kids are grown. This is for me" and "Kids?!? I'm going to be right there watching too!!!" Writes another user: "Need this as a regular cartoon series." The comment received over 3,000 "likes."[32] While Perry's turn to animation is a stylistic reprieve from his usual films, it is clear that he plans to recycle some of the same narrative of Madea's reckless public behavior, her familiarity with and subversion of state-based discipline, and her constant patriarchal mission of transforming the children in the community.

As these new efforts demonstrate, neither Perry nor his fan base has lost an interest or investment in Madea; she appears here to stay as the catalyst in his media efforts. The vision of a close-knit community, pseudo-Christian values, and a matriarch with a gun that Perry has been able to craft around her all remains too fascinating and addictive an image for either the Black intimate viewing public or the man in false disguise to abandon.

Notes

1. Hilton Als, "Mama's Gun: The World of Tyler Perry," *New Yorker*, April 26, 2010, 68.

2. "Tyler Perry: The Birth of Madea," *Tyler Perry Bio*, Biography.com, 2:54, 2014, http://www.biography.com/people/tyler-perry-361274/videos/tyler-perry-the-birth-of-madea-14937667977.

3. Madea Quotes Facebook page, accessed January 22, 2015, https://www.facebook.com/madeafans.

4. Roger Ebert, "Diary of a Mad Black Woman Movie Review (2005)," RogerEbert.com, last modified February 25 2005, http://www.rogerebert.com/reviews/diary-of-a-mad-Black-woman-2005.

5. Editors' note: Also see Rashida Shaw's chapter in this collection.

6. Henry Louis Gates, Jr., "The Chitlin Circuit," in *African American Performance and Theater History*, eds. Harry Justin Elam and David Krasner (Oxford: Oxford University Press, 2001), 141.

7. Roger Ebert, "Who is That Mad Black Woman? (2005)," RogerEbert.com, last modified March 2 2005, http://www.rogerebert.com/rogers-journal/who-is-that-mad-Black-woman.

8. Ibid.

9. "Tyler Perry's Diary of a Mad Black Woman (2005)," *Box Office Mojo*, accessed July 12 2014, http://www.boxofficemojo.com/movies/?id=diaryofamadBlackwoman.htm.

10. "Tyler Perry Movie Box Office Results," *Box Office Mojo*, accessed February 6, 2015, http://www.boxofficemojo.com/people/chart/?view=Director&id=tylerperry.htm.

11. Adam B. Vary, "The 100 Greatest Characters of the Last 20 Years: Here's our full list!" *Entertainment Weekly*, June 1, 2010, http://www.ew.com/article/2010/06/01/100-greatest-characters-of-last-20-years-full-list.

12. Lauren Berlant, *The Female Complaint: The Unfinished Business of Sentimentality in American Culture* (Durham: Duke University Press, 2008), 5.

13. Michael Warren, "Publics and Counterpublics," *Public Culture* 14, no. 1 (2002): 62.

14. Samantha N. Sheppard, "She Ain't Heavy, She's Madea: The Tyler Perry Discourse and the Politics of Contemporary Black Cultural Production," in *Black Cinema Aesthetics Revisited*, eds. Michael Gillespie and Akil Houston, forthcoming.

15. Damon Young, "The Point and Purpose of Tyler Perry," *VerySmartBrothas* (blog), September 12, 2013, http://verysmartbrothas.com/the-point-and-purpose-of-tyler-perry/.

16. Kate Davy, "Fe/male Impersonation: The Discourse of Camp," in *Critical Theory and Performance*, eds. Janelle G. Reinelt and Joseph R. Roach (Ann Arbor: University of Michigan Press, 1992), 233.

17. Roger Baker, *Drag: A History of Female Impersonation in the Performing Arts* (New York: New York University Press, 1994), 15.

18. Timothy Lyle, "'Check With Yo' Man First; Check with Yo Man': Tyler Perry Appropriates Drag as a Tool to Re-Circulate Patriarchal Ideology," *Callaloo* 34 (2011): 943–58.

19. Ibid., 946.

20. Als, "Mama's Gun," 71.

21. Tyler Perry, *I Can Do Bad All by Myself*, directed by Tyler Perry (2005; Santa Monica: Lionsgate Home Entertainment, 2005), DVD.

22. Peter Ackroyd, quoted in Kate Davy, "Fe/male Impersonation," 235.

23. Tyler Perry, *Daddy's Little Girls*, directed by Tyler Perry (2007; Santa Monica: Lionsgate Entertainment, 2007), DVD.

24. Als, "Mama's Gun," 71.

25. Ibid.

26. Judith Butler, *Gender Trouble: Feminism and the Subversion of Identity* (New York: Routledge, 1990), 9.

27. Ibid., 174.

28. I use the term "gender trouble" here as reference to Judith Butler's work on identity and performance.

29. Michael Cidoni, "Perry ponders Madea's demise," *Times Herald*, February, 25, 2009.

30. http://s2smagazine.com/2013/04/15/tyler-perry-calls-orlando-jones-news-not-true-and-not-funny/).

31. Editors' note: for a discussion of how Perry navigates different platforms, see Samantha Sheppard's opening chapter in this collection.

32. Tyler Perry's Facebook page, accessed December 30, 2014, https://www.facebook.com/TylerPerry.

CHAPTER SEVEN

One Man Hollywood: The Decline of Black Creative Production in Post-Network Television

—Aymar Jean Christian and Khadijah Costley White

In 2013, Oprah Winfrey partnered with Tyler Perry to release a drama and sitcom of questionable production value. One critic called them "so clumsily produced, it's difficult to imagine them getting through a table read at any other network."[1] Few people might have predicated such an outcome when the mogul ended her daytime talk show and started her own network, OWN (Oprah Winfrey Network), years before. But an understanding of the new television economy, which privileges corporate partnerships and ownership of intellectual property, might have presaged the network's ignominious start. After releasing a slate of inspirational programs, OWN was having a hard time drawing audiences in a crowded cable TV market. Weak ratings endangered the possibilities of obtaining lucrative retransmission fees, so Winfrey turned to Tyler Perry, known for his ability to attract Black audiences. Perry quickly supplied OWN with *The Haves and the Have Nots* (2013–present) and *Love Thy Neighbor* (2013–present), writing all of the combined forty-two episodes by himself. That was quite a remarkable feat for Perry, all the more notable because he had also released three feature films—*Tyler Perry's A Madea Christmas* (Tyler Perry, 2013), *Temptation: Confessions of a Marriage Counselor* (Tyler Perry, 2013), *Good Deeds* (Tyler Perry, 2012)—along with episodes of *House of Payne* (TBS, 2007–2012) and three filmed plays (*Aunt Bam's Place*, *I Don't Want to Do Wrong*, *Madea Gets a Job*), in the previous year.

Of course, we mean to suggest Perry either did not write all those works, or if he did, his divided attention accounts for their weak plots, reductive characters, and questionable politics. Why not hire help—writers who can earn credits and residuals? Perry insists on owning everything he produces, and he also directs and often stars in those products. In the decade following his film debut in 2005, Perry went from a virtual unknown to one of the highest-paid entertainment moguls, with a fortune estimated at nearly half a billion dollars.[2] He accomplished this by building a following among Black American theatregoers, bringing them into cinemas and inking lucrative partnerships with corporations who could secure and finance his intellectual property, first Lionsgate (and subsidiary Debmar-Mercury) and then OWN.

Academic and popular writers discuss Tyler Perry primarily in two ways: his representations and his industry. While the former sparks lively debates about Perry's portrayal of the Black family, Black women and men, the latter is often cast aside with simple references to his incredible wealth. We argue Perry's multiple roles in entertainment production and his successful self-positioning as a Hollywood outsider compel scholars to grapple with the significance of the ways media corporations have increasingly embraced the "one man Hollywood" niche producer model for its low-cost efficiency in a fragmented marketplace. Like famed director Oscar Micheaux before him, Perry has consistently pointed to the importance of Black audiences, parlaying his grasp of this niche into an ever more powerful and complex production and distribution apparatus. Having this one-man media empire—in theatre, film, and television—gives Hollywood a consistent and safe outlet to market to Black audiences in a creative economy made aggressively competitive by deregulation and conglomeration. But Perry's dominance of the space, and his steely focus on growing his own properties, limits America's range of representations.

Much has been said of the expanding possibilities for storytelling in global creative industries. Yet for marginalized groups this has only been occasionally true.[3] For Black audiences, in particular, a fresh wave of government deregulation at the turn of the twenty-first century paved the way for more media conglomeration, changes which reduced the complexity and diversity of minority stories and producers. As audiences grew harder to organize, studios and networks invested heavily in franchises, established talent, and formulaic storytelling, all of which privileged white male producers. Aware of the size and power of the Black market, but losing sight of diversity off-camera, studios and networks promoted the television stars they had supported in the nineties—Will Smith, Denzel Washington, Jennifer Lopez, Martin Lawrence, Jamie Foxx, and Queen Latifah—to film. At the same time, television shows featuring Black casts and creators declined steeply as major networks aimed to attract broader (or, whiter) audiences. Cable networks targeted smaller but more affluent audiences.

In a fast-changing landscape, Tyler Perry proved a very safe and welcomed bet. Through his theatrical and early cinematic productions, he was one of very few independent producers who had built name recognition among Black consumers. Perry's small but dedicated audience allowed him to ink distribution deals that were lucrative for him but with little room for other Black creators around him. Unlike in the 1990s, when networks hired a critical mass of writing and acting talent, a small network of production and distribution entities—Lionsgate, OWN, TBS, and Debmar-Mercury—went with Perry, the most reliable, albeit problematic, vehicle for garnering audiences in era of hard-to-find niches across platforms. A combination of anti-union labor trends and industry deference to Perry's influence, and indifference to his work, buttressed with heteronormativity, misogyny, and homophobia, yielded a series of profitable products of questionable cultural value: *House of Payne* to *Love Thy Neighbor* (OWN, 2013–present) and *The Haves and the Have Nots* (OWN, 2013–present), as well as *Why Did I Get Married Too* (2010) and *Temptation*.

This essay explains Perry's successful rise as inextricably tied to the growing invisibility of Black labor and audiences in Hollywood, even amidst exponential growth in production and networks for distribution. How is it that, despite hundreds of channels, only Perry and a handful of other Black producers—Shonda Rhimes, Mara Brock, and Salim Akil—were able to profit from the burgeoning new television marketplace? We begin with an explanation of the past and present—the rise and fall—of the Black TV market. We'll then move to discuss how Perry stepped into the void left when growing conglomerates shed Black television shows and creative talent, and how his productions successfully saved or lifted those conglomerates above the fray of a competitive media marketplace. Finally, we will end with an examination of the stories this marketplace supports, focusing on how Perry's cultural politics—based on his perception of what his audience wants—creates damaging narratives that champion patriarchy, heterosexism, and narrow paths to progress within Black communities.

Whither the Black Market?

At the annual conference of the Television Critics Association (TCA), networks promote upcoming programming slates with light and convivial panels with producers and stars. In the generally festive atmosphere of the 2013 conference, there were notable silences as cast members recounted experiences in production. At HBO's panel for *Mike Tyson: Undisputed Truth* (Spike Lee, 2013), Tyson described how the final project differed from his initial vision for the autobiographical piece. He explained that the filming of the one-man Broadway play was originally supposed to include a band and take place in Las Vegas, but was later reshaped by director Spike Lee.[4] What Tyson neglected to mention—but what we can only imagine was on Lee's mind[5] as he listened by his side—was that the two men had pitched another project to HBO. Their scripted drama, *Da Brick* (Spike Lee, 2011), penned by Black screenwriter John Ridley, who wrote the George Lucas-produced *Red Tails* (Anthony Hemingway, 2012) and Steve McQueen's *12 Years a Slave* (2013), was "a contemporary exploration of what it means to be a young, black man in a supposedly post-racial America."[6] HBO, however, decided not to pick up that show. Instead, HBO opted for something far cheaper, balking at the opportunity to break a damning track record: the network, despite numerous chances, had never greenlit a series created by a Black producer.

We narrate the story of *Da Brick* because it reflects the realities of scripted television production in the post-network era: minority producers, despite more buyers for shows (channels), find it difficult to get shows made by networks that could easily support bright new acting talent—*Da Brick* was to be *Attack the Block*'s (Joe Cornish, 2011) John Boyega's breakout US role—and bring in more writers under contract with the Writers Guild. Instead, cable networks, initially launched on the premise they could better reflect America's diverse communities than the three long-standing broadcast networks, focused on cheaper, non-union reality programming and syndicating pre-existing films and TV shows. Indeed, a week before Tyson and Lee's panel, BET announced an unprecedented syndication deal for ABC's Black-led *Scandal* (ABC, 2012–present), paying an undoubtedly hefty price to air the first two seasons in advance of season three, after which it would re-air new episodes within eight days of each episode's broadcast on Disney's broadcast network.[7] While the vast majority of BET's programming was unscripted, it chose to repurpose other scripted content rather than produce more of its own.

The roots of this crisis are complicated but begin with the deregulation of the television industry in the late 1970s, which gave rise to networks like HBO and BET. The founders of cable networks lobbied hard for Congress to break the oligarchy of CBS, NBC, and ABC, arguing, in part, that cable would help bring communities forgotten by television together. As Beretta Smith-Shomade has argued, "for people of color and those concerned with their representation, cable was marketed as the cure all for a very white television world."[8] In reality, cable was a business opportunity for the likes of Ted Turner and Robert Johnson to get a piece of TV's advertising revenue. Turner himself sold cable to advertisers as a way to get *away* from people of color: "We're not wired to the ghettos," he said in 1978.[9] That sell worked, and throughout the 1980s broadcast networks saw periodic declines in viewership, enough to compel them to market to those people of color, who held on to free over-the-air television at higher rates than whites.

The advent of cable, along with Nielsen's implementation of the People Meter in 1987, led to a proliferation of Black stories on broadcast TV.[10] The popularity of *The Cosby Show* (NBC, 1984–92) showed networks white viewers would watch Black stories, and the show's independent production company, Carsey-Werner, grew rich.[11] Soon Rupert Murdoch's upstart broadcaster Fox would take a page from this playbook and invest heavily in Black comedy, providing a platform for a group of stars and producers—among them the Wayans brothers and Martin Lawrence—who would enrich Hollywood companies for decades.[12] Over-the-air network UPN debuted in the 1990s to take advantage of advertiser interest in the Black market and provided dozens of union-contracted jobs for Hollywood's growing community of Black writers. Most notable among these were Salim and Mara Brock Akil, who created *Girlfriends* (UPN, 2000–2008) and later *The Game* (UPN, 2006–2008;

BET, 2011–15). The growth of hip hop as a global music behemoth contributed to this bubble, as evidenced by Will Smith and Queen Latfifah's successful transitions to television, culminating in Viacom's purchase of BET in 2001.

Black audiences thus were integral to the development of cable and the sustainability of broadcast television during the multichannel transition; or, as Robin Means Coleman states, networks during this period perceived Black audiences as "ensuring programmatic successes."[13] Data from Nielsen suggested Black Americans watched these programs and paid for cable as well, both directly and indirectly. By 2005, a comprehensive report on the African American audience reported a greater share of Black audiences watched ad-supported cable and premium channels like HBO throughout their days.[14] This explains the trend of cable channels spearheading successful original programming initiatives with Black-targeted shows after Black broadcast television production slowed: Lifetime (*Any Day Now*, 1998-2002), HBO (*Oz*, 1997–2003), Showtime (*Soul Food*, 2000–2004), Logo (*Noah's Arc*, 2005–2006), VH1 (*Single Ladies*, 2011–present), DirectTV's Audience Network (*Rogue*, 2013-present), and, of course, TBS (*House of Payne*; *Meet the Browns*, 2009–2012; *For Better or Worse*, 2011–present; *Are We There Yet?*, 2010–13). At the same time, throughout television's period of deregulation, Black Americans disproportionately received programming from free over-the-air broadcasts and remained a key viewership of broadcast television programs.[15]

Cable was filling the hole left by the broadcasters, who would become vertically integrated and resistant to pitches from Black producers. Shortly after the passage of the Telecommunications Act of 1996, which allowed networks to own more of their programs, broadcasters premiered a nearly all-white slate of programs, a "virtual whiteout," as the NAACP called it in 1999.[16] Staging direct action, the organization worked to increase diversity by pressuring networks to adopt formal minority development programs, with NBC starting and other networks following suit (this was in addition to Cosby's writing fellowship, which started in the early 1990s and ran through 2012). But the merger of UPN and the WB, creating the CW, and the general trend toward reality television, caused a drastic reduction in the number of Black writers, and other networks soon saw declines.[17] By the 2011–12 season, all minority writers made up just 15 percent of all unionized writers, less than half their representation in the total population.[18] Most of those writers were staffed on majority-white shows, much like the actors forced to play "tokens" on sitcoms and dramas. In this climate, it is no wonder that, when BET revived UPN's *The Game* in 2011, it broke records for the network and cable generally.[19]

When Tyler Perry started producing television in the mid-2000s, Black television was teetering on the brink of crisis. On cable, networks were focused on producing cheaper reality television, and broadcast networks had all but stopped producing majority-minority shows. With many writers and actors finding work hard to come by, and viewers finding decent scripted entertainment even harder, Perry was in an ideal position to get the creative teams he needed at a low cost and the robust distribution deals to make him rich.

How One Man Produces Everything

Tyler Perry achieved success by producing "feel good" comedies and moral melodramas at low cost and rapid pace, organizing large enough audiences to sell them across media platforms. Perry's career grew because he discovered his audience early and secured ownership of intellectual (and physical) property, which gave him power to bypass or accelerate what delayed and complicated production in the post-network era: the hiring of above-the-line creative talent, including writers, producers, directors, and headlining actors. For most of these roles, he simply hired himself.

"Is this sort of selfish anarchy a good thing?" asked Nelson Pressley, a theatre critic writing for the *Washington Post* in 2000, of Perry's *I Can Do Bad All by Myself*, calling it "The Tyler Perry Show."[20] Even after dismissing the play's writing and overall plot, Pressley filed a positive review: "Anything goes, as long as you get the audience's attention and come around to the right message by the end." Inadvertently, Pressley identifies what has always been Perry's modus operandi from the day he self-produced *I Know I've Been Changed* in 1992 by putting up his $12,000 savings to rent and staff a 200-seat theatre, to which only thirty people came.[21] Perry learned he needed the audience, not just ownership, and his break came when he staged the play again at Atlanta's House of Blues, a renovated church. "Promotion was done by word of mouth in Black churches; the eight-night engagement sold out," according to reports.[22] After adapting works from megachurch pastor T.D. Jakes, Perry had a theatregoing audience that generated more than $70 million in box-office and merchandise sales from 1998 to 2004, when Lionsgate announced production on *Diary of a Mad Black Woman* (Darren Grant, 2005).[23] By the time Lionsgate inked *Madea's Family Reunion* (Tyler Perry, 2006) and started releasing official DVDs of the plays, that number was expected to climb to $100 million.[24]

Home videos were a key part of Perry's transition from audience development to master of intellectual property and corporate partnerships. For one, DVDs sales managed by Lionsgate gave him added protection against piracy, which he called a "major issue" when he was self-distributing under the Tyler Perry Company:[25] "Before I could get to my fan base, it had been pirated all over the streets. I knew I needed a bigger machine," he told *Variety*.[26] Lionsgate provided that machine. In 2007, Tyler Perry's success in film, video, and, most significantly, television made him Lionsgate's "favorite son," as vice chairman Michael Burns referred to him in a 2007 quarterly earnings conference call.[27]

Shortly after inking video and film deals with Lionsgate, Perry set his eyes on television and its riches. After the broadcast "whiteout," cable, with its need to fill empty programming schedules, was his savior. In 2003, he was under contract with CBS to write a sitcom pilot, which fell through. The experience of trying to convince a network taught him he needed to produce "on his own terms."[28] Lionsgate had recently purchased syndication firm Debmar-Mercury, and its founders wanted to make a splash. Perry produced ten episodes of *House of Payne* on his own for TBS, and it tested well in ten markets, most notably Atlanta. In mid-2007, it premiered as the highest-rated original sitcom on cable among total viewers and adults 18–49.[29] Debmar-Mercury founders focused exclusively on Perry as self-made brand, his low-cost production model, and built-in audience: "You need someone who has a pre-sold branded element. It can't be an unknown guy with a really good script. You need to be in business with people who have the financial wherewithal to play for the upside," Bernstein said.[30] Tyler Perry's investment in those early episodes paid off. The unprecedented "10/90" deal meant TBS bulk-ordered scores of episodes after Perry's initial ten. TBS paid a $45 million six-year license fee for at least seventy-five episodes; additional licensing fees, estimated at around $40 million, resulted from negotiations with individual stations, mainly from networks owned and operated by broadcasters like Fox.[31] This is on top of advertising revenues. Lionsgate estimated the overall value of the deal at upwards of $200 million, of which Perry pocketed 60 percent to Debmar-Mercury's 30 percent.[32] Perry was explicitly "taking advantage of Georgia as a nonunion state," according to some reports and producing the series for an estimated $500,000 each episode, roughly one-third the broadcast TV average.[33] The series went on to air more than 180 episodes.

Neglected in this cable TV marketplace were the workers who supply the stories. A year after its premiere, *House of Payne*'s writers went on strike after Perry fired them for trying to unionize the room. The writers had been negotiating with Perry for months after having written over one hundred episodes. The final sticking point was residual payments. Writer Teri Brown-Jackson said in a release from Writers Guild of America West, which filed unfair labor practices with the embattled National Labor Relations Board:

> I feel like I was slapped in the face, like we were used.... We were good enough to create over a hundred episodes, but now when it comes to reaping the benefits of the show being syndicated and having other spin-offs from it, he decides to let us go unless we accept a horrible offer.[34]

That week five writers picketed the grand opening of Tyler Perry Studios, the nearly thirty-acre campus which that October night drew the likes of Oprah Winfrey, Will Smith, Sidney Poitier, Patti LaBelle, and other Black luminaries (who all crossed the picket line).[35] Then-Democratic Party candidate Barack Obama was invited but declined to attend.[36] A month after dozens of Hollywood's marquee writers—among them Tina Fey, Shonda Rhimes, Chuck Lorre, and Marc Cherry—publicly chastised Perry for running the only nonunionized scripted production on the air that season, Perry reached an agreement brokered by the NAACP.[37]

The settlement, however, appeared to change little of Perry's production practices. Most of the writers who picketed did not return to the show. On his subsequent sitcoms *Meet the Browns* and *For Better or*

Worse, Perry is credited as the most frequent writer, a questionable claim given his productivity across platforms.[38] After pioneering the 10-90 deal, of which Ice Cube's TBS show *Are We There Yet* and Charlie Sheen's FX show *Anger Management* (2012–present) would take advantage, Perry shifted gears when he got into business with Oprah Winfrey and Discovery Communications. He alone is credited on the OWN prime-time soap opera, *The Haves and the Have Nots,* and sitcom, *Love Thy Neighbor,* allowing him to circumvent paying a staff of union-contracted writers.

Perry's insistence on owning and controlling his own intellectual property has been well-documented and appears consistent. This includes a number of accusations and lawsuits alleging he stole material from other writers and artists, particularly Black women and gay men.[39] Notable among these was CBS local V-103 host and noted Atlanta drag queen Miss Sophia (Joe Taylor), who claimed on an infamous October broadcast that Perry stole Madea from her, showing old footage of her own character playing gay clubs:

> He would come to the show. He would sit up under the spotlight, behind the camera. He never wanted us to take photos of him. He never wanted us to take videos of him ... But after the show Tyler Perry would always come up and tell me, "you know you crazy," "you know you stupid" and "you know I'm going to put such-and-such in the show" ... For all the people asking me, "Miss Sophia, did Tyler Perry steal your stuff" and I used to say, "No, you know, I don't think he stole my stuff." I'm telling you right here on FM digital live: Yes yes yes yes yes yes that nigga stole my character! ... Sophia has been in existence for 20-some years!"[40]

Authorship in media production is more a matter of industrial power than truth; disputing creative ownership is historically a fool's errand for those outside media industries. Nevertheless, Perry's claims of sole authorship on as many properties as possible strains credulity and, at a time when pressure on writers is escalating, betrays his insistence that his work benefits the communities who inspire his works.[41]

Claims to sole authorship have allowed him to profit handsomely from his works and reduce costs for corporate partners desperately searching for cheap, popular content at a time when competition for eyeballs was stiff and consumer options multiplying. Debmar-Mercury and Lionsgate, TBS, and OWN have all built or sustained their enterprises in great part due to Perry. Lionsgate spent years searching for hits, its stock buttressed by Perry's consistent box-office receipts, DVD sales, and television syndication businesses.[42] By the late 2000s, Lionsgate purchased Summit Entertainment, giving it two major franchises (*The Hunger Games* and *Twilight*) and transforming it into a major studio. Perry's early success with TBS gave it the heft it needed to eventually pick up a previously canceled broadcast sitcom in *Cougar Town* (ABC, 2009–2012; TBS, 2013–15). Finally, after OWN's premiere ratings faltered and Perry's planned cable network with Lionsgate, Tyler TV, fizzled, Perry took a small equity stake in OWN and delivered two shows in under a year.[43] OWN followed the same playbook as TBS, banking on Black viewers' appetite for scripted entertainment.[44] Eschewing the pulpy, exploitative reality television that enriched other cable brands—enough to collect generous retransmissions fees—OWN found in Perry a family-friendly alternative that was easy to market. Premiere ratings for *The Haves and the Have Nots* and *Love Thy Neighbor* were strong enough for the network to double the episode order for *The Haves* and pick up the third season of *For Better or Worse* from TBS.[45]

But the numbers only tell the story of tycoons who have profited from an unequal marketplace. What narratives are Black audiences being sold? There have been numerous critiques of Perry's representations in film, which tend to denigrate Black female professional success and valorize traditional, working-class family structures. An analysis of his TBS and OWN shows (Perry's only sole-authored television texts) reveals the pitfalls of when one man guards creative ownership over swathes of programming.

When One Man Produces Everything

Tyler Perry's contribution to television and film extends far beyond the scope of behind-the-scenes battles, plagiarism, and backroom deals. While Perry's approach to the entertainment industry is plagued with accusations of appropriation and lack of originality, the extremely predictable and preachy nature of Perry's texts has also propelled their widespread circulation and consumption among Black audiences, attracted by their Christian overtones and cultural references. A close look at Perry's dominant one-man-band approach to production shows his creative works cohere around his personal ideas about African American identity and behavior. By producing derivative family dramas and situation comedies focusing on the Black experience, Perry does more than promote his brand—he also advances a clear agenda, painting a vexing portrait of Black pathology, values, and norms.

The politics of Black representation on both silver and small screens has been at the center of scholarly and critical analyses (and conflicts) for decades. Most of this work focuses on whether media images provide people with information about racial others that fuel their actions, behaviors, and beliefs; as such, debates over popular on-screen narratives about people of color typically examine whether these narratives vilify (or flatter) Black people, depict their complex identities and roles in society, or present accurate portrayals of Black experiences. Arguably, the tropes represented in Tyler Perry's brand does the work of each, creating accessible and diverse representations of Black characters that venerate working-class people, vilify the wealthy, and adhere to strict pseudo-Christian gender and sexual codes. In his own words,[46] Black women are both the primary subject and audience of his work, and he receives most of his criticism pertaining to their representation. For some detractors, his moralistic texts and humor about their appearances and choices extend the "painful and punishing control over women's bodies" that theorists argue is endemic to modern society.[47] According to his critics, Perry's pieces are "marked by old stereotypes of buffoonish, emasculated black men and crass, sassy black women"[48] and their "image is troubling and harkens back to Amos 'n' Andy."[49] Perry, however, argues that his work is based on real-life personal experiences and, through it, he aims to counsel Black viewers on the challenges they face, especially young women. As he explains in an interview about his film *Temptation*:

> What was more important to me in this film was that I knew there were a lot of people going through things in relationships and I wanted to just raise a flag and say "What happens when you're tempted?" One choice, one bad decision can change your entire future and destiny. That's why I wanted to tell this story and that's why I took the play version to this version and

really extended it and really went into all of those different areas . . . I also wanted this cast, I wanted a younger cast because not only is this message for everyone but its in particular for younger people as well. One decision can change your whole life . . . It's not about trying to make the men more powerful, they're great and moving on and happy and the women aren't. No—it's about the choices that we make and to tell you the truth, I've known some of these women, I know some of these men. I've known a lot of people in my lifetime, in my career and I've seen a lot of these situations and it is pretty sad.[50]

By drawing on what he sees as authentic Black experiences, especially for Black women, Perry's characters and representations function as cautionary tales about success, failure, faith, and power (see, for example, Perry's advice book, *Don't Make a Black Woman Take Off Her Earrings: Madea's Uninhibited Commentaries on Love and Life*).[51]

As the first of Perry's television ventures, *House of Payne* provides a glimpse into the themes, patterns, and ideas pervading his TV work. Typical of the sitcom genre, *House of Payne* focuses on a patriarchal family unit raising children in unconventional circumstances and challenges. In the show, Curtis and Ella Payne (LaVan and Cassi Davis), a middle-class couple in their fifties with a son in college, are forced to take in their nephew and his family after a tragic accident. The spouses of both Payne men are housewives who spend their time volunteering, cooking, cleaning, and otherwise attending to the needs of their husbands and children. Besides common sitcom storylines about aging, financial difficulties, childhood bullies, and school, the show is filled with Black cultural references, like jokes about skin tone, masculinity, layaway, DNA paternity tests, playing the dozens, and referring to various characters with the Black church honorific of "Sister" or "Brother." Like all of Perry's programs, *House of Payne* focuses on issues perceived as facing Black families, most often pointing blame at mothers as responsible for their deterioration. For example, the drug addiction of "stay-at-home mom" Janine (played by Demetria McKinney) nearly rips the Payne family apart.

Irresponsible and neglectful mothers are plot devices in each of Perry's other shows, from another addict mother who loses her children to foster care in *Meet the Browns* to a woman who attacks and regularly threatens her adult children in *Love Thy Neighbor*. This theme echoes popular and historical arguments that blame the poor outcomes of Black people on the pathological behavior of Black women—perhaps most famously in the findings of sociologist Daniel Patrick Moynihan in 1965.[52] The trope almost always neglects systemic injustice and justifies racism by locating Black dysfunction on individuals who should presumably know better and are empowered to change their circumstances.

Perry's work buttresses his intellectual property, along with his preferred themes of religion and individual respectability, by shifting his characters across his theatre, television, and film brands. Abiding by his on-stage vow to only produce Christian, faith-based entertainment, Perry opens the *House of Payne* series with the family returning from a Sunday afternoon at church, padding the show with Scripture, church scenes, and family prayer. Additionally, the first few episodes of the series include two of Perry's trademark characters, Madea (performed by Perry) and Mr. Brown, played by David Mann. Continuing a premise from a 2006's *Madea's Family Reunion*, in which Madea becomes a court-appointed mother, she and her foster daughter appear in *House of Payne* as bullies to the Payne males. The film's star, Keke Palmer, returns to play Madea's daughter on the show. Similarly, Mr. Brown appears as the irritating neighbor in *House of Payne* and also becomes the star of Perry's second sitcom, *Meet the Browns*. Thus, intertextuality in *House of Payne* reflects the ways in which Perry creates and maintains impressive interconnections between his different projects across multiple platforms, frequently using the same characters, actors, and storylines to extend and solidify his brand and extend religious themes and neoliberal politics.

Seven years later, Perry's first shows to premiere on the OWN network continued to draw on his trademark themes and plots. *Love Thy Neighbor* focuses on a family headed by an elderly woman named "Hattie" (Patrice Lovely), who lives with her unemployed college-educated grandson, and her daughter, a former housewife contending with divorce and dating after her husband's infidelity. The Hattie character is explicitly modeled after Perry's Madea—"If you love Madea," he says in one advertisement, "you are going to love Mama Hattie."[53] Perry's other show for OWN, *The Haves and the Have Nots* is a distinctly southern tale depicting the intersecting lives of two wealthy families, one Black and one white, and their domestic servants. Intra-racial and class tensions undergird the show. In one scene, Hanna Young (Crystal R. Fox), an older Black woman character who is a maid and moral compass, remarks, "I can't stand Black people like that . . . who think they're better than us." While Perry continues to display his familiarity with Black vernacular, cultural jokes, and signifiers in the prime-time soap, his work remains plagued with slow pacing, heavy-handed music, awkward camera shots, and stereotypical plots intended to provide moral clarity to an audience he feels desires it. Lacking depth and complexity, *The Haves and the Have Nots* received particularly scathing reviews. Brittney Cooper, noting Perry's predictable reliance on negative Black female archetypes, wrote:

> The fact that Mammy, Jezebel, and Sapphire, along with their remixes (Bad) Baby Mama, Golddigger, Freak and Hood Bitch showed up in under 15 mins is surely a new world record. . . . Tyler Perry is dangerous. He has made Black women mistake hate for love. When his heavy-handedness is still not enough to chastise and discipline us for being independent, driven, and sex-positive, he will resort to straight up distortions of history, and assume that his working class audience will miss the sleight-of-hand.[54]

Ebony's Gerren Keith Gaynor further lambasted the various shortcuts Perry made in storytelling and production value, particularly with regard to sexuality:

> Sticking to his usual formula of mass stereotyping, Perry covers all of his bases. Bourgie Black folk? Check. Hardworking, southern church woman? Check. Privileged Whites? You got it . . . But this time, there's one group Perry threw into the mix that I never thought he'd give the time of day to: gay men. Aside from longstanding rumors about Perry's own sexual preference, it's surprising that he would address homosexuality at all, considering his fan base is predominantly Black Christian women. . . . I suspected Perry would more than likely take the opportunity to do what he does best: drench his character in so many stereotypes that it would turn into a television hate-fest. And that it did.[55]

Despite the largely negative critical reception, however, the two shows gave OWN its largest audience ever. With an average of 1.1 and 1.7

million viewers, respectively,[56] *Love Thy Neighbor* and *The Haves and the Have Nots* pushed OWN into the top five cable networks for African American women aged 25–34[57] among their competition, allowing the network to make its first profits in its four-year history for a show.[58]

Film scholars like Jacqueline Stewart theorize that Black viewers consume Black images in mass media in order to "reconstitute themselves in(to) new public formations."[59] As Black-created representations have been largely marginalized within mainstream media, consuming these types of texts can be seen as a form of resistance. Perry imagines himself as part of this subversive project to generate these images for Black audiences, explaining that "Hollywood thinks that these people do not exist and [this explains] why there is no material speaking to them." While Perry's work depends on easy, familiar plot devices and stereotypical notions of gender roles and Black pathology (i.e., hypersexual or irresponsible Black women and effeminate Black men), it also subverts the veneration of wealth and stigmatization of working-class poor people rife in mainstream media representations. In this way, Perry's work can also be seen as an indictment of the cliquish and exclusionary tendencies of the Black elite, particularly those who actively shun or demean poor Blacks. And while Perry frequently relies on the simplistic vilification of his characters, especially nonconformist women who are ambitious or successful, his texts do introduce some nuance to the portrayals of Black women. In *House of Payne*, for example, while Janine abandons her children due to her drug addiction, her overweight and middle-aged Black aunt Ella is repeatedly constructed as sexually active and attractive. In *The Haves and the Have Nots*, the scheming daughter is both a prostitute and a woman who secretly provides vital financial support to her family. While Perry indeed "hates black women," as Cooper argues, he also does not.

Still, the successful reception and scope of Perry's portraits of Black life displays a major weakness in today's media and cultural environment. Not only has Perry's work perpetuated simplistic and restrictive ideas about gender roles, sexuality, and racial performance, it has been granted a much larger scope and reach than any other producer of color in recent history. With the massive support of loyal Black audiences, Perry has created a media franchise for Black storytelling that serves as a model for successful Black cultural production. As a reliable brand, Perry's work across multiple platforms delivers a cultural product less demanding of production expertise and thus financial investment. That is, its very production implicitly justifies lower expectations and resources given to television programs that center upon protagonists of color, while legitimizing the value of its texts through its consumption among Black audiences. Moreover, by positioning himself as a Hollywood outsider and authentic Black voice, Tyler Perry not only pushes out other voices in his portrayal of Black life, he renders them unviable and unnecessary. At a moment when networks are taking risks in funding and staffing shows led, written, and performed by white peers, Perry's franchising draws attention to the lack of space for innovation and diversity in works by people of color. As Gray argued, "commercial culture operates as both a site of and a resource for black cultural politics."[60] Perry's legacy will consist of more than his steady circulation of controversial Black images. His representations both reflect and degrade the value of Black cultural production in the post-network era.

Notes

1. Mary McNamara, "It's hard to 'Love Thy Neighbor' and the Tyler Perry-Oprah union," *Los Angeles Times*, June 1, 2013, http://articles.latimes.com/2013/jun/01/entertainment/la-et-st-love-thy-neighbor-oprah-tyler-perry-20130601.

2. http://www.forbes.com/profile/tyler-perry.

3. Aymar Jean Christian, "The Black TV Crisis and Next Generation," *Flow*, August 27, 2013, http://flowtv.org/2013/08/the-black-TV-crisis-and-the-next-generation-aymar-jean-christian-northwestern-university.

4. Staff, "TCA: Mike Tyson And Spike Lee On HBO's 'Mike Tyson: Undisputed Truth,'" *Deadline*, July 25, 2013, accessed February 2, 2015, http://www.deadline.com/2013/07/mike-tyson-spike-lee-hbo-mike-tyson-undisputed-truth-tca.

5. Lee was then prepping the infamous $1.2 million Kickstarter campaign for his next feature.

6. Lesley Goldberg, "HBO Not Moving Forward With Spike Lee/Doug Ellin's 'Da Brick,'" *Hollywood Reporter*, March 13, 2012, accessed February 2, 2015, http://www.hollywoodreporter.com/live-feed/hbo-da-brick-spike-lee-doug-ellin-mike-tyson-entourage-299205.

7. Lesley Goldberg, "ABC's 'Scandal' Heads to BET in Early Syndication Deal (Exclusive)," *Hollywood Reporter*, July 15, 2013, accessed February 2, 2015, http://www.hollywoodreporter.com/live-feed/abcs-scandal-bet-syndication-584738.

8. Beretta Smith-Shomade, *Pimpin' Ain't Easy: Selling Black Entertainment Television* (Los Angeles: University of California Press, 2008), 33.

9. Joseph Turow, *Breaking Up America: Advertisers and the New Media World* (Chicago: University of Chicago Press, 1997), 37.

10. Herman Gray, "The Transformation of the Television Industry and the Social Production of Blackness," in *Watching Race: Television and the Struggle for Blackness* (Minneapolis: University of Minnesota Press, 2004), 57–69.

11. Timothy Havens, *Black Television Travels: African American Media Around the Globe* (New York: New York University Press, 2013).

12. Kristal B. Zook, *Color by Fox: The Fox Network and the Revolution in Black Television* (New York: Oxford University Press, 1999).

13. Robin Means Coleman, *African American viewers and the Black Situation Comedy: Situating Racial Humor* (New York: Routledge, 1998), 272.

14. Jana Steadman, "TV Audience Special Study: African American Audience," Nielsen Media Research, Summer 2005.

15. Ibid.; Nsenga Burton, "Nielsen Study: Blacks Watch More TV Than Any Other Group," *The Root*, April 1, 2011, accessed February 2, 2015, http://www.theroot.com/buzz/nielsen-study-african-americans-watch-more-television-any-other-group; National Association of Broadcasters, "Broadcast Television and Radio in African-American Communities," *NAB*, April 2013.

16. NAACP, "Out of Focus—Out of Sync Take 4: A Report on the Television Industry," National Association for the Advancement of Colored People, December 2008.

17. Ibid.

18. Writers Guild of America West, "WGAW 2013 TV Staffing Brief," *Writers Guild*, March 26, 2013, accessed February 2, 2015, http://www.wga.org/uploadedFiles/who_we_are/tvstaffingbrief2013.pdf.

19. Nellie Andreeva, "'The Game' Makes Big Return on BET," *Deadline*, January 12, 2011, accessed February 2, 2015, http://www.deadline.com/2011/01/the-game-makes-big-return-on-bet.

20. Nelson Pressley, "'I Can Do Bad': Wicked Good Fun," *Washington Post*, March 17, 2011, C08.

21. Annette John-Hall, "Writing his own success story; Once, 'home' was a car. Now, it's a 26-room mansion. Tyler Perry, urban theater impresario, has moved to the next frontier, with a first film opening tomorrow," February 24, 2005, *Philadelphia Inquirer*, D01.

22. Ibid.

23. Nicole LaPorte, "'Diary' dear to Lions Gate," *Daily Variety*, July 13, 2004, 01.

24. Nicole LaPorte, "Lions Gate 'Mad' for Perry plays," *Daily Variety*, March 2, 2005, 05.

25. Lena Williams, "'God Must Love Gilt,'" *New York Times*, July 8, 2004, F1.

26. LaPorte, 2005.

27. http://seekingalpha.com/article/26794-lionsgate-f3q07-qtr-end-12-31-06-earnings-call-transcript.

28. Cynthia Littleton, "Innovative deal put syndie pros on map," *Daily Variety*, March 6, 2012, 2.

29. Jay Fernandez, "Tyler Perry prepares to broaden his empire," *Hollywood Reporter*, August 14, 2008, accessed February 2, 2015, http://www.hollywoodreporter.com/news/tyler-perry-prepares-broaden-his-117530.

30. Littleton, 2012.

31. John Dempsey, "Syndies rewrite sitcom script," *Variety*, August 28–September 3, 2006, 24.

32. Ibid.

33. Ted Madger, "Television 2.0: The Business of American Television in Transition," in *Reality TV: Remaking Television Culture*, eds. Murray, Susan and Ouellette Laurie (New York: New York University Press, 2009), 141–64.

34. Nikki Finke, "Tyler Perry Fires 4 Writers For Union Activity; Atlanta Opening Of Perry's New Studio Will Be Picketed; Invited Actors And Guests Being Asked Not To Attend," *Deadline*, October 2, 2008, accessed February 2, 2015, http://www.deadline.com/2008/10/writers-at-tyler-perry-studio-to-take-strike-action-will-picket-grand-opening-and-ask-invited-guests-not-to-attend/#more-7129.

35. Nikki Finke, "Photos: WGA Pickets Tyler Perry Studios," *Deadline*, October 5, 2008, accessed February 2, 2015, http://www.deadline.com/2008/10/photos-wga-writers-picket-tyler-perry-studios.

36. Nikki Finke, "Tyler Perry's Alleged Role As Union Buster Becoming Big Obama Embarrassment?" *Deadline*, October 3, 2008, accessed February 2, 2015, http://www.deadline.com/2008/10/tyler-perrys-accused-role-as-union-buster-becomes-big-obama-embarrassment.

37. Nikki Finke, "TV Showrunners Tell Tyler Perry: Firings For WGA Activity 'Simply Not Acceptable,'" *Deadline*, October 4, 2008, accessed February 2, 2015, http://www.deadline.com/2008/10/big-name-wga-showrunners-send-open-letter-to-producer-tyler-perry; Nikki Finke, "TOLDJA! Tyler Perry Studios And WGA Reach Agreement Mediated By NAACP," *Deadline*, November 26, 2008, accessed February 2, 2015, http://www.deadline.com/2008/11/toldja-tyler-perry-studios-and-wga-settle-naacp-mediated.

38. See IMDb, *Meet the Browns*, http://www.imdb.com/title/tt1319598/fullcredits?ref_=tt_cl_sm#cast; *For Better or Worse*, http://www.imdb.com/title/tt1911883/fullcredits?ref_=tt_cl_sm#cast.

39. Two women, Terri Donald and Donna West, have filed suit against Perry, unsuccessfully, for credit for *Good Deeds* and *Diary of a Mad Black Woman*, respectively. Another writer, William James, sued over authorship credit for the film *Temptation*. See "Madea learns the consequences of allegedly stealing someone's story," *National Post*, November 29, 2012, B6; David Itzkoff, "Tyler Perry Wins Infringement Suit," *New York Times*, December 11, 2008, C2; Sergio, "Screenwriters Sues Tyler Perry Over 'Temptation,'" *Shadow and Act*, April 25, 2013, accessed February 2, 2015, http://www.tmz.com/2013/04/25/tyler-perry-temptation-confessions-marriage-counselor-screenwriter-sues.

40. Sophia said she was speaking out because Perry had promised her a role for years and never delivered. See fmdigitallive, "Miss Sophia's Affair With Tyler Perry," October 29, 2012, http://www.youtube.com/watch?v=Db7qaQ5gixU#at=157.

41. Perry positions his work as giving value to the Black community. In a speech to Al Sharpton's National Action Network, to which he also gave $200,000, he said: "Every other culture in this country knows the value of us as black people but we don't know it ourselves." Nekesa Mumbi Moody, "Tyler Perry honored by Sharpton organization," *Associated Press*, October 20, 2011, accessed February 2, 2015, http://usatoday30.usatoday.com/life/movies/news/story/2011-10-20/tyler-perry-al-sharpton/50842790/1.

42. Etan Vlessing, "Lionsgate Swing to Q1 Profit," *Hollywood Reporter*, August 9, 2011, accessed February 2, 2015, http://www.hollywoodreporter.com/news/lionsgate-swings-q1-profit-220938; Etan Vlessing, "Lionsgate Swings to Fourth Quarter Profit," *Hollywood Reporter*, May 31, 2011, accessed February 2, 2015, http://www.hollywoodreporter.com/news/lionsgate-swings-fourth-quarter-profit-193434.

43. Brookes Barnes, "Lionsgate and Tyler Perry Said to Be In Cable Venture," *New York Times*, August 10, 2011, B3; Brian Stelter, "Tyler Perry Will Produce Shows Exclusively for OWN," *New York Times*, October 2, 2012, B4.

44. D. M. Levine, "OWN Shifting Attention to Its African-American Viewers," *Hollywood Reporter*, December 8, 2011, accessed February 2, 2015, http://www.hollywoodreporter.com/news/own-shifting-attention-to-african-american-viewers-271469.

45. Nellie Andreeva, "OWN Picks Up Tyler Perry's Sitcom 'For Better Or Worse,' Orders Third Season," *Deadline*, February 20, 2013, accessed February 2, 2015, http://www.deadline.com/2013/02/own-picks-up-tyler-perrys-sitcom-for-better-or-worse-orders-third-season; Dominic Patten, "OWN Doubles Order For Tyler Perry's 'The Haves and the Have Nots,'" *Deadline*, June 25, 2013, accessed February 2, 2015, http://www.deadline.com/2013/06/own-doubles-tyler-perrys-the-have-the-have-nots-order.

46. In another interview, Perry explains that his films target and depict Black Christian women: "You're always gonna see a person of faith. Nine times out of ten, it'll be a woman who has problems, who has lost faith or lost her way," Perry explained. "There's always gonna be a moment of redemption somewhere for someone." "Tyler Perry's Amazing Journey to the Top," CBS News, July 26, 2010, accessed February 2, 2015, http://www.cbsnews.com/stories/2009/10/22/60minutes/main5410095.shtml.

47. Turow, 238.

48. Jamilah Lemieux, "An Open Letter to Tyler Perry," NPR, September 11, 2009, accessed February 2, 2015, http://www.npr.org/templates/story/story.php?storyId=112760404.

49. Issie Lapowsky, "Tyler Perry Responds to Spike Lee's Claim that His Work is Comparable to 'Amos N' Andy,'" *New York Daily News*, October 26, 2009, accessed February 2, 2015, http://www.nydailynews.com/entertainment/tv-movies/tyler-perry-responds-spike-lee-claim-work-comparable-amos-n-andy-article-1.380544.

50. iamrogue, "IAR Interview: Tyler Perry Talks 'Tyler Perry's Temptation,'" *I am ROGUE*, March 29, 2013, accessed February 2, 2015, http://www.iamrogue.com/news/interviews/item/8552-iar-interview-tyler-perry-talks-tyler-perrys-temptation.html.

51. Tyler Perry, *Don't Make a Black Woman Take Off Her Earrings: Madea's Uninhibited Commentaries on Love and Life* (New York: Riverhead Books, 2007).

52. Office of Policy Planning and Research, "The Negro Family: The Case For National Action," United States Department of Labor, March 1965, accessed February 2, 2015, http://www.blackpast.org/?q=primary/moynihan-report-1965.

53. http://www.youtube.com/watch?v=I1mavPYCYuc.

54. Brittney Cooper, "Tyler Perry Hates Black Women," *Crunk Feminist Collective*, May 29, 2013, accessed February 2, 2015, http://www.crunkfeministcollective.com/2013/05/29/tyler-perry-hates-black-women-5-thoughts-on-the-haves-and-have-nots.

55. Gerren Keith Gaynor, "[OPINION] Homophobia, 'The Haves and the Haves Nots,'" *Ebony*, August 21, 2013, accessed February 2, 2015, http://www.ebony.com

/entertainment-culture/opinion-homophobia-the-haves-and-the-have-nots-405#axzz2ccsG2ZYj.

56. Press release, "OWN: Oprah Winfrey Network Original Series Premiere to Ratings Highs," *TVbytheNumbers*, July 30, 2013, accessed February 2, 2015, http://tvbythenumbers.zap2it.com/2013/07/30/own-oprah-winfrey-network-original-series-premiere-to-ratings-highs/194753; Carrie Healy, "Tyler Perry's 'The Haves and the Have Nots' breaks 2 million viewers," *The Grio*, August 9, 2013, accessed February 2, 2015, http://thegrio.com/2013/08/09/tyler-perrys-the-haves-and-the-have-nots-breaks-2-million-viewers.

57. Press release, "OWN: Oprah Winfrey Network Delivers Best Quarter in Network History," *TV by the Numbers*, July 2, 2013, accessed February 2, 2015, http://tvbythenumbers.zap2it.com/2013/07/02/own-oprah-winfrey-network-delivers-best-quarter-in-network-history/190128.

58. Liana B. Baker, "Oprah Winfrey Network finally making money for Discovery," *Reuters*, July 30, 2013, accessed February 2, 2015, http://www.reuters.com/article/2013/07/30/entertainment-us-discovery-results-idUSBRE96T0VU20130730.

59. As cited in Stephanie Dunn, *"Baad Bitches" and Sassy Supermamas: Black Power Action Films* (Champaign: University of Illinois Press, 2008), 19.

60. Gray, 5.

CHAPTER EIGHT

Bring the Payne: The Erasure of the Black Sitcom and the Emergence of *Tyler Perry's House of Payne*

—Artel Great

The arrival of the sitcom *Tyler Perry's House of Payne* (TBS, 2006–2012) into the multichannel universe represents a complex contribution to the expansion of Black televisual authorship from both critical and industrial perspectives. At a cultural moment when television programs featuring predominately Black casts and themes had saliently vanished from the small screen, the multi-hyphenate Tyler Perry signed an unprecedented television contract. The TBS network ordered 100 upfront episodes of *House of Payne* in a mega-deal worth $200 million including cable and broadcasting license fees and barter advertising sales.

Perry's deal was the first of its kind and the largest such agreement in cable television history. When *House of Payne* premiered on TBS in June of 2007, the series's first two episodes averaged 5.6 million viewers, becoming the highest-rated cable sitcom ever.[1] Although the ratings steadily declined throughout the show's run, *House of Payne* went on to air an astonishing 264 episodes over eight seasons, surpassing *The Jeffersons* (CBS, 1975–85) as the longest-running Black sitcom on American television. As a medium, television reifies dominant power relations through its visualization of complex codes, signs, and rhetoric. *House of Payne* is more complicated when analyzed within the often conflicting racialized margins of television's hegemonic structure. Despite the show's commercial success, does *House of Payne* celebrate largely one-dimensional mimetic performances of blackness in the twenty-first century that are disturbingly adjacent to the late nineteenth-century and early twentieth-century traditions of minstrelsy?[2] If so, why is the show popular? And what can be made of the show's undeniable achievements in an ever-diminishing Black televisual landscape?

In this chapter, I examine the legacy of the Black sitcom from which *House of Payne* has descended. I explore the foundational trajectory of Black televisual authorship and situate Perry's show, particularly his representations of blackness on screen, as harking back to earlier polarizing Black voices in television. I begin by briefly detailing Perry's political economy, charting his rise to fame and his role as a colossal force in multiple media industries. In doing so, I attend to the shifting industrial conditions that paved the way for the emergence of *House of Payne* on basic cable. Finally, I evaluate the ideological and aesthetic underpinnings of the show as a commodity that does and does not allow for disruptions in television's traditional catalog of, oftentimes, oppressive expressions of Black lives on screen.

The Political Economy of Perry's Media Empire

Tyler Perry's meteoric rise to fame embodies components of a Horatio Alger-style narrative. His triumphant rags-to-riches tale begins with a childhood spent enduring physical and emotional abuse, reportedly suffered at the hand of his father, as well as the torment of sexual molestation by both a male and female neighbor. Filled with frustration and anger, teenaged Perry was kicked out of high school after a heated altercation with a guidance counselor. He later received his GED. After watching an episode of *The Oprah Winfrey Show* (syndication, 1986–2011) detailing the potentially therapeutic properties of writing, Perry began keeping a journal as a method of coping with the pains of his abuse.[3]

Soon thereafter, Perry wrote his first stage play, *I Know I've Been Changed* (1999). He eventually found himself homeless for a short period in Atlanta, Georgia, before he introduced the world to his most famous and enduring character—"Madea," a quasi-religious, gun-toting, pot-smoking, Bible-thumping, foul-mouthed linebacker of a grandmother, played by Perry himself dressed in drag. It was intended for the Madea character to be performed by a stage actress who failed to appear for the opening night of Perry's breakout play, *I Can Do Bad All by Myself* (2000) at Chicago's Regal Theater. As Perry recalls, "There was a person, who was famous, who didn't show up the first night... because she didn't show up, I had to come up [on stage as Madea]."[4] Needless to say, Madea stole the show, so much so that Perry increased her role in his next play, *Diary of a Mad Black Woman* (2001). Madea became a sensation, quickly claiming the throne as the true empress of the gospel stage play arena. Perry's urban-themed Christian tinged plays are situated within a Black theatrical tradition that traces its roots back to the works of the "Chitlin Circuit" and the Theater Owners Booking Association (TOBA) in the early twentieth century.

These institutions emerged as a segregated form of Black entertainment that served as a low-budget equivalent to the white vaudeville establishment, yet characteristics from nineteenth-century blackface minstrelsy did spill over into its method of performance. Consequently, "some may interpret participation [on the Chitlin Circuit] as an acceptance of white America's perceptions of African Americans and a case of self-oppression [or] as Mel Watkins argues, the amusement [of Black audiences] could also have emanated from an acknowledgement of the ridiculous and exaggerated nature of the minstrels' behavior."[5] The performative sites of the Chitlin Circuit and TOBA also allowed for the emergence of talented Black entertainers, including Moms Mabley, Sammy Davis, Jr., Bill "Bojangles" Robinson, and Dewey "Pigmeat" Markham.

The theatrical productions of TOBA and the Chitlin Circuit as descendants of the minstrel tradition stand in stark contrast to the revolutionary works of Black dramatists like Lorraine Hansberry, Ed Bullins, Amiri Baraka, and the "highbrow" Pulitzer Prize-winning plays of Suzan-Lori Parks or August Wilson, who once proclaimed American theatre was "an instrument of white cultural hegemony."[6] In a revealing essay in the *New Yorker*, Henry Louis Gates, Jr., describes the old Chitlin Circuit as a "spawning ground for a good number of accomplished Black actors, comics, and musicians... crisscrossing Black America, the circuit established an empire of comedy and pathos, the sublime and the ridiculous: a moveable feast that enabled Blacks to patronize Black entertainers... The productions were for, by, and about Black folks [but] you don't expect anything fancy from something called the Chitlin Circuit."[7] In this sense, the circuit provided both opportunity and promise for early Black entertainers.

In the twenty-first century, the old Chitlin Circuit transformed into urban Christian-themed melodramas that infused humor, which was sometimes crude, and gospel music into the stage productions. This genre became wildly popular and profitable with the success of such plays as Adrian Williamson's *My Grandmother Prayed for Me* (1996), Vy Higginsen and Ken Wydro's *Mama I Want to Sing* (1983), Shelly Garrett's *Beauty Shop* (1989), James Chapmyn's *Our Young Black Men Are Dying and Nobody Seems to Care* (1993), and David E. Talbert's *Lawd Ha' Mercy* (1989). While many of these plays celebrated Christian motifs, they often contained caricatures of Black religious expression. Nonetheless, these gospel stage plays raked in ticket sales upwards of $100,000 per week.[8] Yet no one on the circuit comes close to rivaling the success of playwright-turned-director Tyler Perry. Between the years of 1999 and 2005, Perry released one new play every year, "selling more than $100 million in tickets, $30 million in videos of his shows and an estimated $20 million in merchandise . . . and the 300 live shows he produce[d] each year [were] attended by an average of 35,000 people a week."[9] As a self-taught businessman, Perry managed to produce, package, and promote his entertainment brand with such dexterity and financial success that he was able to invest his stage profits into his first film production.

Perry teamed with Lionsgate, an independent film and television studio and distribution company, in 2005 to co-produce and distribute his first film. He wrote, produced, and starred in *Diary of a Mad Black Woman* (Darren Grant, 2005) based on his stage play. The film was shot on a $5 million budget (meager by Hollywood standards) and went on to earn the number one spot at the box office with a $33 million opening weekend, beating out the films of two Hollywood heavyweights: Will Smith's *Hitch* (Andy Tennant, 2005) and Keanu Reeves's *Constantine* (Francis Lawrence, 2005). *Diary of a Mad Black Woman* went on to gross $50 million in theatres and sold 2.4 million DVDs during the first week of its release.[10]

Perry's next film, his directorial debut, *Madea's Family Reunion* (2006), was also based on his stage play. *Madea's Family Reunion* grossed $65 million on a $6 million budget and ranked number one at the box office for two consecutive weeks. While Perry's box-office victories took Hollywood by surprise, "his success [was] hardly news to the devout theatre fans who have followed him since 1998, when the multi-hyphenate became a *tour de force* among African American communities through his plays."[11] With his first two feature films taking the top box-office spot, Perry displayed a keen ability to produce content that resonated within largely underserved African American audiences.

In spite of his commercial success, Perry's work drew strong criticism. The *New York Post* warned of his first film: "Stay clear of this mess."[12] And *Chicago Sun-Times* film critic and TV personality Roger Ebert wrote: "I've been reviewing movies for a long time, and I can't think of one that more dramatically shoots itself in the foot [than *Diary of a Mad Black Woman*]."[13] The most common criticism leveled against Perry within Black communities is that his work repackages regressive tropes conceived in the attics of white imagination and proliferated through Hollywood's persistently racist media discourses.

For Todd Boyd, Perry's work became the blackface version "of an increasingly visible right-wing evangelical Christian culture."[14] Perry's next two films, both released in 2007, *Daddy's Little Girls* (Tyler Perry, 2007) and *Why Did I Get Married?* (Tyler Perry, 2007), generated profitable returns, although the former film made only $31.6 million, his lowest-grossing film at that point. Having successfully conquered the stage and the silver screen, Perry's next move was to try his hand at television. From a business perspective, Perry had established himself as a strong and recognizable entertainment commodity. Positioning his brand in the landscape of television would offer Perry an even greater opportunity to permeate the daily lives of his constituency and further corner an underserved market segment of African American audiences.

Blackness in Prime Time

The announcement of Dick Robertson's retirement as president of Warner Bros. Domestic Television in 2006 signaled change, particularly in the industrial logic of television syndication. In fact, "during [Robertson's] three decades as a top syndication exec, Robertson had a big influence on shaping the traditional major-studio model of how to sell programs to cable networks and TV stations."[15] News of Robertson's retirement and the sale of *House of Payne* as a first-run sitcom for syndication to TBS were announced within days of each other, leading to speculation within the industry that Robertson did not support Perry's unprecedented deal. Nevertheless, both TBS and Perry were eager to promptly broadcast the program. Perry understood the dearth of Black sitcoms available for African American viewers, and he was eager to fill this void.

Since the inception of television as a widespread form of American culture and communication, its on-screen depictions of Black lives have been marked by restrictive racial boundaries. Initially, World War II delayed the mass production of commercial television in order to prevent its overlapping radar technology from falling into the hands of America's enemies. In the postwar period, television quickly "penetrated American homes faster than any previous domestic technology. While in 1948 less than 2 percent of U.S. homes had a television set, by 1960 almost 90 percent of U.S. households had one or more TV[s]."[16] The situation comedy became one of television's dominant genres that aided in achieving what Jacques Rancière calls a "redistribution of the sensible."[17] In other words, the sitcom was used as an instrument to shift postwar social dynamics and promote a culture of consumerism. By focusing largely on white domestic spaces, early sitcoms like *Burns and Allen* (CBS, 1950–58), *The Honeymooners* (CBS, 1955–56), and *Make Room for Daddy* (ABC, 1953–57) offer visual metaphors and hierarchical arrangements that emphasize patriarchy, traditional gender roles, and Black exclusion.

The structural template for the sitcom, which primarily consists of "simplistic plots with little dramatic depth . . . [and] a cyclical story formula that moves from establishment of a situation, through complication and confusion, to resolution"[18] served as a guide for audience expectations. The first Black sitcoms to penetrate the televisual landscape, *Beulah* (ABC, 1950–52) and *Amos 'n' Andy* (CBS, 1951–53), were both adaptations of successful radio programs created by whites and performed by white male actors. The arrival of these shows on primetime television featuring African American actors initiates what Robin Means Coleman argues is the beginning of the Black situation comedy as a subgenre of the sitcom "not only because of the featured performers, but also because the humor is based on race and a parody of Blackness"[19] where African Americans become "securely positioned in popular culture as the aberrant Other, with little space for conflicting images."[20] These early Black sitcoms exhibit vaudeville-style mimicry of so-called "ethnic" humor that emphasized minstrel-era stereotypes of the nurturing mammy (*Beulah*) or the shiftless sambo exemplified by Kingfish (*Amos 'n' Andy*). Because these shows were the only Black sitcoms on the air in the 1950s, they carried an even heavier burden of representation. Although *Amos 'n' Andy* enjoyed ratings success, the show was the subject of harsh criticism. Soon, the NAACP launched stringent protest campaigns against both programs.

The 1960s saw new racial attitudes reflected on television. Both Bill Cosby and Diahann Carroll were able to break through as TV stars: Cosby's dramatic role was the cool Rhodes Scholar secret agent on *I Spy* (NBC, 1965-68), and Carroll's was the widowed nurse and single mother raising a son on the sitcom, *Julia* (NBC, 1968-1971). Each show offers pristine depictions of its lead characters, however, the program's Black voices are shorn of their soul and ritual intonation. The characters of Carroll and Cosby represent a safe ideological stance of assimilation during a time of sweeping antiwar protests and sociopolitical turmoil. In this sense, neither show truly reflects the spirit of its cultural moment. After the cancellation of *I Spy* in 1968, *The Bill Cosby Show* (NBC, 1969-71) was Cosby's first foray into the Black sitcom. He portrayed a high school physical education teacher in Los Angeles as an all-around good guy. In this program, Cosby operates with what Mantiha Diawara would describe as "transtextuality,"[21] in the sense that he functions as the visual embodiment of a new emerging Black middle class.

In the mid 1970s, American television attempted to reflect the social and cultural struggles of the moment, particularly in relation to race, class, and gender issues. Still, African Americans held no executive roles as television decision-makers. As a result, African American talent continued to conform to dominant typologies of character in white-produced shows, such as Norman Lear and Bud Yorkin's *The Jeffersons* (CBS, 1975-85), *Good Times* (CBS, 1974-79), *Sanford & Son* (NBC, 1972-77), or *That's My Momma* (ABC, 1974-75). The Black characters featured in these programs are primarily contained within working-class urban ghettos. The exception, of course, is *The Jeffersons*, in which lead character George is allowed to "move on up" to the ritzy Upper East Side of Manhattan with his family as a result of his success as an entrepreneur.

The shift toward conservatism during the late 1970s and early 1980s, away from the Carter administration and into the logic of the Reagan era, saw the arrival of Black-oriented sitcoms like *Gimme a Break* (NBC, 1981–87), *Benson* (ABC, 1979–86), *Diff'rent Strokes* (ABC, 1978–85), Amen (NBC, 1986–91), and *The Cosby Show* (NBC, 1984–92). These 1980s programs became breakout hits while "depict[ing] Black upward social mobility and middle-class affluence replac[ing] Black urban poverty as both setting and theme [of the shows in the previous decade]."[22] Contemporaneously, Reagan's social policies further marginalized Black communities. Herman Gray argues that "although blackness was explicitly marked in these shows, it was whiteness and its privileged status that remained unmarked and therefore hegemonic within television's discursive field of racial construction and representation."[23] The next decade would witness an extraordinary expansion in Black media authorship.

The 1990s provide fond memories for many Black Americans who enjoyed the presence of a "hyberblackness"[24] in television programming during this period. The 1990s also offered viewers a hyper sense of political correctness and a wave of multiculturalism that presented the promise of social progress on television. As the multichannel cable television universe quickly expanded, the Fox network emerged to challenge the big three, CBS, NBC, and ABC. Executives at Fox implemented a strategy of radical individuation (i.e., focusing on and targeting specific segments of the television market). Fox's niche was young audiences, particularly those in large urban cities. By specifically, "'counterprogramming' against other shows to suit that audience's taste, Fox was able to capture large numbers of young, urban viewers. By 1993, [Fox] was airing the largest single crop of Black-produced shows in television history."[25] The new Fox shows included *In Living Color* (1990–94), *Roc* (1991–94), *The Sinbad Show* (1993–94), *Martin* (1992–97), *New York Undercover* (1994–98), and *Living Single* (1993–98).

In contrast to the Black sitcoms of the previous four decades, 1990s programming allowed for multivalent voices to emerge in the television discourse. Black entertainment creatives held more decision-making positions and were able to offer audiences new perspectives on-screen. Prime examples include the female-centered voice of *Living Single*, developed by Yvette Lee Bowser (who became the first African American woman to develop a prime-time series), and Ralph Farquhar's social problem sitcom, *South Central* (Fox, 1994). These programs "explicitly engaged the cultural politics of diversity and multiculturalism within the sign of blackness . . .

position[ing] viewers, regardless of race, class, or gender locations [as participants] in Black experiences from multiple subject positions."[26] Fox's quest to disrupt the oligopoly of the big three television networks, along with the further development of the cable universe, unwittingly allowed for an expansion of Black televisual authorship. Black entertainment creatives—producers, writers, directors, and actors—were allowed a short-lived but unprecedented access to mainstream Hollywood. In this regard, their programs (most notably, *A Different World* [NBC, 1987–93], *Roc*, and *South Central*) more often than not delivered progressive and polysemic representations of blackness on screen.

By the mid 1990s, however, the Black sitcom was becoming confined to what Darnell Hunt termed "televisual ghettoization."[27] Hunt refers to the launch of the WB and UPN networks with their trademark "lowbrow" Black sitcoms like *The Wayans Brothers* (WB, 1995–99), *The Jamie Foxx Show* (WB, 1996–2001), *Malcolm & Eddie* (UPN, 1996–2000), and *Homeboys in Outer Space* (UPN, 1996–97). With the backing of sitcom actor-turned-producer, Kelsey Grammer, UPN also aired the feminist-leaning sitcom, *Girlfriends* (UPN/CW, 2000–2008) as an exploration of Black female success, friendship, sexuality, and love. This was followed by its companion program, *The Game* (CW/BET, 2006–present) a popular but un-ambitious comedy that revolves around the exploits of Black professional football players and the women who date them, and *Everybody Hates Chris* (UPN/CW, 2005–2009), a sitcom depicting the teenage experiences of comedian Chris Rock.

Unfortunately, "once established both Fox and the WB dropped their Black shows in favor of programs that appealed to white youth, who advertisers consider a more upscale demographic. UPN continued Black programming until it merged with the WB in 2006 to become the CW network."[28] *Girlfriends*, *The Game*, and *Everybody Hates Chris* represented the last Black situation comedies on network television. These shows continued to air on the CW after the merger, until *Girlfriends* was canceled in 2008 and the latter two were canceled in 2009. Broadcast television's shift away from the production of Black sitcoms coincides precisely with the increase in popularity and media visibility of Tyler Perry. Understanding the current industrial climate, Perry bypassed traditional avenues of broadcast television production and set his sights on the world of basic cable.

Let's Make a Deal

The harsh reality of the new millennium's erasure of Black sitcoms from the small screen stands antipodal to the proverbial land of milk and honey television was thought to be for Black creatives in the previous decade.

The decline of Black sitcoms in the 2000s represents a collapse of catastrophic proportions considering that in "1997 twenty-one prime-time network shows had Black lead characters."[29] By 2006, the number of Black-themed shows on network television was down to three programs. By 2009, that number dwindled to zero, and the erasure of the Black sitcom on major networks had been achieved. While there are several reasons for this, the industrial shift away from scripted sitcoms toward (un)scripted "reality" television programming featuring nonprofessional celebrity seekers (and washed-up former stars) was a major factor. Ghen Maynard, the CW's reality television chief, points out "reality series have better odds than sitcoms or dramas of becoming breakout hits, and they appeal to families and young adults, who command higher ad rates."[30] In this respect, many cable networks, including MTV, Bravo, VH1, and A&E, began to change their programming schedules to consist primarily of reality television shows as an inexpensive alternative to garnering target demos. But what became of the once highly sought-after Black demo that created so many stars in the previous decade? Were Black dollars no longer desirable? Tyler Perry certainly didn't think so.

Having solidified himself as a colossal media figure with a *New York Times* best-selling book, a strong presence at the Hollywood box office, continual dominance of the gospel stage play circuit, and a high-traffic Internet talk show, Perry saw an opportunity to increase his empire. As television network executives' infatuation with the direct pursuit of Black audiences lost its luster, Perry saw a void in Black content that desperately needed to be filled. By promoting his message of sin and redemption, Perry sought to capitalize on what Mark Anthony Neal describes as "a segment of the Black community that would define itself as churchgoing, and that has no interest in what Hollywood, the stage, and, to a certain extent, the music industry was offering."[31] Recognizing the inclinations of this underserved audience, Perry enlarged his brand by creating, producing, writing, directing, and acting in ten episodes of a new sitcom he called *Tyler Perry's House of Payne*.

The program aired a test run in ten television markets during the summer of 2006. When the results were analyzed, *House of Payne* received "an 'A' on the Nielsen report card for all 10 markets, and the show was off and running."[32] Perry expanded his business relationship with Lionsgate by partnering with its subsidiary, Debmar-Mercury, a media corporation that specializes in network, cable, syndication, VOD/pay-per-view, and pay TV. The company is best known for producing and distributing such programs as *South Park* (Comedy Central, 1997–present), *American Chopper* (Discovery Channel/TLC, 2003–2010), *Deadliest Catch* (Discovery Channel, 2005–present), and *The Dead Zone* (USA, 2002–2007). Debmar-Mercury struck a deal with Perry and TBS that is unique in the history of television. The deal stipulated Perry would retain complete ownership of *House of Payne*, possess creative autonomy regarding the show's content, and deliver 100 episodes to TBS (then to other networks) straight out of the gate—thus becoming the first-ever originally produced syndicated comedy to garner an upfront 100-episode order. The agreement for *House of Payne*, which was to be distributed by Debmar-Mercury and licensed by TBS, was worth a record $200 million.

The contract between Perry, Debmar-Mercury, and TBS is also remarkable because "in the past sitcoms ordered by cable or syndication came in short bursts of 13 episodes or, at most 22 episodes, suitable for play once a week. The hope, which rarely materialized, was that the comedy would draw an audience and get renewed every year until it reached the magic 100 episode quota [typically required for syndication]."[33] For TBS, the Perry deal was extremely significant in that it allowed the network the opportunity to immediately begin airing *House of Payne* anywhere from five to ten times per week, potentially generating advertising revenue of upwards of $25 million a year.[34]

The acquisition of *House of Payne*, according to co-president of Debmar-Mercury, Ira Bernstein, signaled that "TBS is saying to sitcom distributors 'treat us like the big guys'—and the industry is [now] definitely paying attention."[35] TBS' partnership with Perry's program was not a radically original business strategy. The network merely put a syndication spin on the broadcast programming model exemplified by Fox, WB, and UPN back in the 1990s. However, Perry's shrewd acumen to acknowledge the underserved Black audiences—instead of (white) television executives—engendered this and led white media corporations down a path toward increased profit margins.

Bringing the Payne

House of Payne first aired on TBS June 6, 2007. The series portrays a Black extended family living under one roof in Atlanta, Georgia. Curtis Payne (LaVan Davis), the show's protagonist, is the cantankerous, loud-mouthed patriarch who works as a fire chief. His wife, Ella (Cassi Davis), is a deeply religious homemaker. Curtis and Ella are the rotund parents of Calvin (Lance Gross), a ne'er-do-well slacker who rarely attends his college classes. CJ (Allen Payne) is Curtis's nephew and a devoted husband to Janine (Demetria McKinney), and father to Malik (Laramie "Doc" Shaw), Jazmine (China Anne McClain), and twins Jayden and Hayden (uncredited).

House of Payne's protagonist, Curtis, brims with aggression often directed at his son, Calvin, and nephew, CJ. Yet the show never explores the origins of Curtis's anger. Is he mad because he's a Black man in America tired of being beaten down by "the man?" Or perhaps it is the growing economic hardships that have emerged during the Great Recession? *House of Payne* never reveals these vital details. Instead, the show depicts Curtis as a "bitter cynic whose anger management issues border on emotional abuse."[36] Perry claims the show provides a refreshing spin on the sitcom genre by depicting the workings of a strong Black family; yet Curtis the patriarch "always has something negative to say about everyone and constantly lets his nephew, CJ, and his wife, Janine, and their children know they are not welcome in his home."[37] There is an abundance of sophomoric humor exercised through signifying, or "verbally putting down or berating another person with witty remarks, also called ranking, sounding, or dissin.'"[38] This "lowbrow" form of mocking is deeply polarizing and serves as *House of Payne*'s most frequently employed comedic tool.

The pilot episode reveals CJ, Janine, and their children as a solid working-class family, but when their house unexpectedly burns down they are forced to move in with the cantankerous Uncle Curtis. The plot of the second episode focuses on the deterioration of CJ and Janine's relationship. CJ notices bills aren't being paid even though he gives Janine money to pay them. Janine's behavior becomes increasingly passive-aggressive and she begins vanishing for hours on end, with her whereabouts unknown to the family. When she is home, Janine constantly asks for money, or is given money to buy groceries or pay bills, but nothing is ever accomplished and the money is never retrieved. CJ suspects Janine is having an affair with another man and confronts her. Janine, of course, denies the allegations, professes her love, cons CJ into giving her more money, and quickly leaves the house. By the third episode, Janine is revealed to be strung out on crack cocaine and responsible for burning down her family's house while in a drug haze. Her ephemeral presence is the result of her spending extended periods of time at a local "crack house." Uncle Curtis finds Janine's drug addiction amusing. He discloses her condition to CJ in a crude and cynical fashion when he blurts out:

CURTIS: Janine's a crackhead.
CJ: A crackhead? A crackhead? What are you saying?
CURTIS: I'm saying if you want your wife to stay at home, go get some crack!

This anemic attempt at humor falls flat and gives the scene an awkward tone. Ella suggests the family join hands in prayer to ask God to help Janine. Curtis leads the family in prayer using a rich melodic tenor reserved for Black ministers in the pulpit—half-singing and half-preaching, he moans: "Father, we wanna thank you. Thank God for chicken, you gave 'em two legs, two thighs, and two breast-eses, and two wings, little hot sauce on 'em, and I can hear that chicken today, offer up a sacrifice of praise. I'm gonna fry up today." This stultifying monologue, with its exaggerated churchliness, exemplifies *House of Payne*'s ambivalence toward the recirculation of derisive tropes.

Curtis's imitation of an old Baptist preacher turns into an inexplicable caricature of Black religious expression, and instead of actually praying for help to ameliorate Janine's addiction, he merely rambles on ridiculously. In response to his antics, the family walks away, leaving Curtis alone with his poultry prayers. This form of jocularity hearkens back to the old-style "ethnic humor" popularized by early Black sitcoms like *Beluah* and *Amos 'n' Andy*, created in the imaginations of white TV executives. This polarizing brand of "ethnic humor is one of the sitcom's original and most stable aspects. It exists in comedy 'as a function of social class feelings of superiority and white racial antagonisms.' Extending itself particularly from minstrelsy, ethnic humor allows racialized hierarchical positioning to institute itself without commitment."[39] Ultimately, this scene amounts to an opportunity wasted. Nothing is resolved, and the viewer is left bearing the immense weight of such a heavy topic without the necessary comedic or dramatic catharsis.

House of Payne is not the first Black sitcom to attempt to address the issue of drug addiction. Nor is Perry the first writer to use humor to shed light on serious topics. However, in addressing the issue of Janine's addiction to crack cocaine *House of Payne* does not offer viewers an opportunity to truly contemplate the gravity of her condition or the immensity of the subject matter. Instead, her drug abuse is introduced in jest and disregarded for the quick fix of a punch line. "What makes the Black situation comedy unique is its regular core cast of African American characters that works to illuminate the Black cultural, artistic, political, and economic experiences";[40] in this regard, humor can be a very useful tool in dealing with topics largely considered taboo. But Perry's employment of humor in this instance does little to complicate the issue of addiction or the psychosocial conditions of its occurrence; instead, it reinforces well-worn racist conceptions. Perry's apparent lack of concern for the mechanics of minstrelsy and its potent cultural ramifications presents an unfortunate expansion to a legacy of devalued Black media discourses that promote inequality and the adverse role this type of Black vocality plays in shaping the perceptions of Black folk in the national and global imaginary.

House of Payne's reinforcement of racialized identity formations demonstrate, as Ed Guerrero suggests, "the comic darky has risen from his plantation grave where the social protests of the civil rights movement and the following insurgency of Black Power nationalism last dumped him, to once again joke, dance and shuffle across the American screen, stage, tube, [and] internet."[41] While *House of Payne*'s comedic discourse offers broader audiences a myopic view of Black Americans, the program also reveals a stark divide within many Black communities regarding an indifference towards history and basic comprehension of the role Black culture plays in the global marketplace. The show brings to bear issues of class in relationship to materialist and ideological systems such as economics and cultural politics that are rarely discussed in Black communities. For instance, Perry appears on the show as Madea, the foster mother to a young girl, Nikki (KeKe Palmer), who has been bullying CJ's son, Malik. In order to reconcile the children's differences, Madea and Uncle Curtis agree to supervise them while they help each other with their homework. When the children are stumped on a history question Nikki asks the adults for help:

NIKKI: We stuck. Name two great kings.
MADEA: Oh, I got that. I can answer it, two great kings for two hundred. Okay, the first great king is smo-king and the second one is drin-king. Smoking and drinking. Write that down on the paper.

This mode of jocularity inadvertently serves to rearticulate racist conceptions of Black cognitive inferiority and exalts traditionally deleterious working-class habits (smoking and drinking) at the expense of Black working-class viewers.

Although the show's characters appear to be an upwardly mobile middle-class family, the show's content, subject matter, and brand of humor is more aligned with a working-class sentiment. Berratta E. Smith-Shomade argues that "assumptions [in many Black communities] of class are coded in words, looks, behaviors, [and] dress. Community members on all sides of the class prism know how 'no home training,' 'bougie,' 'keeping it real,' 'ghetto,' and 'siddity' translate. They are covert ways to separate and distinguish folks."[42] In this respect, the appeal of *House of Payne* to poor and working-class Blacks evinces Perry's strategy of employing so-called ethnic humor (reminiscent of the polarizing Black sitcoms of the 1950s) in his efforts to cater to poor and working-class segments of Black audiences that have been rendered all but voiceless in dominant media culture.

The Politics of Thirst

The supposition that *House of Payne*'s comedic style and distorted performances are politically neutral belies the ideological dimensions of media content and aesthetic choices as a form of maintaining the status quo. James Lull contends that "dominant ideological streams must be subsequently reproduced in the activities of our most basic social unit," and "hegemony requires that ideological assertions become self-evident cultural assumptions. Its effectiveness depends on subordinated peoples accepting the dominant ideology as 'normal reality or common sense.'"[43] In other words, television functions culturally as an important medium to advance dominant ideological assertions.

Through the presentation of Perry's Black televisual discourse, *House of Payne* attempts to reify the behavior of its characters as culturally "authentic" and approaches a form of nouveau racism. There is no monolithic "Black community" nor is there any one way to be "Black." Blackness is fluid, hybrid, and can emerge from a multitude of experiences and in multiple modes of expression. Still, if Perry does, at times, engage old-style ethnic humor that celebrates denigrating Black stereotypes, why are viewers watching? Are viewers laughing subversively or because they truly find pleasure in these images? A part of the human experience necessitates stories and the practice of the art of storytelling. James Baldwin explores this concept and reminds us of the human requirement for stories when he writes, "in order for a person to bear his [or her] life, he [or she] needs a valid re-creation of that life."[44] Consequently, the epistemological function of television in the process of American socialization cannot be overlooked. Television provides stories and images of our humanity that help shape our understanding of *being-in-the-world*, as does media in general

In this respect, the philosophy of difference (in Deleuzian terms) exposes the operation of every screen image as intrinsically political. Moreover, television "extends beyond an affirmation to create a doubled production that mutates and creates and causes specific differences to affected images and objects ... [These] appearances are clearly demonstrated to be linked to systems of judgment."[45] Therefore, the regressive Black voices operating in *House of Payne* present a rather dangerous set of problematics, particularly, since the show has gone on to air more episodes than any other predominantly Black sitcom in history.

House of Payne's success relies most significantly on the dearth of Black televisual representation. This Black voice/image/story deficiency has created a condition that I have termed the "politics of thirst," a concept that suggests, in the absence of a variety of voices and interlocution that speaks to the plurality of experiences of a particular group, members of that group will cling to any emergent voice that is heard and appears familiar even if that voice goes against their own interests. In this sense, the removal of the Black sitcom from the small screen creates an intensified "thirst" for Black voices, stories, narratives, and discourses from members of Black communities, which has caused some to accept voices that marginalize and/or disempower. The process of eliminating blackness on television (which began once the upstart networks Fox, WB, and UPN established their positions in the mainstream) created a deep chasm in the lives of many Black viewers. By 2009, the number of Black shows in prime time shrank to zero from twenty-one shows in 1997. Means Coleman argues that "the domination of and subordination over African Americans, through cultural representation, results in objectification, caricatures, or an exotic casting of Blackness that calls racial identity and relevancy into question. When African Americans are presented 'rarely as subjects,' cultural representation becomes a political hotbed when the potential for shaping societal discourse and social and economic treatment is considered."[46] To that extent, television's systematic Black diminutization brings to bear important questions regarding the social value of blackness in the nation-at-large and also generates unarticulated class tensions within Black communities.

When *House of Payne* emerged (even with its coarse humor and stale malapropisms), Black people watched. Having been deprived, rendered invisible, and undervalued for so long, Black viewers in many communities have developed a "thirst" for Black voices, images, and stories so insatiable that they are willing to "imbibe" any mainstream product that is made available, in order to quench their thirst. At the same time, many members of Black communities perceive Perry's commercial success with *House of Payne* as a mark of achievement, while others view the show as promoting racial inequality. This illuminates the complex and paradoxical manners in which *House of Payne* is accepted or rejected in Black communities through various prisms of class. The politics of thirst engenders feelings for Perry by some Blacks who believe that, regardless of what voices he brings to bear, "if he's getting money, it's cool." Conversely, other Blacks view Perry's capitalist-driven media empire as destructive to Black solidarity and cultural survival. For these latter Black folk, "there is a tremendous ambivalence expressed toward the effects of materialism on the community, as well as toward wealthy Blacks who are believed to have struck it rich by exploiting stereotypical Black cultural representations of gangsta and ghetto lifestyles—that is, by selling aesthetics and values associated with poverty."[47] For these reasons, Perry's televisual offerings, which are created and consumed within the dynamics of the politics of thirst, remain inevitably problematic.

Payneful Resolution

As television continues to rapidly change, media culture still remains a highly active site for the production and circulation of complex power relations. *Tyler Perry's House of Payne* represents a remarkable industrial success and an expansion of Black media visibility. The show's content attempts to ostensibly address subject matter of importance to poor and working-class Blacks, although it does so in ways that are quite problematic. While achieving the lofty status as the longest running Black sitcom in television history, *House of Payne* rarely addresses existing power hierarchies. The permanence of racism or the impact of institutionalized white supremacy never arises in Perry's all-Black world.

Yet his industrial success is undeniable, and his business acumen and achievements must be recognized. Perry remains an interesting case study that reveals how capitalist-driven economic prosperity remains the benchmark for social value in American culture. In spite of this, the unenlightened pursuit of capitalist imperatives undermines the collective interests of the majority of Black folk by privileging material acquisition over cultural affirmation and unity. In other words, "capitalism functions by keeping most of its participants in debt, incarcerated, enamored with things, and ostensibly enslaved... [and] specifically African-Americans find themselves a large part of the building blocks for the wealthy of the system,"[48] yet most do not have access to that wealth.

In the vast landscape of media culture where Black sitcoms are marginalized to the point of near invisibility, the yearning for new Black media voices has never been greater. For the first time in nearly a decade, a sitcom featuring a predominately Black cast has found its way back onto network television with Anthony Anderson and Tracey Ellis Ross's prime-time program *black-ish* (ABC, 2014–present). Perry has also continued to extend his televisual brand with the *House of Payne* spin-off, *Tyler Perry's Meet the Browns* (TBS, 2009–2012) and *Tyler Perry's For Better or Worse* (TBS/OWN, 2011–present). In 2012, Perry entered into an exclusive partnership with the Oprah Winfrey Network (OWN) to bring scripted content to the fledgling cable channel.

After the cancellation of Perry's *For Better or Worse* on TBS, he quickly renewed the show on OWN, and introduced another sitcom, *Love Thy Neighbor* (OWN, 2013–present). Perry's partnership with Winfrey has also allowed him to expand beyond the Black sitcom genre into one-hour dramas with such series as *The Haves and the Have Nots* (OWN, 2013–present) and *If Loving You Is Wrong* (OWN, 2014–present). Many more multivalent Black voices are needed within media culture to counteract Hollywood's aesthetics of domination. Black image-makers and lobbyists must demand a radical overhaul of the current network television "white-out," and relentlessly challenge what James Snead describes as the three devices "whereby Blacks have been consigned to minor significance on screen: *mythification, marking,* and *omission* . . . [which permits] elevation of the dominant and the degradation of the subordinate."[49] In many ways, Perry has—wittingly or not—led a charge to increase Black media visibility. However, the existence of a singular voice cannot foster the type of media discourse necessary to challenge television's well-defined racial margins, or to achieve a substantive multivocality that goes against the grain of socially constructed inequalities. Television continues to represent the locus of mainstream acceptance in our society, and contemporary Black media authorship cannot be defined merely by the presence of Black performers on-screen; rather, a truer impression of Black media authorship would evince the disruption of the status quo in ways that make room for a wide range of Black voices to be heard with full resonance. In this sense, there is still much work to be done.

Notes

1. *House of Payne* would later relinquish its distinction as the highest-rated cable sitcom on January 11, 2011, when *The Game* premiered on BET with 7.7 million viewers.

2. The stylistic standard for this anthology is to capitalize "Black" and use lowercase for "blackness"; this contributor has graciously complied but personally and politically prefers to capitalize both.

3. Margena A. Christian, "Becoming Tyler," *Ebony*, October 2008, 76–78.

4. Ibid., 80.

5. Christine Acham, *Revolution Televised: Prime Time and the Struggle for Black Power* (Minneapolis: University of Minnesota Press, 2005), 11.

6. Henry Louis Gates, Jr., "The Chitlin Circuit," *New Yorker*, February 3, 1997, 44.

7. Ibid., 49.

8. Ibid., 53.

9. Brett Pulley, "A Showbiz Whiz," *Forbes*, September 15, 2005.

10. Ibid.

11. Nicole LaPorte. "Perry Paves Way for Hollywood Crossover," *Variety*, February 19–25, 2007, 56.

12. Pulley, "A Showbiz Whiz."

13. Roger Ebert, "Diary of a Mad Black Woman," *Chicago Sun-Times*, February 24, 2005.

14. Ruth La Ferla, "Sometimes Piety Isn't Squeaky Clean," *New York Times*, October 14, 2007.

15. John Dempsey, "Syndies Rewrite Sitcom Script," *Variety*, August 28–September 3, 2006, 24.

16. Lynn Spigel and Max Dawson, "Television and Digital Media," in *American Thought and Culture in the 21st Century*, eds. Martin Halliwell and Catherine Morley (Edinburgh: Edinburgh University Press, 2008), 275.

17. Jacques Rancière, *The Politics of Aesthetics* (London: Bloomsbury, 2013), 43.

18. Robin R. Means Coleman, *African American Viewers and the Black Situation Comedy: Situating Racial Humor* (New York: Garland Pub, 1998), 66.

19. Ibid., 68.

20. Ibid., 73

21. Manthia Diawara and Silvia Kolbowski, "Homeboy Cosmopolitan," *October* 83 (Winter 1998): 51.

22. Herman Gray, "The Politics of Representation in Network Television," in *Channeling Blackness*, ed. Darnell Hunt (London: Oxford University Press, 2005), 161.

23. Ibid., 161.

24. Ibid., 155–75.

25. Kristal Brent Zook, *Color By Fox: The Fox Network and the Revolution in Black Television* (London: Oxford University Press, 1999), 4.

26. Ibid., 169.

27. Darnell Hunt, "Making Sense of Blackness on Television," in *Channeling Blackness*, ed. Darnell Hunt (London: Oxford University Press, 2005), 18.

28. Yuval Taylor and Jake Austen, *Darkest America: Black Minstrelsy from Slavery to Hip-Hop* (New York: W. W. Norton & Company, 2012), 187–88.

29. Ibid., 187.

30. Gary Levin, "Simple Economics: More Reality TV," *USA Today*, May 9, 2007.

31. La Ferla, "Sometimes Piety Isn't Squeaky Clean."
32. Dempsey, "Syndies Rewrite Sitcom Script."
33. Ibid.
34. Ibid.
35. John Dempsey, "Stations Aren't Laughing at Turner Comedy Buys," *Variety*, July 30–August 5, 2007, 15.
36. Ken Parish Perkins, "Looking for Laughs in Tyler Perry's House of Pain," *Chicago Defender*, June 13, 2007, 9.
37. Linda Armstrong, "Perry's 'Payne' Lacks Laughs," *New York Amsterdam News*, June 7–13, 2007, 19.
38. Mel Watkins, *On the Real Side: A History of African American Comedy* (Chicago: Chicago Review Press, 1999), 64.
39. Beretta E. Smith-Shomade, *Shaded Lives: African American Women and Television* (New Jersey: Rutgers University Press, 2002), 25.
40. Means Coleman, *African American Viewers and the Black Situation Comedy*, 68.
41. Ed Guerrero, "Bamboozled: In the Mirror of Abjection," in *Contemporary Black American Cinema: Race, Gender and Sexuality at the Movies*, ed. Mia Mask (New York: Routledge, 2012), 114.
42. Beretta E. Smith-Shomade, *Pimpin' Ain't Easy: Selling Black Entertainment Television* (New York: Routledge, 2008), 12.
43. James Lull, *Media, Communication, Culture* (New York: Columbia University Press, 2000), 13–73.
44. James Baldwin, *The Devil Finds Work* (New York: Random House, 1976), 63.
45. Felicity Colman, *Deleuze & Cinema: The Film Concepts* (Oxford: Berg, 2011), 148.
46. Means Coleman, *African American Viewers and the Black Situation Comedy*, 9.
47. Avi Santo, "Of Niggas and Citizens: The Boondocks Fans and Differentiated Black American Politics," in *Satire TV: Politics and Comedy in the Post-Network Era*, eds. Jonathan Gray, Jeffrey P. Jones, and Ethan Thompson (New York: New York University Press, 2009), 260.
48. Smith-Shomade, *Pimpin' Ain't Easy*, xvii.
49. James Snead, *White Screens, Black Images* (New York: Routledge, 1994), 4.

CHAPTER NINE

Spike and Tyler's Beef: Blackness, Authenticity, and Discourses of Black Exceptionalism

—Karen M. Bowdre

Spike Lee made a name for himself inside and outside of Hollywood with the 1986 release of his independent film, *She's Gotta Have It*. Since that time, he has become one of the most prolific African American directors with films such as *Do the Right Thing* (1989), *Malcolm X* (1992), and *Bamboozled* (2000). In May 2009, during the Black Enterprise Entrepreneurs Conference held in Detroit, Michigan, Lee was the keynote speaker at the Small Business Award Luncheon. During a discussion about Black media, Lee commented, "I think there's a lot of stuff out today that is coonery and buffoonery. I see ads for 'Meet the Browns' and 'House of Payne' and I'm scratching my head. We've got a black president and we're going back. The image is troubling and it harkens back to Amos 'n' Andy."[1]

Though Lee did not mention him by name, he was singling out *Meet the Browns* and *House of Payne*'s creator Tyler Perry in his criticism. Perry has captivated film audiences with his work since the introduction of his first scripted movie, *Diary of a Mad Black Woman* (Darren Grant, 2005). Perry's origins in Black theatre or the "Chitlin Circuit," his humor, and his often troubling class politics have irked many media critics.[2] However, Perry's success on stage (ticket sales, videos of the plays, and merchandise) provided him with the income, an estimated $150 million a year, to create films. For the past ten years, Perry has directed, produced, and starred in at least one film a year, and most of these movies have been commercially successful earning over $765 million to date. Perry's box-office receipts, along with his theatre ticket sales and television deals—most recently with the Oprah Winfrey Network (OWN) and previously with TBS—have made him a media mogul and someone who cannot be ignored.[3]

Though there were other ways Lee's critique of Perry could have been framed, media outlets circulated a narrative which cast the comments as a type of problem or beef he has (or had) with Perry's work. Beef, according to the urban dictionary, is "to have a grudge or start one with another person."[4] Yet professional jealousy, if this was indeed the case, is only part of the story. Though this may have been the first time Lee publically disparaged Perry's media productions, there are other issues at work here, including where his statement was made, in terms of both the type of the event and where the conference was held, and Lee's comments coming from a place of his expertise as a film and media director.

The months following Lee's statement, not surprisingly, brought a response from Perry. One of his early remarks elucidates the different approaches of the filmmakers. Perry observes that "it's attitudes like [Lee's] that make Hollywood think that these people do not exist and that's why there's no material speaking to them."[5] Perry creates plays, films, and television shows that speak to his audience—mostly southern, Christian, African American women—in ways that Hollywood does not. While one can argue, as many have, that Perry's work lacks "quality," a term loaded with issues of class and taste, and trades on stereotypes, his films clearly have audiences, and those revenues have allowed him to make a number of films since his first in 2005. Perry's ascendance in several media venues should have engendered a more complicated examination of his products in relation to other directors. Instead, between 2009 (when Lee's comments about Perry first begin to circulate in the media) and 2013 (when the two state they reconciled), their comments were framed as a typical tabloid type of beef. Through an overview that focuses on these directors and the popular discourses that surround filmmakers in general, as well as how these conversations affect Black directors specifically, I argue that the beef between Lee and Perry is rooted in director discourses and the ways a director's blackness can often pivot around ideas of authenticity, region, and Black exceptionalism.

Where's the Beef?

The term "beef" was introduced in a Biggie Smalls song, "What's Beef," from his 1997 CD *Life After Death*. Since 1997, others have given their definitions of the term, thereby expanding its meaning. In his examination of the term, Eli Sweet notes that while Smalls understood beef to be a "life or death battle that endangers even those around you," rapper Royce 5'9" describes beef as a "literary game written in rhyme and validated through belief."[6] Sweet goes onto to consider other nuances of beef:

> Beefs are conflicts expressed through texts, but they are also conflicts about texts. In a song attacking another artist, a "beef track," a rapper often acknowledges the beef track of the other artist, as well as his magazine interviews and second hand comments. This recognition and response to texts is the essence of the discourse of beef—and the source of its power.[7]

Similar to the worlds of hip hop and rap, discussions that surround the beef between Lee and Perry are where power, notoriety, and potential marketability are located. Their beef, which uses films and other media products, along with interviews and comments about one another, feeds into a media construction of an exaggerated antagonism between two African American directors with a significant media presence. Since the late 1980s, Lee has been one of a handful of directors who has gotten "press, media, and academic attention to the point of saturation," as Wahneema Lubiano noted over thirty years ago.[8] Currently, Perry incurs the same type of attention, though he is not the focus of a great deal of academic discourse. Moreover, their disagreement and the verbal shots that they made at one another and its coverage further illuminated how each man often overshadows the ability of other filmmakers to gain considerable media attention.[9] And while this media scrutiny works well for both men, it obscures the creative work of several other Black directors.

Returning to the meaning of beef as a life and death battle, let's briefly consider that Lee does in fact view Perry as a threat. Perry's rise to prominence takes place at the same time Lee is having challenges with his films. Lee's recent movies have not done well at the box office, and the planned sequel to his biggest hit to date, *Inside Man* (2006), and a James Brown biography never came to fruition.[10] Recently, Lee used Kickstarter, a platform for funding creative projects, to raise the money for *Da Sweet Blood of Jesus* (2014). He was able to raise $1.25 million for the project and recently decided to distribute the film using Vimeo, a streaming service, a month prior to the film's theatrical debut. Lee explained that he went with Kickstarter so he would have the freedom to make the film he desires, not one dictated by a studio. Though Lee does remain a creative force, his declining box-office and media presence make it understandable that he could be jealous of Perry's monetary success and media coverage. Moreover, based on his position as *the* Black director, he is well aware that his diminished media power could impact his ability to get future projects.

Using another definition for beef, it being more of a game than a life and death struggle, one could argue that Lee, who describes himself as an instigator, uses this aspect of his persona to maintain media attention as he publically criticizes the work of others.[11] Anyone who has followed Lee knows that he has had public squabbles with Quentin Tarantino, Clint Eastwood, Michael Rapaport, Samuel Jackson, and others. Thus, his "attack" on Perry could be more of a tactic to bring attention back to him. Lastly, Lee could have been offering commentary on Perry's work based on his "expertise" as a filmmaker and teacher with an extensive knowledge pertaining to historical Black images. If his comments had not been made in a public forum, they could have been interpreted as Lee trying to teach Perry how his media products replicate older forms of Black humor that are often associated with minstrelsy. Though the public nature of Lee's criticism makes it difficult to frame this as a potential teachable moment, if either man had utilized a different approach, this conversation could have been kept between them and not fodder for tabloids.

Perry's responses to Lee align more with traditional notions of beef—that is, a grudge against another person. He was upset about Lee's comments and, like Lee, made his feelings known in public media venues. His initial response to Lee occurs in 2009 during a *60 Minutes* interview with Byron Pitts. During the course of that interview, Perry mentions how he is "pissed" and "insulted" by the attitudes of Lee and others about his work.[12] He also makes the insightful observation, quoted earlier, that those who belittle his work also ignore and disregard his audience. Then, two years later, while promoting the film, *Tyler Perry's Madea's Big Happy Family* (Tyler Perry, 2011), Perry reacts to Lee much more aggressively, stating, "Spike can go straight to hell!"[13] It appears that Perry had become exasperated not only by Lee's comments but also by how his press junket for *Madea's Big Happy Family* becomes an occasion to focus on Lee's opinion and not his film. During this response, Perry discusses Lee and his tendency to talk unfavorably about others: "I'm so sick of hearing about damn Spike Lee," Perry said. "Spike can go straight to hell! You can print that. I am sick of him talking about me, I am sick of him saying, 'this is a coon, this is a buffoon.' I am sick of him—he talked about Whoopi, he talked about Oprah, he talked about me, he talked about Clint Eastwood. Spike needs to shut the hell up!" From his outburst, it's clear both Lee and his critique have touched a nerve due to his re-articulation of Lee's criticism. Then, Perry adds that Lee should stop talking about others and stop talking altogether. Finally, Perry's "allowing" the press to print and circulate his comments speaks to his own awareness of the media and their framing of the beef. Needless to say, Perry's response this time garnered more media attention, and the beef between these two Black directors continued.

Discourses of Authorship

Even among people who do not study or review films, there is an understanding of the importance of the role of the director in the film process. This notion has circulated in popular culture for over fifty years and exists today because of academic and critical reconsiderations of the director in the 1950s and '60s.[14] French critics, after viewing Hollywood films from the 1930–50s, developed the idea that film is the creative vision of one sole author or auteur: the director.[15] Since film is a collaborative process, this particular view has been and continues to be contested. Though the dispute over auteur theory continues in both academic and non-academic circles, its influence on popular discourses about directors is germane to this discussion because Perry and Lee are Black directors and, as such, have influence in Hollywood in ways that producers or writers often do not.

One of the problematic aspects regarding the cultural logic of director discourses is who is "allowed" to be labeled as such. French film critics who later became directors, such as François Truffaut and Jean-Luc Godard, felt that certain directors created art in spite of Hollywood's studio system. However, there were also directors who were not worthy of the term.[16] For many film critics, Perry is not a *real* director because his films lack technical savvy and/or creativity. But as TreaAndrea M. Russworm mentioned in the introduction to this book, for Perry to be considered for critical praise and potential awards, his work would have to conform to "bourgeois aesthetic judgments."[17] Perry has stated in an interview that he is not making his films for critics or critical acclaim; he is more than content to cater to his fan base than consider critics and their awards.[18] Yet Perry's exclusion also reveals the slippery definitions of who is deemed extraordinary and does his/her work have distinct characteristics according to the taste of media critics.

Since Lee went to film school at New York University and his work has been praised as unique and highly stylized, his inclusion in auteur conversations is typically not contested. Yet, in spite of his films conforming to particular aesthetics, he has not received many award nominations for his work. Whereas Perry's lack of education and his affiliation with urban theatre or "Chitlin Circuit," which is often considered lowbrow, essentially eliminates him from significant director discourses. However, based on the control that Perry has over his films, his distribution deal with Lionsgate meant that he was free in creating his own content without studio interference. Within the studio system, most directors are given feedback from studio executives, but only important directors—auteurs—are allowed to disregard producer notes or are not given any notes at all. Thus, while some feel Perry's artistry is lacking, the power he wields places him in a conversation with other powerful and influential directors.[19]

The last troubling element of the centrality of the director within film discourses, especially when analyzing African American directors, is the media's tendency to focus almost all attention on one Black director, with other Black directors elided from conversations. There is a rich history of Black directors, including Julie Dash, Charles Burnett, Euzhan Palcy, Gordon Parks, and Sidney Poitier, to name just a few; many worked outside of Hollywood, a fact which gets eliminated from conversations about directors because of the focus on great men/individuals.[20] Moreover, the myopia of this mindset not only erases past African American directors, it also gives way to a "there can only be one" mentality about Black directors.[21] While other African American directors get some media coverage if their films do well in festivals, with critics, or at the box office, they can still lack notoriety in spite of strong revenues, as in the case of Tim Story, director of Barbershop (2002), *Fantastic Four* (2005), *Fantastic 4: Rise of the Silver Surfer* (2007), *Think Like a Man* (2012), *Ride Along* (2014), and *Think Like a Man Too* (2014).[22] Thus, Lee was *the* Black director, but his recent production struggles, coupled with the rise of Perry, have made the latter *the new* Black director, a kind of warped succession that continues focusing most media attention on one director and giving other African American filmmakers very little or significantly reduced coverage for their films.

Conflating Blackness

The idea of the director has had an interesting trajectory in African American communities because some were viewed as early race men as they combated the ways film was used as a tool of racist propaganda against Blacks. *The Birth of a Nation* (D. W. Griffith, 1915), an adaptation of *The Clansman*, is the highly problematic and lauded film that propelled many African Americans to increase their filmmaking efforts to tell stories about Black people from a Black perspective.[23] Pioneers such as Oscar Micheaux and George and Noble Johnson established their own companies and produced their own films outside of the dominant system. The work of these independent Black filmmakers later becomes what historians classify as race films. Race films are movies that employed African American actors to tell stories about Black people. Though some companies that produced these films were controlled by whites and had white directors, the draw for many African American communities was seeing films that placed people who looked like them at the center of the narrative. Due to lack of capital and other resources, the production values for race films were not strong, but they did provide an alternative to mainstream films that would exclude Blacks most of the time or place them in secondary or tertiary roles.

The naming of motion pictures about African Americans as race films is reflective of the time and race relations. It also exposes the tendency in both commercial and academic communities, as well as industries like music, to pigeonhole products that do not feature white men as "other"—e.g., women's films and films categorized based on race, ethnicity, or nationality.[24] Hence, Black films become a genre unto themselves, and in the latter part of the twentieth century, and when African Americans did direct films, most of those films are about blackness.[25]

Films helmed by Blacks often presented a hope to African American audiences that blackness would be dealt beyond stereotypical stories and characters. Blackness is not a fixed term; as Herman Gray articulates, it is a "constellation of productions, histories, images, representations, and meanings associated with [a] black presence in the United States."[26] Although there is fluidity as well as competing claims to blackness and how it is defined, there is also a desire among some African Americans to rehabilitate or reimagine blackness outside of notions of white supremacy. Those hopes usually embody an eagerness to see a more "authentic" blackness that would portray positive and/or more complicated examinations of Black humanity that transcended what Stuart Hall calls a regime of racialized representation, racial stereotypes that persist over time.[27] Not surprisingly, Black audiences did not always view films from African American directors as steps towards making more productive images of blackness; these tensions inform another dimension concerning Lee and Perry's conflict.

Authenticity and Region

Debates about imagery also inform discussions about how directors qualify their blackness or demonstrate their credibility to tell stories about Black people. When Black directors create images that some deem to be questionable or contributing to the myriad of troubling Black characters and/or stories, his or her blackness is interrogated by critics and audiences. Hence, the question of what is Black, the positive/negative image dispute, moves to who is or is not truly Black. Similar to blackness, Black identity is also a contested definition. Sometimes "true" Black identity is defined on whether one dwells in the city or rural areas; one's class background or skin color; or one's ability to promote blackness through his/her talent and work.[28] When Lee aired "the dirty laundry" of colorism within the Black community in his film *School Daze* (1988), many felt he tore down African Americans and questioned his blackness.[29] For Perry, his use of comedy (a genre with a complicated history and links to minstrelsy), Madea, and his class politics have been among the reasons why critics question his blackness.

Though blackness is a complex constellation, this fact does not stop people (including directors) from positioning themselves in relation to blackness or other markers of race or ethnicity (as well as excluding others). When critics question Perry about his legitimacy, he can claim an authentic blackness, or at least a relationship to blackness, due to his success in cultivating an audience that is largely African American and female. Obviously, this audience existed before but few media outlets were able to tap into it. Perry's financial success with this market now makes him the point of contact for other organizations wanting to financially capitalize on this group.[30]

While Perry's associations with markets/audiences link him to a type of blackness, Lee's insistence of authenticity often lies in his claim that his films "tell the truth" about Black life in ways that most films, particularly those from white directors, do not.[31] Lubiano interrogates Lee's position by illuminating how his truth claims purport to be "reality," when in fact reality within the context of narrative is "inherently problematic" because "realism poses a fundamental, longstanding challenge for counter-hegemonic discourses."[32] Lee believes he is telling stories from a vantage point that privileges blackness, and in some cases parts of his films do this; however, realism "enforces an authoritative [or hegemonic] perspective."[33] Moreover, when Lee posits that his films are reality, his past position as *the* Black director with the greatest media presence has meant that other Black realities, especially those from African American women directors, are marginalized and greatly obscured.

In addition to these more commercial claims of Black authenticity, audiences, and filmic realism, there are also aspects of "true blackness" that come from a place of individual identity such as region. Important discussions about region have not factored into an analysis of blackness often due to the problem of African American communities being framed as singular without variation until recently. Riché Richardson demonstrates the significance of region in her book, *Black Masculinity and the U.S. South: From Uncle Tom to Gangsta*, through an examination of how Black men from this region have been constructed as problematic from the days of enslavement. Extremely negative discourses about

African American men started after slavery ended with the myth of the Black rapist being used in earnest later to counter Harriet Becher Stowe's Uncle Tom character.[34] Though these formulations started in white communities, Richardson maps how pathological perceptions of Black masculinity also circulate in many African American communities.[35] Her observations about Malcolm X and his construction of southern African American men provide insight about Lee and Perry, especially since Lee often frames his persona as a Black nationalist significantly influenced by Malcolm X.

Using his speeches, Richardson delineates how Malcolm X created a "discourse on authentic blackness and maleness" that established a "hierarchy of Black masculinity through a north-south binary."[36] He differentiated himself from Martin Luther King, Jr., and the civil rights movement, which was based in the south, by constructing King and the movement with its focus on nonviolence and integration as "alien, inferior, and ineffective" for true liberation of African Americans. Though Malcolm X was born in Omaha, Nebraska, and lived briefly in Lansing, Michigan, before moving to Boston, the rural parts of his background are no longer an important part of his narrative once he joins the Nation of Islam. Malcolm X distinguished himself through his speeches as a "field Negro," with King and his allies drawn as "house Negroes" or "Uncle Toms."

Consciously or not, Lee, in his admiration of Malcolm X, appears to promote a hierarchical and regional view of authentic blackness in his films. Moreover, this particular notion of Black authenticity motivates his attacks on Perry. For Lee, Perry represents the southern Black man, an inauthentic "house Negro," making films that are not grounded in realism and in fact often are fantastic or escapist and cater to women. Returning to Lee's description of Perry's work as trafficking in stereotypes, it becomes evident that his initial concern about Perry operates on multiple levels. Perry can be a threat to Lee's media presence, as discussed earlier, as well as a danger because Perry does not, in Lee's opinion, create media products that promote the right type of blackness.

After his first public critique of Perry, Lee talked about Perry with Oprah Winfrey in November 2013. A few years removed from his back and forth with Perry, Lee told Winfrey that the two had resolved their differences and that "one day [they] might work together." Before this revelation, Winfrey asked him about Perry, showing a segment with Perry and pointing out that their backgrounds are different from one another. Specifically, Perry is from the rural south and his parents were not highly educated, while Lee was raised in New York, his father was a musician, and his mother an educator. Interestingly, Lee did not want to affirm that their dissimilarities are motivated by regionalism; during the interview, Lee emphasized the southern influences in *his* life. Lee mostly explained that their difference in imagery is a matter of taste and style. As sociologist Pierre Bourdieu articulates, taste is linked to educational status and social origin; rarely is this term interrogated in venues outside of the academy.[37] Lee's attempt to mark his uniqueness from Perry as merely a stylistic choice elides his education and training as a filmmaker. While I am not suggesting that a film degree automatically makes one an exceptional director, it would be disingenuous to act as if Lee's training is not a factor in his style and a reason for his concern about Perry's. Comparatively, Perry's formal "training" was his early forays into theatre, specifically "urban theatre" or the "Chitlin Circuit." While Perry and Lee are indeed separated by their styles, Lee's candid conversation with Winfrey attempted to elide the class implications of taste, regional training, and style.

Directing Black Exceptionalism

The director discourses that often separate Lee and Perry from other Black directors function as a media-inspired form of Black exceptionalism. This trope or view of a Black woman or man as "exceptional" when compared to the rest of the race occurs when a person of African descent, who is gifted in intellect, musically and other arts, or in sports, is celebrated not only in African American communities but also in mainstream and white ones. Though this unique status may seem similar to the ways gifted people of European descent are written about, it is not. Black exceptionalism at its core espouses the notion of innate Black inferiority and is an unfortunate product of racism and white supremacy. According to this mindset, African Americans who accomplish notable feats are rare, and, in order to perpetuate the idea of these individuals being distinct from other Black people, exceptional Blacks are almost never contextualized as products of their environment, particularly when their surroundings are composed of other people of color.[38] Importantly, this causes a type of erasure of other successful African Americans who were/are gifted in the same area as the newly discovered "exceptional Negro."

These ideals are also, of course, evident in the notion of talented tenth. Though W. E. B. Du Bois writings on the talented tenth are more well known, the idea originated with Henry Lyman Morehouse, a white man who developed this concept in response to Booker T. Washington's insistence that African Americans should only be exposed to an industrial or vocational curriculum and not college education. Morehouse, for whom Morehouse College is named, argued that there were some outstanding Blacks who needed to be college educated so they would be prepared for leadership.[39]

Even before Du Bois elaborated further on the talented tenth in his essay from 1903, he and Washington were framed as leaders in the African American community by whites. To be clear, I am not saying these men were not leaders; rather, I intend only to stress that there were several Black leaders, some of whom were women, who had great influence among African American communities. Giving attention to one or two exceptional Black men further contributes to the ideology of exceptionalism because the majority of African Americans are understood as not only simply unremarkable but unintelligent and disposable. In the past, most mainstream newspapers focused exclusively on Du Bois and Washington as the leaders of the Black community because of their opposing views on education. In the 1960s, Martin Luther King, Jr., and Malcolm X were cast as opponents to one another; also note that Du Bois and Malcolm X are aligned with the north, and Washington and King with the south. More recently, Professor Cornel West and media commentator Tavis Smiley have been viewed as foils and in opposition with President Barack Obama. This focus on one great Black man (maybe two) for a monolithic "Black community" continues to the present in politics and other social arenas. The notion of being extraordinary also has a specific resonance in Black communities aside from leadership. Since African Americans are familiar with structural inequality and racism, several generations of parents often taught/teach their children that in order to obtain employment, they must be twice as good as their white counterparts to get hired.[40]

Though discourses of exceptionalism are sometimes intended to be complimentary to African American people, the persistence of these discourses perpetuates racial bias and deep-seated inequality. For example, the "exceptional Negro" also shares characteristics of a more recent media trope, the "Magical Negro," or Black characters with supernatural powers whose sole purpose are to assist the main (white) protagonist.[41] Such characters mysteriously appear and disappear from the story so that it can be noted that "multicultural casting" has been achieved.

In Lee's early days as a filmmaker, he was framed using a similar logic and rhetoric. For example, reviews of his first film, *She's Gotta Have It*, place his work in conversation with white independent filmmakers like Woody Allen and Jim Jarmusch. In most of these reviews, there is no mention of other Black directors such as Oscar Micheaux, Melvin Van Peebles, or Gordon Parks.[42] Though, as I have argued elsewhere, this may have been a strategy critics used to make Lee more palatable to arthouse audiences, it still results in these same audiences not being educated about the breadth of African American directors. Further, during Lee's "discovery," there was no real acknowledgment of the LA Rebellion filmmakers and their work that began in the late 1960s and early 1970s.

Similarly, almost twenty years after Lee's debut film, Perry's first film, *Diary of a Mad Black Woman*, was released. Perry did not direct this film but he wrote the screenplay and starred. The film ranked first in its opening weekend, and he became a compelling story of exceptionalism because the film's success took Hollywood insiders by surprise. Granted, two of the key reasons why most of Hollywood did not anticipate Perry was because they consistently ignored his audience of African American women, and because few knew of his success in theatre.

Lines of Symmetry

Beyond the discourses of exceptionalism that have informed their careers, Lee and Perry are more similar than dissimilar in various ways. While Lee believes his differences from Perry are extreme and aesthetic, neither director has successfully portrayed complicated Black women. Though Perry verbally praises Black women, Madea (Tyler Perry) and many of his other female characters often exacerbate racial regimes of representation or gloss over severe trauma. Perry often dramatizes extreme trauma such as child molestation, generational sexual abuse, and domestic violence as obstacles his female protagonists can overcome through the love of a good man. *Tyler Perry's Madea's Family Reunion* (Tyler Perry, 2006) offers some crystallizing examples of Perry's typical representation of Black women. The film's protagonists are sisters, Vanessa (Lisa Arrindell Anderson) and Lisa (Rochelle Aytes), who are negotiating their romantic and family relationships. Vanessa despises her mother, Victoria (Lynn Whitfield), seemingly because her mother constantly belittles her and her young children. Later, audiences learn that Victoria allowed her husband, Vanessa's stepfather, to sexually abuse Vanessa as a child in order for Victoria to maintain her lifestyle. This knowledge is unveiled during a confrontation between Vanessa and Victoria where Lisa learns about her parents' behavior and her sister's abuse. Victoria also confesses that her mother was a prostitute and drug addict, who traded her for $10 and some drugs. Vanessa admits she constantly worries about her children's safety and has difficulty allowing herself to be loved. She states that she has forgiven her mother, though the latter refuses to apologize for her behavior; later, the two physically fight one another after another one of Victoria's vicious comments. At the close of the film, Vanessa marries Frankie Henderson (Boris Kodjoe). When her mother approaches the bride and groom dance, Vanessa is able to hug/bless her in return.

In *Madea's Family Reunion* Vanessa's ability to truly forgive her mother and permit love into her life only occurs after her impromptu marriage. Though her boyfriend Frankie was present and physically pulls Vanessa away from her mother as they are fighting at the family reunion, a few scenes prior to the wedding, it appears the magic of marriage or at least the wedding enables supernatural forgiveness on Vanessa's part. Perry's use of marriage or love as a type of cure-all for serious trauma is part of his style; nevertheless, it could be beneficial for his audiences if he would use the didactic elements of his films to expand the possibilities, beyond catharsis and testimony, for those who have suffered from abuse.[43] Many of his viewers attend church, and though the stigma surrounding mental illness is decreasing in religious circles, Perry's suggestion of their behavior could encourage more engagement. Frankly put, women who have gone through the trauma that Vanessa, her mother, and sister experience in the film should seek mental health treatment. And while being in loving relationships is important, learning how to cope with past abuse and anxiety from that abuse, as Vanessa has regarding the safety of her children, typically cannot be addressed by loved ones alone.[44]

Similar to Perry, Lee often demonstrates his misunderstanding of powerful Black women. His breakout film, *She Gotta Have It*, masquerades as a woman's narrative of sexual empowerment when in actuality the film frames its protagonist, Nola Darling, through the eyes of her sexist suitors, who desire to date her exclusively and control her sexually. The film is consistently described as a romantic comedy yet it also features the protagonist being raped. Years later, Lee still struggles with female portrayals. The character of Sloan Hopkins (Jada Pinkett-Smith) in *Bamboozled* (2000) is clearly very intelligent and professional. She is the assistant of executive Pierre Delacroix or Dela (Damon Wayans), and Lee has described her character as being strong.[45] In this film, her boss, Dela, comes up with an idea that he hopes will get him fired so that he can be released from his contract. His twenty-first-century minstrelsy show becomes a runaway success, and Dela and Hopkins have to deal with the consequences. Throughout most of the film, Hopkins attentively keeps Dela abreast of his appointments, goes to meetings with him, and gets him coffee. She recruits the program's principal characters, Womack/Sleep 'n' Eat (Tommy Davidson) and Manray/Mantan (Savion Glover), and assists Dela in other aspects of production. Yet in spite of her hard work, when Hopkins and Dela clash over the program and the fact that he and his boss, Thomas Dunwitty (Michael Rappaport), feel she has gotten too close to Manray, he fires her. When Manray questions Dela about her dismissal, the latter disregards her past diligence for him and reveals she only obtained her job by sleeping with him.

Though Lee could have been trying to replicate a real-life problem in the entertainment industry, as Beretta E. Smith-Shomade suggests, it tremendously undermines the character.[46] Later in the film, Manray accuses Hopkins of only wanting to be with him to get his money, belittling her for sleeping with Dela. Whatever the reason Lee had for having Hopkins sleeping with Dela, the ramifications made her open to ridicule from her co-workers, Dela and Manray. And in the film's final sequence, where Manray is kidnapped and killed because his capturers believe he is a sellout, Hopkins completely unravels. She shows up at Dela's office with a gun. When he tries to disarm her while she is telling him not to approach, she shoots him. But her reaction seems more passive and hysterical; he made her shoot him—instead of her intentionally shooting him for not complying with her demands. So, while the character may have started off as a different type of female character for Lee, Hopkins ends in madness and is therefore more consistent with Lee's problematic depictions of Black women in such films as *School Daze* (1988), *Mo' Better Blues* (1990), and *She Hate Me* (2004).

These similarities help better contextualize and complicate the war of words between Tyler Perry and Spike Lee. Whether their perceived differences have been informed by region, class, education, or a combination of all three, discourses of exceptionalism continue to eclipse some of the more interesting lines of symmetry between the two. Since both Lee and Perry are aware of the power they wield, as evidenced by their producing the work of other directors as well as their strategic deployment of media during their "beef," hopefully in the future, when/if they are pitted against one another or against the latest Black director, they (and others) will take care to enlarge the conversation to include directors and media-makers who are less well-known. This broader inclusion of both established and newer talent will distance analyses of film and culture from the ideology and discourse that privileges *the one* African American director over the diverse field of others.

Notes

1. Issie Lapowsky, "Tyler Perry responds to Spike Lee's claim that his work is comparable to 'Amos 'n' Andy,'" *Daily News*, October 26, 2009, accessed February 5, 2015 http://www.nydailynews.com/entertainment/tv-movies/tyler-perry-responds-spike-lee-claim-work-comparable-amos-n-andy-article-1.380544.

2. In her chapter on Perry, Rashida Z. Shaw makes connections between Perry, the Chitlin Circuit, and Black theatre history extending back to the nineteenth century. See Shaw, "From the Margins to Center Stage: Tyler Perry's Popular African American Theatre." Other critics of Perry include Brittany Cooper, Latoya Peterson, Roxane Gay, and Andisheh Nouraee.

3. Paul N. Reinsch compares Perry with George Lucas and considers the similarities in their media empires, while Aymar Jean Christian and Khadijah Costley White examine Perry's effect on media production as a singular production entity. Also Artel Great discusses

Perry's prominence in television in connection with the "thirst" Black television audiences have for seeing programing reflective of their communities. See Reinsch, "The Case for Calling George Lucas the 'White Tyler Perry'"; Christian and White, "One Man Hollywood: Tyler Perry and the Limits of Niche Marketing"; Great, "Bring the Payne: The Erasure of the Black Sitcom and the Emergence of *Tyler Perry's House of Payne*."

4. Urbandictionary.com, http://www.urbandictionary.com/define.php?term=Beef, accessed January 21, 2015.

5. Lapowsky, "Tyler Perry responds."

6. Eli Sweet, "Bullet on the Charts: Beef, the Media Industry and Rap Music in America" (Senior Thesis, Haverford College, 2005).

7. Ibid.

8. Wahneema Lubiano, "But Compared to What? Reading Realism, Representation, and Essentialism in *School Daze*, *Do the Right Thing*, and the Spike Lee Discourse," in *The Spike Lee Reader*, ed. Paula J. Massood (Philadelphia: Temple University Press, 2007), 31.

9. The range of sources that report on the feud or its aftermath reflects Lubiano's idea of media saturation. Some of the articles on the Perry/Lee beef include: Keith Josef Adkins "Spike Lee Blasts a Hole into Tyler Perry," *The Root*, June 1, 2009, accessed February 5, 2015, http://www.theroot.com/blogs/on_the_dig/2009/06/spike_lee_blasts_a_hole_into_tyler_perry.html; Jimi Izreal, "Tyler Perry Vs. Spike Lee: A Debate Over Class And 'Coonery,'" NPR, April 22, 2011, accessed February 5, 2015, http://www.npr.org/blogs/tellmemore/2011/04/22/135630682/tyler-perry-vs-spike-lee-a-debate-over-class-and-coonery; Allison Samuels, "Inside Tyler Perry's Tantrum," *Daily Beast*, April 22, 2011, accessed February 5, 2015, http://www.thedailybeast.com/articles/2011/04/22/madea-movie-inside-tyler-perrys-tantrum-spike-lee-feud.html; Perez Hilton, "Tyler Perry Responds Heavily To Spike Lee Criticism," Perezhilton.com, April 20, 2011, accessed February 5, 2015, http://perezhilton.com/2011-04-20-tyler-perry-responds-to-spike-lee#.VNqZNS4kT6A; "Tyler Perry: 'Spike Lee Can go Straight to Hell,'" *Hollywood Reporter*, April 19, 2011, accessed February 5, 2015, http://www.hollywoodreporter.com/news/tyler-perry-spike-lee-can-179972; Todd Gilchrist, "Tyler Perry Says Spike Lee 'Can Go Straight to Hell,'" *Wall Street Journal* blog, April 20, 2011, accessed February 5, 2015, http://blogs.wsj.com/speakeasy/2011/04/20/tyler-perry-says-spike-lee-can-go-straight-to-hell/; Ken Tucker, "Tyler Perry rips Spike Lee on '60 Minutes': 'I'm insulted' and 'pissed off' by Lee's 'insults,'" *Entertainment Weekly*, October 25, 2009, accessed February 5, 2015, http://www.ew.com/article/2009/10/25/tyler-perry-spike-lee-60-minutes; Aisha Harris, Dan Kois, and Derreck Johnson, "Poster for the Upcoming Spike Lee-Tyler Perry Movie," *Slate*, November 14, 2013, accessed February 5, 2015, http://www.slate.com/blogs/browbeat/2013/11/14/spike_lee_and_tyler_perry_to_collaborate_maybe_now_friends_lee_tells_oprah.html.

10. Lee's latest films have grossed the following: *Oldboy* (2013) $2,193,658; *Red Hook Summer* (2012) $338,803; *Miracle at St. Anna* (2008) $7,919,117; and *Inside Man* (2006) $88,513,495. His affiliation on a James Brown biography was mentioned in Adkins, "Spike Lee Blasts a Hole into Tyler Perry." In 2014, Tate Taylor, director of *The Help* (2011), helms a James Brown project, *Get on Up*. Meanwhile, Perry's lowest-grossing film was *Tyler Perry's The Single Mom's Club* (2014), which grossed $15,973,881; and his highest-grossing film was

Tyler Perry's Madea Goes to Jail (2009), which grossed $90,508,336; the other Madea films grossed at least $50 million, http://www.boxofficemojo.com/people/chart/?view=Director&id=spikelee.htm; http://www.boxofficemojo.com/franchises/chart/?id=tylerperry.htm.

11. *Oprah's Next Chapter*, Oprah Winfrey, November 10, 2013.

12. *60 Minutes*, Byron Pitts, October 25, 2009.

13. Todd Gilchrist, "Tyler Perry Says Spike Lee 'Can Go Straight to Hell.'"

14. Melvin Donalson and Steve Neale posit that, due to the dissemination of auteurism in college film classes and film criticism in the early 1970s, the importance of the director has become a framework that the general public understands and engages. Donalson, *Black Directors in Hollywood* (Austin: University of Texas Press, 2003), 2; Neale, *Genre and Hollywood* (London: Routledge, 2000), 10.

15. American critics Pauline Kael and Andrew Sarris debated auteurtism, the latter being credited with bringing the term to the US. Kael's concerns were the seeds to later critiques by media scholars who questioned why certain directors were being elevated and on what basis. Kael was an opponent of the auteur theory. Andrew Sarris, "Notes on the Auteur Theory in 1962," *Film Culture* 27, no. 27 (Winter 1962/63): 1–8; Kael, "Circles and Squares," *Film Quarterly* 16, no. 3: 12–26.

16. Kael, 12–17.

17. TreaAndrea Russworm, "Introduction: Media Studies has Ninety-Nine Problems . . . But Tyler Perry Ain't One of Them?"

18. Gilchrist, "Tyler Perry Says Spike Lee 'Can Go Straight to Hell.'"

19. In an article for *Slate* magazine, Doree Shafrir discusses the problem with auteur theory in the case of the films *Amores Perros* (2000), *21 Grams* (2003), and *Babel* (2006) from director Alejandro González Iñárritu and writer Guillermo Arriaga. http://www.unz.org/Pub/Slate-2006oct-00290.

20. Donalson examines sixty-seven African or African American directors in his book *Black Directors in Hollywood*, and he notes that when the book was finally published in 2003 there were others he was not able to include because of press deadlines. Donalson, x.

21. In their reporting on the Lee/Perry reconciliation, Aisha Harris, Dan Kois, and Derreck Johnson have created a fictional poster for their future collaboration titled "Mookie vs. Madea," with the following subtitle: "There can only be one [in very large font] 'mainstream' Black writer/director in the minds of the public, thanks to institutionally biased entertainment media [in much smaller font]." See Harris, Kois, Johnson, "Exclusive Poster for the Upcoming Spike Lee-Tyler Perry Movie." I had not seen their mock poster and my description of "there can only be one" comes from the television show *Highlander* (syndication, 1992–98).

22. In spite of the box-office success of his films, over $690 million, which comes very close to Tyler Perry's total box office of $765 million, Patrick Goldstein was concerned about his job security and future. Two years later, Tambay A. Obenson notes that Story is still not known to broad audiences. See http://latimesblogs.latimes.com/movies/2012/05/tim-storys-filmmaking-career.html; http://blogs.indiewire.com/shadowandact/tim-story-the-top-grossing-black-director-many-apparently-still-arent-familiar-with despite.

23. Thomas Cripps delineates the various men and companies to spring up in the wake of *The Birth of a Nation*. Cripps, *Slow Fade to Black: The Negro in American Film, 1900–1942*

(Oxford: Oxford University Press, 1993), 70–89. Anna Everett details the development of Black film criticism and how the film sparked an increase in writing and activism. Everett, *Returning the Gaze: A Genealogy of Black Film Criticism, 1909–1949* (Durham: Duke University Press), 59–106.

24. In my book, I elaborate more on the problem of racial erasure in genre. Karen M. Bowdre, *Shades of Love: African Americans and Hollywood Romantic Comedies*, chapter 2 (University of Illinois Press, forthcoming).

25. Cripps's book about Black film being a genre follows the historical trajectory of films about those who are not white as understood as others. Thomas Cripps, *Black Film as Genre* (Bloomington: Indiana University Press, 1978), 1–12.

26. Herman Gray, *Watching Race: Television and the Struggle for "Blackness"* (Minneapolis: University of Minnesota Press, 1995), 12.

27. Donalson, 6–7.

28. Todd Boyd articulates the authenticity problem within race and media studies when he notes that there are scholars who believe that Black identity is synonymous with working-class politics and those who cannot identify with this are not Black enough. Boyd, *Am I Black Enough for You?: Popular Culture from the 'Hood and Beyond* (Bloomington: Indiana University Press, 1997), 22.

29. Toni Cade Bambara mentions how Lee's film put issues such as colorism and sexism into the open, although some thought it was dirty laundry. Bambara, *Deep Sightings and Rescue Missions: Fiction, Essays & Conversations* (New York: Vintage, 1996), 179–200.

30. Christian and White, 2.

31. Lubiano, 34.

32. Ibid, 37.

33. Ibid.

34. Being able to trace particular ideas and ideologies back through centuries is important because though blackness is not fixed, one can see elements of the past in many present formulations.

35. Riché Richardson, *Black Masculinity and the U.S. South: From Uncle Tom to Gangsta* (Athens: University of Georgia Press, 2007), 1–22.

36. Richardson, 159.

37. Pierre Bourdieu, *Distinction: A Social Critique of the Judgment of Taste* (Cambridge: Harvard University Press, 1984), 1.

38. Robin D. G. Kelley, *Thelonious Monk: The Life and Times of an American Original* (New York: Free Press, 2009).

39. Evelyn Brooks Higginbotham, *Righteous Discontent: The Women's Movement in the Black Baptist Church, 1880–1920* (Cambridge: Harvard University Press, 1994). Also on a blog post, Henry Lewis Gates posits that President Lincoln may have been the first to articulate the idea of an unusual class of African Americans. http://www.pbs.org/wnet/african-americans-many-rivers-to-cross/history/who-really-invented-the-talented-tenth/.

40. For one recent article about minorities being twice as good as whites in order to get half the opportunities, see http://www.theguardian.com/commentisfree/2012/jul/04/graduates-ethnic-minority. For employment statistics, see http://www.pewresearch.org

/fact-tank/2013/08/21/through-good-times-and-bad-black-unemployment-is-consistently-double-that-of-whites/.

41. Scholars either feel the Magical Negro is an extension of older stereotypes or a new distorted image. See Audrey Colombe, "White Hollywood's New Black Boogeyman," *Jump Cut* 45 (2002): 1; Matthew W. Hughey, "Cinethetic Racism: White Redemption and Black Stereotypes in 'Magical Negro' Films," *Social Problems* 56, no. 3 (August 2009): 543–50; Cerise L. Glenn and Landra J. Cunningham, "The Power of Black Magic: The Magical Negro and White Salvation in Film," *Journal of Black Studies* 40, no. 2 (November 2009): 135–40.

42. Bowdre, forthcoming.

43. Ben Sher's chapter unpacks Perry's love of film, cinephilia, and penchant for trauma in his films. Brandeise Monk-Payton posits that Perry's films create a worship type of experience in the movie theatre. Finally, Keith Corson defines Perry's style as Gospel Cinema. Sher, "'All My Life I Had to Fight': Domestic Trauma and Cinephilia in Tyler Perry's Archive of Feelings"; Monk-Payton, "Worship at the Altar of Perry: Spectatorship and the Aesthetics of Testimony"; Corson, "Tyler Perry, TD Jakes, and the Birth of Gospel Cinema."

44. Scholarly articles, as well as those in popular media, catalogue the hesitancy of African Americans to reach out to mental health professionals. The reasons for this resistance include lack of health insurance, distrust of the medical community, negative attitudes about mental illness, and churchgoing communities' distrust of mental health professionals.

45. Lee believes the Hopkins character is multilayered as well as the most intelligent and sympathetic character in the film. See Gary Crowdus and Dan Georgakas, "Thinking about the Power of Images: An Interview with Spike Lee," *Cineaste* 28, no. 2 (2001): 6.

46. Beretta E. Smith-Shomade, "'I be Smackin' My Hoes': Paradox and Authenticity in *Bamboozled*," in *The Spike Lee Reader*, ed. Paula Massood (Philadelphia: Temple University Press, 2007), 240.

CHAPTER TEN

The Case for Calling George Lucas the "White Tyler Perry"
—Paul N. Reinsch

> But if I can break through with this movie, then hopefully there will be someone else out there saying let's make a prequel and sequel, and soon you have more Tyler Perrys out there.
> —George Lucas on his plans for *Red Tails*

> What a guy! For him to believe so strongly in this story is amazing. I think we should pull together and get behind this movie. I really do! . . . George, I just want to say, thank you for having the courage to do this.
> —Tyler Perry's open letter to George Lucas after hosting a screening of *Red Tails*

Introduction

Tyler Perry's stature and reputation have expanded to the point where his appearance as a presenter at the 2012 Tony Awards was a surprise to few observers. Though his power is acknowledged in this occasion, Perry is still regarded as something of a problem in much of the discourse about him. Can a problem like Tyler Perry be solved? Does his expanding cultural presence suggest that an answer needs to appear soon? Any potential solution must include careful thinking about Tyler Perry, "Tyler Perry," and the various texts associated with his media empire. A number of journalists, critics, and scholars from a variety of disciplines have already begun to situate Perry's work in theatre, cinema, and television in its industrial and cultural contexts. These authors often compare Perry to other media figures in the past and present. This scholarship helps contextualize and explain the cultural acceptance of Perry's work. Yet for an artist of his power, the list of media figures to which Perry is linked and/or compared is unfortunately concise. Tyler Perry is typically linked to a small set of friends (Oprah) or foes (Spike Lee, Todd Boyd).[1] These figures can be grouped into broad categories wherein they share affinities with Perry: race and genre. Writers link Perry to Lee and Oscar Micheaux, for example, because they are Black Americans. Writers link Perry to Douglas Sirk and Pedro Almodóvar, for example, because these filmmakers deal in (female) melodrama. As Wesley Morris states plainly in *Film Comment*: "After Pedro Almodóvar, no working director has committed himself so completely to the emotional lives of women."[2]

Other pieces cast a somewhat wider net in attempting to situate Perry's films in popular culture. Some authors seem almost bewildered by the challenge. In his review of *For Colored Girls* (Tyler Perry, 2010), Matt Zoller Seitz offers a laundry list of influences, remarking that the film "seems equally influenced by sitcoms, Douglas Sirk melodramas, Pedro Almodóvar pictures and early-'60s social problem dramas such as Sidney Lumet's *The Pawnbroker* and the old CBS series *East Side, West Side*."[3] Seitz also claims that Perry has "a touch of the vibrant renegade looniness that [critics] prize in directors such as Sam Fuller," before concluding, "the only thing standing between Tyler Perry and a spot alongside Fuller in the pantheon of great American primitivists is half a year of film school."[4] Despite the apparent differences between the filmmakers' personas and films, Fuller's independence (and not just "looniness") makes this comparison somewhat apt. Fuller is indeed lauded as a "renegade" and "primitivist" in part because he loudly criticized Hollywood while also at times taking its money. Perry has famously not taken Hollywood's money and remains independent at the level of production. Seitz's proposed solution to the "problem" of Tyler Perry—sending Perry to film school (a place high school dropout Fuller could not and did not attend)—would almost necessarily tie Perry to the very thing he works to disrupt: mainstream Hollywood. This industry training would, apparently, make Perry's films less unwieldy, less frustrating, and more readily linked to the work of other mainstream filmmakers of the past and present.

What follows is a modest proposal for a reframing of, or adjustment to, the discourse around Perry. Without rejecting the suggestions of Seitz and others, what additional independent American filmmakers can help deepen the Perry discourse? Charlie Chaplin might be an option that has not been adequately explored. Like Perry, Chaplin wrote, directed, produced, performed in, and created music for his films. Like Perry, whose work often features Madea, Chaplin's empire featured a familiar and distinctive character at the center: the Tramp.[5] Discussing Chaplin and Perry together has the additional benefit of expanding the discussion beyond the present dominant parameters of race and genre.

This chapter, however, proposes to discuss Perry's work and career alongside that of the one contemporary figure with comparable cultural ubiquity, success, and freedom: George Lucas. If we must link Perry to other filmmakers—and it seems we must—I suggest we compare arguably the two most important independent American filmmakers of the past several decades. One cannot study American cinema of the 1970s and '80s without taking Lucas into account. One should not study American cinema of past two decades without taking Perry into account. Furthermore, this is a comparison at least suggested by the filmmakers themselves, particularly in the discourse around the Lucas-produced *Red Tails* (Anthony Hemingway, 2012), a film about African American fighter pilots in World War II. Long before the release of this film, Perry arguably cemented himself as the next singular, successful, and independent filmmaker behind Lucas. Perhaps no two filmmakers of the past few decades are more successful and yet also so highly criticized. The following discussion of Perry does not give equal attention to Lucas and *Red Tails* but rather intends to use these materials to suggest potential new avenues in Tyler Perry scholarship. A case study of the discourse around Perry's *For Colored Girls* helps make the discussion more concrete.

Origin Stories and Myth-Making

The careers of Perry and Lucas can be analyzed and compared as contrasting studies of moguls negotiating the peril-fraught status of "independent" in the age of global capital. Each has the unique freedom that comes only with success. Both create media centers physically removed from Hollywood and brands that are ubiquitous in the media landscape. Each also builds an empire around the troubling figure of a Black man (Darth Vader/Madea). Though free of Hollywood funding at the production stage, each creator makes populist work designed to please and assure large audiences. If Lucas's entertainments lean toward escapism and release, Perry's more commonly offer uplift and lessons (if not didacticism). Both create works steeped in nostalgia. Each has cinema at the center of his empire but a large stake in other forms. For Lucas, these include special effects (Industrial Light & Magic), novels, DVDs, games, licensing deals for a host of products, and more. For Perry, these include a book, plays, DVDs of his plays, soundtracks, DVDs, and more.

Each has been able to establish himself as an outsider to Hollywood, even while their careers began in different cultural and industrial spaces. Lucas famously graduated from USC in 1967. He is also the target audience for most definitions of Hollywood: an (upper-) middle-class white male. Lucas did not learn on the job but instead learned the job in Los Angeles from the industry. He also benefitted from witnessing firsthand the failures of would-be mentor Francis Ford Coppola's attempts at becoming an independent filmmaker who could use Hollywood for his own ends. To regard Lucas as an independent filmmaker who "sells out" to Hollywood is a common reading strategy, but it is not the only way to interpret his career.[6] Lucas's first efforts were youthful endeavors, and his student films demonstrate the freedoms and luxuries that come with a film school education. He also achieved the dream of many student filmmakers in getting the chance to turn a student work into a feature film. His *Electronic Labyrinth THX 1138 4EB* (George Lucas, 1967) then became the Warner Bros.-backed *THX 1138* (George Lucas, 1971). When this feature failed to turn a profit, Lucas responded to the market, or, to be more precise, created something for the market. *American Graffiti* (George Lucas, 1973) is a populist text; it peddles nostalgia to upper-middle-class whites for the time when they could spend days eating fast food, listening to pop songs, and cruising.[7]

Tyler Perry's background and ascendancy to media mogul is well-documented and a core part of his mythology. Roy S. Johnson's piece for *Ebony*, "His Own Man," confides: "Of course, you know by now that Perry was homeless almost two decades ago before his comedic stories of faith, family and confronting life's challenges—all gleaned from his own experiences."[8] Perry famously began on the outside, and not simply as a Black man without the money to attend USC.[9] He moved into cinema only after establishing himself in the world of theatre and built his film empire squarely on the back of his theatre work. Once in the realm of media production, Perry looked to the careers and legacies of Micheaux, Louis Jordan, and other African American artists who worked within and outside of the mainstream film industry. He tips his hat to several through his choices in names for soundstages at Tyler Perry Studios (Micheaux, Cicely Tyson, Ruby Dee and Ossie Davis, Quincy Jones, and Sidney Poitier).

Having achieved economic independence, each mogul is in a sense a victim of his own success, at least in the sense that each becomes the target of heated rhetoric from those who consume their product. Much of the discourse around both Lucas and Perry expresses frustration, and often a sense of betrayal. Writing on Perry, for example, often takes on the language and tone of disappointment. Stephanie Zacharek asks: "And is it a sin to wish the filmmaking, and the overall storytelling, in Perry's movies were better?"[10] Robert J. Patterson chastises Perry throughout his essay, writing, "familiarizing himself with the nuances of (black) feminist inquiry might behoove him."[11] Others ostensibly speak directly to the filmmaker: "Mr. Perry, you owe your audience something better."[12] While most of the writing on Perry offers valid critiques and gives voice to legitimate concerns, perhaps more writing on Perry should take account of what he is doing, and focus a bit less on what he could, or should, be doing.[13]

There is a considerable amount in repetition in the discourse on each filmmaker, and there is a considerable amount of repetition within each mogul's products. Both artists build and protect their empires in part by selling consumers essentially the same product again and again. The most common put-down of Perry refers to his tendency to place his name at the beginning of all his film and television show titles. And there are many products whose first two words are "Tyler Perry's." But "Lucasfilm," "LucasArts," and even "THX" and the other (trademarked) names Lucas provides for his products serve the same purpose in the marketplace. Each creator turns his name into a brand and a promise to consumers about the quality of, and similarity to, previous products. If Perry peddles versions of what is basically the same film (featuring Madea), Lucas actually sells the same film (*Star Wars* was shown in theatres a number of times before various home video versions, "special" editions, and, most recently, the 3D variations). While Tyler Perry Studios operates tirelessly to produce more (of the same), Lucasfilm produces nearly only the same (with minor variations). Perry does, however, build his empire by selling audiences the same text in multiple forms; most of his properties begin in the theatre, become DVDs, and then feature films for cinema exhibition (that later appear as DVDs and Blu-ray discs as well as appearing through streaming services). A Tyler Perry film is therefore often a pre-sold property. Lucas continues to release and sell versions of the same handful of texts (the six *Star Wars films*) while offering little new content beyond accessories (novels, games, toys).

The branding has worked, and continues to work, for each man and company. Lucas's empire rests on a mere six feature films and for decades relied on only three films to hold its center. As a writer and producer, Lucas is involved with the *Indiana Jones* films (Steven Spielberg, 1981–2008), *Howard the Duck* (Willard Huyck, 1986), *Radioland Murders* (Mel Smith, 1994), the TV series *The Young Indiana Jones Chronicles* (Amblin, 1992–93), with two iterations of *Star Wars: The Clone Wars* (Lucasfilm, 2003–2005, 2008), and more.[14] Perry has written and directed over ten feature films, more than ten plays, more than ten video releases (of his own plays), and the majority of episodes of *Meet the Browns* (TBS, 2008–2011), *House of Payne* (TBS, 2007–2012), *Love Thy Neighbor* (OWN, 2013–present), *The Haves and the Have Nots* (OWN, 2013–present), and *For Better or Worse* (TBS, 2011–2012; OWN, 2013–present). Each company also works to ensure the best profit from all products. Before concluding in early 2014, Perry's distribution deal with independent Lionsgate gave him a healthy percentage of theatrical box office. Lucas has famously bullied both Fox and exhibitors to give his films more money and more time in the largest and best theatres, and his licensing deals are justly famous.[15]

While Lucas's films as a producer have grossed well over $3 billion domestically in theatrical release, Perry's films have earned almost three quarters of a billion at this point in theatres (and both men have earned even more from other ventures). This is a substantial disparity, but Perry is not making action films or selling board games. Whether labeled "women's pictures," melodramas, Black evangelical Christian celebrations, or pseudo-musicals, Perry's films are not blockbuster material. Also important is the fact that those sorts of films—blockbusters, tent-pole films, and even Pixar films—make well more than half of their theatrical box-office revenue overseas. A cursory glance at the numbers for each creator's film reveals that while 99.9 percent of the gross of Perry's films comes from the US, more than half of the gross for Lucas's films comes from overseas.[16] Though Denene Millner claims that Madea "has become an international sensation," there is actually little evidence of audiences outside the US embracing Madea or Perry's films more generally, at least at the theatrical exhibition stage.[17] Perry's funding is similarly based in the US, which contrasts readily with the packages put together that allow David Lynch, Jim Jarmusch, and other more-lauded American independent filmmakers to continue working. Tyler Perry, for better or worse, is perhaps the most American independent filmmaker of recent decades.

In sum, here are two similar yet very different empires. Lucas names the companies and technologies and he stands alone as overseer of all things *Star Wars* (at least until the 2012 sale to Disney). He chooses what products will bear the "Star Wars" logo. Perhaps these words are the center of the empire, and have more power to circulate than one man can control. Perhaps Darth Vader is the center (episodes 1–3 work hard to re-imagine the later films as his story). Or perhaps the center of the Lucas empire is the technology itself. Though at least one scholar argues "no one has closed the gap between art and technology more successfully than George Lucas," one might counter that the true heart of the Lucas empire and legacy is the ultimate ascendancy of ones and zeros.[18] If Lucas fetishizes technology and demands that audiences do the same, it is worth noting that Perry seems willfully to ignore the trappings of modern, or at least digital, filmmaking. No contemporary media-maker with similar success and productivity relies less on technology than Perry. It is not simply the absence of explosions or CGI effects in Perry's films; it seems Perry has no desire to explore the malleability of the film image. Just as likely is the idea that Perry's faith in the image is total. His films are records of actors performing. At the center of his empire are performances. Perhaps the center of the Perry empire is his own performance as Madea—a figure as troubling in its racial implications as Darth Vader and doubly so because she is done in drag. Each appearance of Madea is a reminder of whose work we are seeing, whose dialogue we are hearing, who decided to put the camera just there. If the Lucas empire has data for a heart, the Perry empire at least claims to have "real" people there instead.

Representing (the Race)

Comments from each filmmaker on the occasion of the release of the Lucas-produced *Red Tails* encourage a comparison of their careers. I will briefly explore the reception of *Red Tails* and Perry's *For Colored Girls*—perhaps the two most ambitious films from each media mogul in that both films move the filmmaker away from the characters that have created their wealth and influence. To do so, I will first explore the discourse around the release of *Red Tails*, especially some striking comments from Lucas about the film, contemporary cinema, and Black cinema. Lucas's comments to Bryan Curtis are interesting here in particular, and not simply because he mentions Perry more than once. Lucas claims that with the $65–100 million used to finance the film he "realize[s] that by accident I've now put the black film community at risk," because if the film is not profitable, "there's a good chance [Black filmmakers] stay where [they] are for quite a while."[19] In other words, Black filmmakers will continue making only low-budget films. Lucas claims to place the future of Black film, and the Black film "community," in jeopardy. He does not claim to speak for "them," but ties the future of Black cinema to his need for a large audience to see *Red Tails*. His plea for ticket sales then becomes more overt: "But if I can break through with this movie, then hopefully there will be someone else out there saying let's make a prequel and sequel, and soon you have more Tyler Perrys out there."[20] In the midst of these proclamations, Lucas seems to inadvertently admit that he has quite likely never seen a Tyler Perry film. Perry's oeuvre is unconcerned with American history or action cinema (though he did take on the titular role in the Rob Cohen-directed *Alex Cross* [2012], played a small role in J. J. Abrams's *Star Trek* [2009], and has recently appeared in David Fincher's *Gone Girl* [2014]).

In the weeks around the film's release, Lucas claimed repeatedly that he could not talk Hollywood studios into funding or being involved with the film. One studio's executives even declined to attend the screening of the completed film. Wesley Morris begins his review of *Red Tails* with this anecdote and notes that we have no reason to doubt the veracity of Lucas's tale.[21] There is certainly no history of Black film blockbusters or recent examples of profitable PG-13-rated Black action films. But if we agree to believe Lucas, then we should also consider his pitch for the film. Our ability to second-guess the executives' decision becomes more challenging. Lucas readily admits that he described the film as "like *The Color Purple*, only they're in airplanes. It's sort of like a Tyler Perry movie, only without jokes."[22]

Putting aside the box-office potential of a WWII variation on *The Color Purple* (Steven Spielberg, 1985) or a joke-free Tyler Perry film, what exactly is Lucas selling here? The references here are understandable, at least partially. Lucas wants to link his film to other successful American films featuring Black actors. But this cannot have been appealing to most studio executives. By mentioning *The Color Purple*, Lucas opens the door to comparing his film to sometime-collaborator Steven Spielberg's similar foray into fictionalized treatments of the historical oppression of Black Americans. Most troublingly, what exactly does Lucas here claim these three (types of) films have in common beyond the presence of Black actors? Does *Red Tails* present Black southern women in airplanes? Does *Red Tails* present contemporary Black Americans negotiating trying family relationships or tacking problems like drug addiction or crises of faith?

Just as there is little evidence that Lucas is familiar with Perry's work, his casual mentions of other films to promote *Red Tails* betray little awareness of Black cinema, or even films featuring Black performers. Curtis also quotes Lucas's financial ambitions for the film and here again Lucas asserts links between his film and another: "If we can get over $20 million in our first weekend ... we're kind of in the game. We're in *The Help* category."[23] Here again, Lucas links his action film (which he says is targeted at teenagers) to a very different sort of text. *The Help* (Tate Taylor, 2011) is the modestly budgeted film of the quite successful book of the same name, whose sales were driven by the book's incorporation into countless reading circles around the country. *Red Tails* is a not a novel, or even a graphic novel, and so lacks the "pre-sold" characteristics of *The Help* (and many Tyler Perry films). Lucas does not stop at $20 million however: "If it gets $30 (million) in the first weekend then those guys get to make their movies without even thinking about it." After this quote, Curtis injects an explanation: "Here Lucas meant Spike Lee or Lee Daniels or whoever else might direct the *Red Tails* prequel and sequel."[24] This is a logical interpretation because, as Curtis recounts, Lucas explicitly mentioned these two filmmakers from the stage at a Times Square theatre screening of the film. But Lucas's easy conflation of "personal" films (Daniels/Lee get to make "their" movies) with a project that is his (Lucas's) is troubling. Lee and Daniels have established film careers that exist without the patronage of Lucas.[25]

Lucas's vision for the future of Black filmmaking is grim but not in exactly the way he claims. He seems to envision a Black cinema where Black directors make large-budget films produced and owned by Lucas himself that also help create yet another franchise for a man with almost unimaginable wealth. If one of the goals of *Red Tails* is to prove that there is an audience for films made by, and for, Black Americans, Lucas here and throughout his promotion for the film does a poor job of acknowledging the contributions of director Anthony Hemingway or screenwriters John Ridley and Aaron McGruder (creator of *The Boondocks* and a vocal critic of both Lucas and Perry). Though *Red Tails* has Black talent behind, as well as in front of, the camera, the Lucas-driven discourse around the film manages to almost completely obscure this fact. While certainly drumming up publicity with his name and comments, the Lucas media blitz also allows him to claim not just ownership but authorship of the film. It is to the credit of most film reviewers that the film is not more often compared to other white films about the Black experience like *Mississippi Burning* (Alan Parker, 1988). Michael Phillips, for example, actually compliments *Red Tails* for avoiding "the aggravating Hollywood strategy of telling an African-American story by way of a mass-marketable white protagonist, a la the Civil War drama *Glory*."[26] While taking Phillips's point, like most critics, he regrettably gives Lucas credit/blame for the film and openly discusses Lucas as the film's author. This "authorship" of a Black story is something the film does share with *Glory* (Edward Zwick, 1989) and *The Color Purple*. *Red Tails* and Lucas's comments around the film foreground some key questions for contemporary cinema and media scholarship, especially how we define Black cinema and who gets to create this definition.

The status of Perry's *For Colored Girls* as a Black film is relatively unquestioned, and critics read the film in relation to its source play and other films. Perry created a film of Ntozake Shange's 1975 play *For Colored Girls Who Have Considered Suicide When the Rainbow Is Enuf*. Adapting (adequately or not) theatre works for the cinema is (arguably) what Perry has been doing for his entire film career. In this sense, *For*

Colored Girls is in keeping with his general cinema project except for the fact that he has turned someone else's play into a film rather than performing a translation of one of his own works. Though the act of adaptation is familiar, the source is more complex and famous than Perry's own stage work. Perry at times seems unsure how to describe the film. In an interview with Miki Turner he calls it "an art house movie ... with an all-Black cast," but after the interviewer questions this description, Perry claims, "if you look at all the dramas I've done, it fell somewhere in line with them."[27] *For Colored Girls*, and the play before it, is concerned directly with the unique experiences of Black American women. Perry adds characters, provides proper names for characters, adds dialogue, and locates the play in and around a single building in contemporary Harlem. The film also provides further evidence of Perry's emerging aesthetic. The melodrama remains persuasive but Perry manages mostly to smooth over the transitions between Tyler Perry Studio's Atlanta backlot and helicopter shots of New York City.

In terms of cinematography, Perry's film also plays with planes of focus to a larger degree than his earlier works, and this potentially serves to remind the audience that they are watching a film, and helps preserve the combination of intimacy and distance built into the play. Some critics argue that the film shows Perry's growing confidence as a film director. Others argue that, even if it is improving, Perry's command of film technique is not up to the task presented by this material. Most reviewers compare the film to the play with varying degrees of specificity and many compare the film to Lee Daniels's *Precious* (2009). For some, *For Colored Girls* must be read as a deviation from the Perry brand and an admirable effort to put an important piece of Black theatre on the film screen, though even in favorable reviews, Perry is regularly denigrated in comparison to Daniels and/or Shange.

Having briefly commented on the reception of *For Colored Girls*, what follows is a brief survey of how a handful of established film critics for major American publications reviewed both *For Colored Girls* and *Red Tails*. This survey does not begin to account for the totality of the reception of either film. However, I highlight these reviews because they sketch out how each film was received and suggest the genesis of the critical discourse around each film. Specifically, I draw on comments from Jake Coyle, Roger Ebert, Lou Lumenick, Claudia Puig, and Peter Debruge.

Jake Coyle offers negative comments on both films while linking each to the creator's earlier work. Coyle regards *For Colored Girls* as similar to Perry's previous work, writing that the film "plays very much like a typical Perry soap opera, with the exception that every now and then his characters spout a poetic soliloquy."[28] Although it is an adaptation, Coyle sees links between the film and Perry's life and work: "Perry, himself an incredible rags-to-riches story, is intractably drawn to characters who survive hardship, often through faith."[29] But here Perry's inadequacies as a filmmaker are exposed: "he doesn't have the filmmaking talent for anything more than low-rent television."[30] Coyle also notes a number of failings of *Red Tails*. In his review, Coyle mentions the earlier HBO project *The Tuskegee Airmen* (Robert Markowitz, 1995), noting that *Red Tails* is a "pet project" of Lucas.[31] He also comments on the film's troubling nostalgia: "Instead of creating something authentic and new, *Red Tails* superimposes the tale of the black World War II pilots on a dated, white genre of 1940s patriotic propaganda."[32] The film is finally "blatantly old-fashioned, just with a change in color."[33]

Roger Ebert's remarks on both films indicate ambivalence about the ambitions of each. In his remarks on *For Colored Girls*, he writes, "Perry tries to be faithful to the play and also to his own boldly and simply told stories, and the two styles don't fit together."[34] He concludes that the play was not fully transformed into a film, and that Perry might not be capable of this endeavor: "[Perry] seems more at home with everyday, human-comedy types of people, and here I think he is, if anything, too wary of his material."[35] Like Coyle, Ebert mentions the HBO film in his review of *Red Tails* and notes that Spike Lee's *Miracle at St. Anna* (2008) more directly, if briefly, deals with the racism Black soldiers face. More importantly, Ebert gets to the heart of one of the film's most troubling aspects: "Lucas begs the question: Did this have to be an expensive movie? Was the purpose to make a blockbuster, or to make a statement?"[36] He even admits expecting too much: "I imagined a film that contained more history and drama—and that was angrier."[37] This admission suggests that Ebert has perhaps forgotten his experience of other Lucas films, and that he is susceptible to Lucas's marketing rhetoric.

Lou Lumenick's reactions to the two texts are very different. Lumenick does not think very highly of Perry's film or his directing ability, stating that *For Colored Girls* features "flat, TV-style direction and ... highly variable performances of an all-star cast."[38] He concludes by linking the film to Daniels's: "*Precious* worked partly because it did not wrap its sordid tale in Christian uplift and dime-store psychology—elements that have made Tyler Perry a rich filmmaker but have turned *For Colored Girls* shrill and manipulative."[39] His response to *Red Tails* is very different, however, and Lumenick offers one of the most spirited defenses of the film. He notes the film's ongoing tension between history and pastiche but regards this as a positive value, calling it "an inspiring, rousing tribute to the heroic, history-changing Tuskegee Airmen and World War II movies of the '40s."[40] Lumenick regards the film as "well-directed," mentioning Hemingway by name. The film in his estimation succeeds in leaving audiences "thirsting to read more about the Tuskegee Airmen."[41] He argues that many others will "dump on" the film simply because they are upset with Lucas "for desecrating their childhoods with the *Star Wars* prequels" instead of embracing this film which "Lucas personally poured $60 million into after trying to sell it to Hollywood studios for 20 years."[42] Lumenick seems persuaded by Lucas's marketing comments and so does not ask why Lucas needed Hollywood at all, or why it should take $60 million to tell this particular story (especially since it was told for much less by the makers of the HBO production). Though complimenting Hemingway, he also does nothing to suggest that the film be read as the work of someone other than Lucas.

Claudia Puig offers largely negative remarks on each film, though her comments on *Red Tails* include praise for Hemingway. Like many reviewers, Puig favors Shange's play over Perry's film, writing that where Shange offers "poetry, drama and dance to explore black female identity," Perry can only deliver "strained soap opera."[43] And this extends to his aesthetics: "Perry repeatedly employs tight, soap-opera-style camera angles that are awkwardly edited and distracting blends of sharp and soft focus that serve only to take the viewer out of the movie."[44] Puig, like Lumenick, mentions director Hemingway and says the film "is paced at just the right pitch to maintain excitement without becoming frenetic."[45] The film succeeds as an action film but once "those dogfighting planes land, the story trips up by skimming the surface of history."[46] Unlike Lumenick, she feels the film falls short of Lucas's claims, and wishes the film was invested in "delving deeper beneath the surface of what these intrepid men faced from the military's then-entrenched racism."[47]

Finally, Peter Debruge compares each film unfavorably to other texts. He begins his comments on *For Colored Girls* by mentioning *Precious* and says that Perry's film "falls squarely in familiar territory, better acted and better lit, perhaps, but more inauthentically melodramatic than ever."[48] He qualifies his compliments of the aesthetics by stating that Perry fails to put the camera in the right place to capture performances and that his editing prowess is lacking. He concludes that Perry's ideology does not combine with Shange's, arguing that Perry has "impos[ed] diva worship where nuance is called for and a pleasure-punishing Christian worldview where a certain moral ambiguity might have been more appropriate."[49] In his review of *Red Tails*, and like Ebert and Coyle, Debruge mentions the HBO film, and states that it offers better "human-interest material." He even unfavorably compares *Red Tails* to the 1927 Best Picture winner *Wings*.[50] While that earlier film set "the gold standard," for aerial combat photography, *Red Tails*, "by contrast, feels as if it were shot against greenscreens and rendered on an elaborate videogame engine."[51] Debruge's comments point to how these works connect to film history and differing ideologies about what cinema should be doing.

Nostalgia for the Classical Era

Outside the major reviewers just mentioned, the reception of each film includes numerous complaints that *For Colored Girls* and *Red Tails* both offer simplistic filmmaking technique, and worse, old-fashioned ideas. These critiques have been made about the previous work of both Perry and Lucas as well. Within many of these critiques is the specter of classical Hollywood cinema. Tom Long writes that *Red Tails*, "is the equivalent of a 1940s World War II flying aces movie with black characters instead of white characters. At times, you expect John Wayne or William Bendix to make cameos."[52] Several critics, including Puig, label Perry's film a reduction of a complex play and one whose aesthetics are too much like television soap operas. More generally, Perry's oeuvre is defined by its cultural conservatism. Timothy Lyle argues that Perry "is not trying to subvert the gender apparatus at all; rather, he highlights conventional gender roles and maintains the conservative status quo."[53] Few of the critiques of *Red Tails*, *For Colored Girls*, or of the career of either filmmaker consider or even mention Black films made in the 1920s, '30s and '40s, and instead focus only on contemporary mainstream Hollywood. This decision signals the need to explore Black film history in more detail, and also suggests that Perry's work in particular should be discussed more directly in relation to classical Hollywood cinema.

Without defending the gender politics of Perry's films, the conservative content, traditional aesthetics, and production circumstances of his work might be productively interpreted as enacting a critique of earlier cinematic forms. Or, to be more specific, if *Red Tails* and *For Colored Girls* each feel somewhat "old," is that necessarily (only) a negative quality? Each film is, overtly or not, linked to classical Hollywood in reviews, and this linkage is almost always regarded as a fault. Yet each film might be regarded as necessitating a consideration of classical Hollywood cinema, in part, through the lens of nostalgia. Perry's nostalgia for old Hollywood is a transforming nostalgia. More than Lucas's work, Perry's output expresses a critical nostalgia for a cinematic America that has unfortunately never existed, and a Hollywood whose flaws are as important as its positive attributes. Perry's cinematic work—in part because much of it begins as theatre work—embraces the conservative aesthetics of classical Hollywood cinema while insisting that the ideology of classical Hollywood cannot be remembered fondly.

Though the debate about when and how the classical era of American film ended is ongoing, film historians have, for the most part, settled on the narrative of Lucas and Spielberg spearheading Hollywood's movement into the blockbuster and/or postmodern era. For Thomas Schatz, the "post-1975 era best warrants the term 'the New Hollywood,'" because of the move to narratively deficient and star-driven blockbusters that stabilized an economically unstable industry.[54] The New Hollywood includes changes in business practices and in the product being offered to the public. In his canonical essay on spectatorship, narrative, and history, Tom Gunning locates Lucas as offering a return of the repressed spectacle of early cinema when he mentions the "Spielberg-Lucas-Coppola cinema of effects."[55] For Kenneth Von Gunden, Lucas is a "postmodern auteur" worthy of a chapter alongside Coppola, Spielberg, Martin Scorsese, and Brian De Palma.[56] Though independent of Hollywood, the Lucas empire is emblematic of the rise of media conglomerates and the turn of Hollywood to fewer, more expensive, and more special effects-dependent releases. These films have, as many scholars argue, an ideal audience of the "global teen"—or 12–14-year-old boys, to be more precise.

For Fredric Jameson in the various versions of "Postmodernism and Consumer Society," *Star Wars* is also evidence of the cultural turn towards nostalgia and the inability of society to live within, and coherently process, the present. The success of *Star Wars* demonstrates not simply Lucas's love for "Flash Gordon" and "Buck Rogers" but the culture's desire to return to a simpler time. Just as much as Lucas is in the business of selling technology, he is also in the business of apparently avoiding the present. Whether diegetically looking back (*American Graffiti, Radioland Murders*, the *Indiana Jones* films, *Red Tails*) or ahead (*THX-1138, Star Wars*—despite its claims to be set "a long time ago"), his films work to avoid gazing at the present. More importantly, and regardless of diegetic temporality, Lucas's works express nostalgia for childhood and a world where good and evil are clearly marked and truly separate. The possible advance offered by *Red Tails* is that here he at least wants to tell stories about a past neglected by American cinema. Though he uses a major studio (Fox) for distribution, Lucas remains financially aloof from Hollywood and his practices are the logical outcome of the United Artists-based model of utilizing existing production power to dictate favorable distribution terms. Lucas's power allowed *Red Tails* to be made but could have resulted in the film's production years (if not decades) before 2012.

Like Lucas, Perry does not extend his business interests into film distribution, and for years he enjoyed a stable and mutually beneficial relationship with an established distribution organization. Though no longer part of an exclusive partnership with Lionsgate, both sides benefited enormously from the relationship.[57] Here, he follows the New Hollywood example of Lucas by using Hollywood's tools to distribute and exhibit his work. But more than Lucas's work, Perry's films are dismissed for their aesthetic and ideological similarity to (old) Hollywood products. For example, Seitz insightfully argues that Perry is attacked not simply because his films lack polish but "because he mixes moods and genres with the blithe confidence of an old Hollywood filmmaker, switching from dumb slapstick to three-hankie melodrama and back again within minutes."[58] Though aesthetics are central when taking account of Perry's films, where and how he creates these works is equally relevant. With respect to Rich Cohen's claim that NFL Films should be called the "last Hollywood studio," a stronger and more interesting case can be made for referring to Tyler Perry Studios by that label, provided one critiques just what "Hollywood" means.[59]

Perry resists the model of the "Spielberg-Lucas-Coppola cinema of effects," and its expensive handful of yearly releases, not simply by resisting the use of the latest special effects technology, but, just as importantly, by returning to the old Hollywood practice of creating a steady stream of moderately budgeted and reasonably profitable product. He also embraces the iconography of old Hollywood. His logo (and the Madea character) is a promise of quality and comfort not unlike MGM's roaring Lion. Atlanta's Tyler Perry Studios looks like his dream of a 1930s Hollywood studio and backlot.[60] Perry has created a real movie studio of the sort that barely exists anymore. Structurally it is also the sort of movie studio correctly associated with pre-World War II Hollywood. At Tyler Perry Studios, there are standing interior sets and exterior street sets with various, and barely convincing, storefronts. To view the facilities is less like a tour of Universal Studios and more like a nostalgic return to an era that seemed permanently gone. But in recreating this bygone era, Perry offers a radical transformation, and not simply in terms of the sort of films produced by the studio. According Roy S. Johnson, "Tyler Perry (TP) Studios is a vibrant place with more than 100 full-time employees who are Black, Hispanic, Indian, Cuban, White, you name it, making it unlike any studio you'd find in Hollywood."[61] Though working outside the Hollywood system, Perry's work recreates (on-screen and off-) the first fifty or so years of Hollywood with one central difference: the presence of Black bodies, Black faces, and Black voices in front of and behind the camera. To see and hear classical Hollywood aesthetics transformed into a cinema of Black faces and Black voices is a radical project, and one for which Perry has not been properly praised.[62] Both in terms of aesthetics and production practices, classical Hollywood cinema is not simply what it includes and who it represents. Classical Hollywood cinema is equally what it excludes and who it refuses to represent; classical Hollywood cinema is who is kept off the soundtrack and out of the frame. Intentionally or not, Perry's practices should remind film and media observers and scholars that classical Hollywood cinema hinges on the systematic exclusion of non-white humans, even more than the exclusion of demonstrations of Christian faith.[63]

The nostalgia for classical Hollywood that Perry expresses in interviews, his production facilities, and throughout his oeuvre is not naïve nostalgia. Though Jameson and others regard the nostalgia of post-1975 cinema as wholly negative sense, other scholars like Pam Cook note a radical potential. For Cook, nostalgia can be used to explore the past and shape a culture's future: "Rather than being seen as a reactionary, regressive condition imbued with sentimentality, [nostalgia] can be perceived as a way of coming to terms with the past, as enabling it to be exorcised in order that society, and individuals, can move on."[64] For sociologist Janelle L. Wilson, it is imperative to note that nostalgia consciously transforms the past: "the nostalgia we experience is often for a past that did not exist (at least not exactly the way our nostalgic vision would suggest)."[65] She continues: "The head knows that what is being fondly recalled *wasn't really* that way, but the heart finds comfort in the feeling."[66]

In the same book, Wilson discusses a research project where she interviewed adults about the 1950s, and while most respondents remember the era fondly, the results vary significantly according to race: "White informants were most nostalgic for the fun they had in the '50s (e.g., drag racing, drive-in movies, school activities), whereas African Americans were more apt to express nostalgia for the institution of the family, the close-knit communities, the role of the church, and segregated entertainment."[67] The African Americans surveyed by Wilson, for the most part, remember the era fondly, but as she notes, these respondents do not ignore the very real, and often government-sanctioned, racism they faced in the period. The list of seemingly lost institutions and ideas—family, church, community, entertainment—overlaps with a list of what Tyler Perry's work valorizes throughout his career on stage, film, and television. The last item here is worth noting in particular: a nostalgia for specifically Black entertainment.

Perry does not blithely desire a return to Old Hollywood; Perry twists Hollywood to meet his needs.[68] He also does not simply provide entertainment featuring and addressing Black Americans. Perry remembers Hollywood fondly, wishes that Hollywood was more like his memories than its historical reality. In these terms, Perry does the very thing for which Tom Long criticizes *Red Tails*: he takes an old form (and often its old ideas), populates it almost exclusively with Black actors, and employs non-whites to create the finished work. His films, plays, and television programs are populist, more comforting than not, directly address female audiences, and are committed to presenting an idealized vision of the world. This is a workable definition of classical Hollywood cinema both in terms of form and content. Perry's revision of classical Hollywood cinema, however, is one where Black Americans get to be in, and work to create, movies.

Conclusion

The news in 2012 that Disney purchased Lucasfilm for over $4 billion (which Lucas immediately donated to charity) was breathlessly followed by the announcement that there would be more official *Star Wars* films. The sale was equally surprising and overdetermined. *Star Wars* was created by Lucas and he owned the universe outright. His decision to direct episodes 1, 2, and 3 (1999–2005) marked his first official directorial efforts since the 1970s but also reasserted his authorial control of the franchise. His alterations of episodes 4, 5, and 6 are more clear demonstrations of ownership. Lucas changes, alters, amends, and meddles with these films to increase his wealth but also, perhaps, simply because he can. Though Lucas directed only *Episode 4: A New Hope* (1977), the various "special editions" of the first three films (released in 1997) are undeniably authored by Lucas, regardless of their director. After guarding and continually reworking and repackaging these items for decades, Lucas finally chose to walk away.[69] Yet, for his part in creating the "new" Hollywood, Lucas's independence from Hollywood was perhaps always only temporary.

Lucas and Disney join forces as arguably the most mercenary "media" giants of the past fifty years. Each company has partially built its empire on claims that one must buy a product (usually a film) right now or one's children will never know its supposed majesty. Disney's use of the "vault" to scare consumers into immediate purchase is shameful, and not simply for suggesting that its products are too precious to freely circulate. By purchasing Lucasfilm, Disney acquires lasers and spaceships to put on the shelf next to its Marvel superheroes. Media power changes hands but does not move. The story of Disney's rise from independent production company to massive conglomerate is not unlike that of the company it purchased. Certainly neither Disney nor Lucasfilm ever targeted or desired a portion of the marketplace but instead sought the entire public, or at least asked the public to be children. In their pursuit of the "average" American, both companies have ignored Black Americans. On the other hand, Perry's films assert a conservative normalcy, but address audiences and concerns that Lucas and Disney deny.

Finally, if critics and scholars want Perry's and/or Lucas's films to be "better," perhaps they (and we) should equally desire that the cultural environment in which these products circulate be "better." The purchase of Tyler Perry Studios might actually signal cultural progress. A few months prior to Disney's acquisition of Lucasfilm, Oprah Winfrey teamed up with—but did not buy—Tyler Perry Studios. Though Perry has in the past expressed a desire to create his own network, the collaboration with Winfrey benefits both moguls.[70] For Jameson and other media critics, the conglomeration of media is all but inevitable, and simply part of the flow of global capital. The proliferation of media products and channels is always joined by the consolidation of media power into fewer and fewer companies. We might actually hope for a world where Disney (or Warner Bros., or Sony) tries, and even fails, to bring Tyler Perry Studios into the fold. The end of Perry's truly independent media empire could be mourned, and perhaps should be if purchased like Lucasfilm. But such a move would indicate that the major media corporations regard texts with Black casts, that are concerned with the lives of contemporary African Americans, as mainstream; such a move would suggest that major media conglomerates think of Black texts as at least potentially profitable investments. That is a revision of "Hollywood" to be desired.

Notes

1. Lee's works like *Inside Man* (2006) or the Michael Jackson documentary *Bad 25* (2012) show him doing (personal) work for hire. His documentaries tied to HBO, such as *4 Little Girls* (1997) and *When the Levees Broke* (2006), allow him to put real stories on the (small) screen and he continues to make low-budget independent films like *Red Hook Summer* (2012), where he cannot resist mocking Perry. Much of his fiction cinema—independent

or not—operates in the registers of melodrama. Certainly the exchanges through the press between Perry and Lee allow one to compare their work though Lee continues to work very much within the established systems of media, especially film.

2. Wesley Morris, "The Year of Tyler Perry. Seriously," *Film Comment*, January–February 2011, 60.

3. Matt Zoller Seitz, "'For Colored Girls': Tyler Perry's Misunderstood Genius," *Salon.com*, http://www.dev8.salon.com/2010/11/04/defense_of_tyler_perry/.

4. Linking Perry to Fuller is perhaps a unique gesture on the part of Seitz and might be explained by noting that the often independent Fuller dealt in (largely male) melodrama throughout his career whether ostensibly making war films (*The Steel Helmet* [1951], *The Big Red One* [1980]), crime films (*The Crimson Kimono* [1959]), or something harder to define (*Shock Corridor* [1963]). A few of his films—most notably *The Naked Kiss* (1964) and *White Dog* (1982)—feature a female protagonist negotiating a world of violence and turmoil created by men.

5. In 1919, Chaplin banded together with other powerful white film figures to create United Artists, a company independent of the major studios but one that also showed the industry how to survive going forward (package talent and focus on distribution). UA did nothing to truly redistribute power in the film industry, and this was not the goal of its creators. Chaplin's power and ability to embark on the UA project was acquired in large part through his Tramp persona, one that can still be evoked instantly and quickly by filmmakers. As of this writing, the Tramp sits atop the Society for Cinema & Media Studies website alongside Apple icons, the *I Love Lucy* (1951–57) logo, Pac-Man (and ghost), and Audrey Hepburn from *Breakfast at Tiffany's* (Blake Edwards, 1961). Perry's Madea character has not yet attained such a level of media ubiquity.

6. For example, see David E. James, *The Most Typical Avant-Garde: History and Geography of Minor Cinemas in Los Angeles* (Berkeley: University of California Press, 2005), 209–213.

7. If Lucas "sells out," he does so here, rather than later with *Star Wars*. Lucas's legacy to the world is also *Happy Days* (Paramount, 1974–84) and not simply lasers in space. *Star Wars* simply builds on the model of *American Graffiti*, and sells nostalgia not for cars and a "pre-racial" America but instead for Westerns, war films, and *Flash Gordon* serials (1936–40).

8. Roy S. Johnson, "His Own Man," *Ebony*, August 2011, 82.

9. In an interview with Oprah Winfrey, Perry sounds very much like Kevin Smith when describing how he learned filmmaking on the job. For example:

PERRY: But here's the thing: Steven Spielberg got to start messing around with a camera as a kid, and Jason Reitman got his father to help. Me, it took nine films to be ready.
WINFREY: You just sort of taught yourself how to be a director. How did you do that?
PERRY: I learned in progress. My first time directing was *Madea's Family Reunion*, which I cannot watch.
WINFREY: Why not?
PERRY: Because I didn't know that the cameras should actually move! The camera is the eye of the audience. But it's all a part of learning, and I'm grateful for the journey, and I'm proud of the work—every bit of it.

Interview with Oprah Winfrey, *O, The Oprah Magazine*, December 1, 2010, http://www.oprah.com/entertainment/Oprah-Interviews-Tyler-Perry_1.

10. Stephanie Zacharek, "Meet the Browns," *Salon.com*, http://www.dev8.salon.com/2008/03/21/browns/.

11. Robert J. Patterson, "'Woman Though Art Bound': Critical Spectatorship, Black Masculine Gazes, and Gender Problems in Tyler Perry's Movies," *Black Camera, An International Film Journal* 3, no. 1 (2011): 15.

12. Courtney Young, "Tyler Perry's Gender Problem," *Nation*, http://www.thenation.com/article/tyler-perrys-gender-problem.

13. The same might also be said of the discourse on Lucas.

14. For one example, consider *The Star Wars Holiday Special* (Steve Binder, 1978), which is probably Lucas's most mocked and perversely revered endeavor.

15. Amy Wallace and Marla Matzer, "Lucas Cuts Deal With Fox for Next 'Star Wars,'" *Los Angeles Times*, April 3, 1998.

16. See http://boxofficemojo.com/people/chart/?view=Director&id=tylerperry.htm; http://boxofficemojo.com/people/chart/?id=georgelucas.htm.

17. Denene Millner, "The Unstoppable Tyler Perry," *Essence*, August 2007, 97.

18. Camille Paglia, "George Lucas's Force," *Chronicle Review*, October 19, 2012, B12.

19. Bryan Curtis, "George Lucas is Ready to Roll the Credits," *New York Times Magazine*, http://www.nytimes.com/2012/01/22/magazine/george-lucas-red-tails.html?_r=1&seid=auto&smid=tw-nytmag&pagewanted=all.

20. Ibid.

21. Morris, "The Year of Tyler Perry. Seriously." Perhaps the most interesting feature of the review is that Morris unwittingly contributes to Lucas's narrative of neglect and passive oppression. Though Morris claims that no studio representatives attended Lucas's screening, the *Times* piece reports that only one studio's executives failed to attend. Morris's version turns Lucas's tale of woe into one of almost unfathomable neglect.

22. Curtis, "George Lucas."

23. Ibid.

24. Ibid.

25. While this is not to suggest that these filmmakers could not create a blockbuster, neither has attempted a pure action film to this point. Lee Daniels's filmography is not nearly as extensive as Lee's and at least begins with *Shadowboxer* (2005), a film with action, suspense, and violence—though it is not a summer would-be blockbuster.

26. Michael Phillips, "Heroism Loses to Hollywood," *Chicago Tribune*, January 19, 2012, http://www.chicagotribune.com/entertainment/movies/sc-mov-0117-red-tails-20120119,0,1748740.column.

27. Miki Turner, "Tyler Perry: Show Business His Way," *Jet*, 34.

28. Jake Coyle, "Review: Tyler Perry's 'For Colored Girls,'" November 3, 2010, www.boston.com/ae/movies/articles/2010/11/03/review_tyler_perrys_for_colored_girls/.

29. Ibid.

30. Ibid.

31. Jake Coyle, "Review: The Laudable 'Red Tails' Misses its Target," January 18, 2012, www.boston.com/ae/movies/articles/2012/01/18/review_the_laudable_red_tails_misses_its_target/?rss_id=Boston.com+--+Movie+news.

32. Ibid.

33. Ibid.

34. Roger Ebert, "Review of *For Colored Girls*," Rogerebert.com, November 3, 2010, http://rogerebert.suntimes.com/apps/pbcs.dll/article?AID=/20101103/REVIEWS/101109992.

35. Ibid.

36. Roger Ebert, "Review of *Red Tails*," Rogerebert.com, January 18, 2012, http://www.rogerebert.com/apps/pbcs.dll/article?AID=/20120118/REVIEWS/120119986/-1/RSS.

37. Ibid.

38. Lou Lumenick, "'Colored Girls' Blind to Subtlety," *New York Post*, November 4, 2010, http://www.nypost.com/p/entertainment/movies/colored_girls_blind_to_subtlety_VT4aDZX9c2zLg7d8WQH5sI.

39. Ibid.

40. Lou Lumenick, "'Tail' Blazers," *New York Post*, January 19, 2012, http://www.nypost.com/p/entertainment/movies/tail_blazers_uwLwlfaNBXW3CIMAxJmHzO?CMP=OTC-rss&FEEDNAME=.

41. Ibid.

42. Ibid.

43. Claudia Puig, "Tyler Perry Turns Poetic 'For Colored Girls' Into a Soap Opera," *USA Today*, November 6, 2010, http://usatoday30.usatoday.com/life/movies/reviews/2010-11-05-Forcoloredgirls05_ST_N.htm.

44. Ibid.

45. Claudia Puig, "'Red Tails' Only Soars in the Air," *USA Today*, January 19, 2012, http://usatoday30.usatoday.com/life/movies/reviews/story/2012-01-19/red-tails-review/52684758/1.

46. Ibid.

47. Ibid.

48. Peter Debruge, "Review: *For Colored Girls*," *Variety*, October 22, 2010, http://www.variety.com/review/VE1117943896/.

49. Ibid.

50. Peter Debruge, "Review: *Red Tails*," *Variety*, January 18, 2012, http://www.variety.com/review/VE1117946848?refcatid=31.

51. Ibid.

52. Tom Long, "'Red Tails' Biopic Doesn't Reach Heights of WWII Unit," *Detroit News*, January 20, 2012, http://www.detroitnews.com/article/20120120/ENT02/201200318/1034/Review-Red-Tails-biopic-doesn-t-reach-heights-WWII-unit.

53. Timothy Lyle, "'Check with Yo' Man First; Check with Yo' Man': Tyler Perry Appropriates Drag as a Tool to Re-Circulate Patriarchal Ideology," *Callaloo* 34, no. 3 (2011): 948.

54. Thomas Schatz, "The New Hollywood," in *Film Theory Goes to the Movies*, eds. Jim Collins, Hilary Radner, and Ava Preacher Collins (New York: Routledge, 1993), 9.

55. Tom Gunning, "The Cinema of Attractions: Early Film, Its Spectators and the Avant-Garde," in *Critical Visions in Film Theory: Classic and Contemporary Readings*, eds. Timothy Corrigan, Patricia White, and Meta Mazaj (New York: Bedford/St. Martin's, 2011), 75.

56. Kenneth Von Gunden, *Postmodern Auteurs: Coppola, Lucas, De Palma, Spielberg and Scorsese* (Jefferson, NC: McFarland, 1991).

57. Borys Kit, "Tyler Perry, Lionsgate End Long-Term Relationship (Exclusive)," February 28, 2014, http://www.hollywoodreporter.com/news/tyler-perry-shutting-down-la-684483.

58. Seitz, "For Colored Girls."

59. Rich Cohen, "They Taught America How to Watch Football," *Atlantic Monthly*, October 2012, http://www.theatlantic.com/magazine/archive/2012/10/they-taught-america-to-watch-football/309083/?single_page=true.

60. The presentation of the studio on Perry's website endorses such a reading. See http://www.tylerperry.com/studio/; http://www.tylerperry.com/studio/#modal_tps-gallery.

61. Roy S. Johnson, "His Own Man," *Ebony*, August 2011, 83.

62. Lenore Skenazy, however, does: "What's mind-blowing about these hit-you-over-the-head movies is how fun and fresh they are, thanks to Perry's presence, yes, but also his casting. It's just amazing to walk through the looking glass into a movie where almost everyone, including the extras, is African-American." "Tyler Perry's 'Madea' Offers Lessons for Media, Marketers," *Advertising Age*, http://adage.com/article/lenore-skenazy/tyler-perry-s-madea-offers-lessons-media-marketers/135054/.

63. Lucas's *Star Wars* films may tap into cultural myths along the lines described by Joseph Campbell. They also offer the new normal for Hollywood's treatment of religion and spirituality: an incoherent mixture of "Eastern" and "Western" mysticism, faith in the unprovable, destiny or pre-destination, the power of biology, the necessity of a journey, and life after death (even if it only means that you glow with a blue light). While classical Hollywood cinema is nearly always vaguely Christian, at least since the mid-1960s Christian films are a niche market and overtly Christian films are usually independently produced and distributed. Perry's appeal to Christian audiences is in some ways not unlike that of the *Left Behind* (2000–2005) films, *Fireproof* (Alex Kendrick, 2008), or other low-budget productions produced specifically for a market that regards itself as neglected by mainstream media. Here, Perry offers a return, or the approximation of a return, to a world where Christianity is the default ideology of the populace.

64. Pam Cook, *Screening the Past: Memory and Nostalgia in Cinema* (New York: Routledge, 2005), 4.

65. Janelle L. Wilson, *Nostalgia: Sanctuary of Meaning* (Lewisburg: Bucknell University Press, 2005), 23.

66. Ibid.

67. Ibid, 73.

68. Perry named the division of his enterprise that handles films he does not write "34th Street Films" after the Christmas film *Miracle on 34th Street* (George Seaton, 1947). This naming is more evidence of his love for old Hollywood and its idealized America. But to his credit, Perry wants more. He wants a world where *Miracle on 34th Street* could have been made a few years earlier and featured Cicely Tyson (b. 1933) instead of Natalie Wood (b. 1938). In the last word, Perry's films are something like Hollywood fan fiction. He loves Hollywood but wants the films to be different, to be more like his experiences, and for the people on screen to look and sound more like himself. Note that with the end of his Lionsgate partnership in February 2014, Perry also closed the Los Angeles office of 34th Street Films.

69. And yet the *Star Wars* product has always been the result of significant collaboration. From Ralph McQuarry's sketches, to the sound design of Ben Burtt, and to the voice work of James Earl Jones, the *Star Wars* universe—long before it became officially "expanded"—was always a kingdom of many members with Lucas as the undisputed ruler and king. To sell *Star Wars* and legally part with Lucasfilm is a final act of control, and a gesture that ultimately claims authorship and demonstrates ownership. Lucas, in a sense, "owned" the work of McQuarry, John Williams, James Earl Jones, Alan Dean Foster, Timothy Zahn, and many others, but sells the results of their labor to Disney. He cedes control with a gesture that underlines exactly how much control he has wielded over all things *Star Wars*. *Star Wars* is/was Lucas's.

70. For example, see Roy S. Johnson, "His Own Man," *Ebony*, August 2011, 80–85; and also Sonia Murray, "The Talented Mr. Perry," *Essence*, February 2009, 112–17.

CHAPTER ELEVEN

To Brand and Rebrand: Questioning the Futurity of Tyler Perry

—Leah Aldridge

As scholars, fans, and critics, many of us were introduced to the polyhyphenate performer-writer-director-producer through his feature film debut, *Diary of a Mad Black Woman* (Darren Grant, 2005). The backstory to Perry's brand and self-branding is as dramatic as any of his movies, including *Diary*. His is a tale that includes a rags-to-riches story of a Black southerner whose formative years were laced with poverty, child abuse and molestation, attempted suicide, and homelessness. These setbacks, trials, and storms, according to the Perry folklore, were all overcome by his strong sense of purpose, determination, personal accountability, and Christian faith. It is against this backdrop of triumph that Perry's media successes loom especially large: feature films, numerous syndicated television shows, stage plays, books, DVDs, film studio mogul, and a partnership with Oprah Winfrey and the OWN cable channel. Perry has made it very clear that these aspects of his personal story and star persona are very much related to his "brand" of entertainment and to the ways his media properties function as brand. For example, in an interview with *Men's Health Magazine,* Perry explains:

> When I started doing plays, there were a million shows out and a lot were really bad. I had to have something to set mine apart. So I would make sure my name was on the tickets and the marquee. I wanted people who had never heard of me to become familiar with this name. When I went into film, I wanted to do the same thing. It's not that I'm narcissistic—I'm very aware of brand building. When you see that name, it gives you a good feeling, like Coke or Disney or Oprah/Harpo.[1]

As these comments indicate, Perry's focus is on his name recognition and the creation of a self-titled brand has been intentional. He further illustrates the usefulness of his name-in-the-title branding strategy in a section of the same article called: "A Man's Guide to Becoming a Brand." In this section, Perry carefully details how he used the Madea character as "bait on the hook" to lure audiences in to films which do not feature her prominently within the diegesis in hopes that the audience will appreciate the rest of what the films have to offer. Relatedly, an overt part of Perry's brand identity has been to foster a "one-on-one great relationship" with his core audience: fans commiserate with him regarding his mother's death, feel free to ask him for money and jobs, and castigate him for having a child out of wedlock.

With his unprecedented successes, unique backstory, and self-conscious branding in mind, we might all wonder: What's next? What are some of the future potentialities and possibilities of Perry's media and branding machine? In this neoliberal moment, what is the market logic of Perry's celebrity and how does race as commodity complicate that logic? Further, what might Perry have to do to find success on the international film stage?

As a celebrity, Perry's name represents a brand of media and media practices. The American Marketing Association (AMA) defines a brand as a "name, term, sign, symbol or design, or a combination of them intended to identify the goods and services of one seller or group of sellers and to differentiate them from those of other sellers."[2] Brands promise to provide a particular quality of product. Using a combination of shorthand and semiotics, brands communicate to consumers how they can distinguish between products that are materially the same. Taste, values, economics, politics, and other variables are actively addressed and referenced within a brand, and this is then marketed to a core demographic in ways that include but can also signal beyond or grow past that core group. Typically, celebrities who become established by performing their primary talent extend themselves by aligning their image, and what that image is perceived to stand for, with products ancillary to their primary talent. Traditionally, there has been a clear line of demarcation between celebrity-as-spokesperson and the pitched product. Tiger Woods offered one such example with his relationship with Tag Heuer, Gillette, and Gatorade, until his infidelity scandal "sullied" the quality of his image and self-brand, thus endeding the alignment of those products with his persona. Other celebrities such as Britney Spears, Beyoncé Knowles, Jennifer Lopez, Sean Combs, and Carlos Santana, trading in similar ways on their identity, have moved beyond mere spokesperson status by creating consumer products such as perfumes, clothing, alcoholic beverages, and women's shoes. In this way, the brand extends the star persona beyond corporeality. Similarly, Perry's name signifies a specific kind of product that is marketed to audiences, particularly Black women.

Related to the branding of celebrity is the fact that race also functions as a commodity. In her investigation into brand culture and its relationship to neoliberal capitalism, Sarah Banet-Weiser explains that changes in constitutive elements between consumers, capitalism, branding, and citizenship "make sense" given neoliberalism's economic imperative to commodify, but not without compelling us first to ask whether "racial or gender identity [is] a commodity"?[3] Given the hegemonic centrality of whiteness, "selling" blackness turns race into a commodity. bell hooks describes this process in globalized culture as the "commodification of difference" where "whatever difference the Other inhabits is eradicated, via exchange, by a consumer cannibalism that not only displaces the Other but denies the significance of that Other's history through a process of decontextualization."[4] Banet-Wiser and hooks variously discuss the relationship between "context" (a set of social and/or historical conditions) and its relationship to "identity." This process informs discussions of cultural currency and the high premium consumers place upon "authenticity" and "realness." Anne Friedberg's work is a helpful heuristic here for understanding how "identification [is] made through recognition, and all recognition is itself an implicit confirmation of the ideology of the status quo" or as that which can be identified as material or verifiable within an established landscape.[5] Thus, in today's media culture, Tyler Perry functions at the center of a brand by using himself as a point of familiarity whereby audiences identify with him and the worlds which he creates on screen and stage.

In the contemporary neoliberal moment, where the preferred path to self-determination is "bootstrap empowerment," Perry's brand of self-help is importantly individualized and lacks an engagement with social and cultural institutions of oppression. As such, Perry's niche products of melodrama and extreme hijinks comedy have sidestepped what Isaac Julian and Kobena Mercer identify as "representational democracy, [which] like the classic realist text, is premised on an implicitly mimetic theory of representation as correspondence with the 'real'" that circumvents the trappings and "burden of racial representation."[6] This means that by not representing the "burden" of racial history, Perry's characters can pose no threat to whiteness as their neo-Black uplift messages are ultimately aimed at getting Black folks to fall in line; his works animate an aspect of religiosity that has historically been used to curb resistance. Once bell hooks's perception of the "other" is deracinated, then, the brand of blackness which Perry's corporeality symbolizes, is recontextualized to exemplify a pseudo-version of what Raymond Williams called "structures of feeling," a context which collectivizes a particular contemporary Black experience and delivers an illusion of empowerment and catharsis which assuages rather than alters dysfunction and masks structures of dominance.[7] In line with neoliberalism's market logic and Hollywood's dismissive attitude toward Black representation, Perry has recontextualized—branded and rebranded—his own Black body into a commodified image of blackness that is less characterized by misery, lack, oppression, or resistance (pre-Blaxploitation-era associations with blackness) and more associated with full affect.

What might all of this indicate about Perry's ability to market his brand abroad in the future? The terms and tenets of capitalism would dictate that the entrepreneurial and enterprising Perry will only find new ways to cater to his market. A capitalist logic would also support the idea that Perry will seek additional markets to whom he can sell his existing cultural products, and for whom he can develop new ones. As discussed throughout this collection, Perry's current core consumer constituency is typically understood to be Christian, African American, middle-aged women, a demographic that is diffused somewhere across mainstream Hollywood's four-quadrant schema (if targeted at all). As such, Perry's cultural production is considered to be too niche for a larger US market saturation, much less international consumption. Any aspirations for capturing an international market share are further compounded by the persistent industry lore that most Black films/actors do not generate big box-office dollars globally. This notion is frequently treated uncritically by Hollywood and international buyers, despite the fact that the careers of Josephine Baker, Paul Robeson, and Will Smith are evidence that there have certainly been Black American international film stars.

Yet what are Perry's chances for transforming the saturation of his core demographic into broader market saturation? As a self-made "every(wo)man," Perry's conflation of his persona with his brand becomes problematic when gesturing toward international markets. Will his fan engagement translate to talk-show circuits in Germany and Japan? Will his do-it-yourself to achieve upward mobility play in Australia and Brazil? Will his Madea as "bait-and-switch" strategy for morality tales work in the Netherlands and Hong Kong? Without the benefit of conducting longitudinal audience reception research, the educated guess is a qualified "maybe."

As it relates to the wider US market and territories and regions beyond the US, Perry will have to attend to the demands of local buyers and distributors who, in addition to recognizable star power, prize "universal" themes, and "cultural proximity," which according to Timothy Havens in his discussion of international circulation of the Black televisual, is "the primary programming consideration" for non-television-producing territories who import from abroad.[8] As an illustration of this theory, continental distributors Ster Kinekor, Nu Metro, and Gulf carry Perry's products more than other independent distributors, with his films receiving theatrical releases in East and South Africa, and the UAE respectively, earning him negligible yet consistent revenue. Other frequent territories that carry Perry's media products consistently include Russia, Kuwait, Serbia, and Poland, all of which are fairly consistent buyers but again generate limited returns. To this point, DVD premieres allow for a wider distribution across various territories while reducing the financial risk for buyers who are unfamiliar with Perry's brand (persona and themes). International bias against Black cultural production will continue to be a hurdle for Perry to overcome without the benefit of having had a pre-film career to precede him abroad (as was the case for Eddie Murphy, Jamie Foxx, Martin Lawrence, Denzel Washington, and most notably Will Smith). Interestingly, Perry's "crossover" films that starred white performers who have some international name recognition garnered some of Perry's highest international box-office returns: *Alex Cross* (Rob Cohen, 2012), $8,700,00 million with the widest release; *Temptation: Confessions of a Marriage Counselor* (Tyler

Perry, 2013), $1,150,000; and *Madea's Witness Protection* (Tyler Perry, 2012), $1,246,000.

The good news for Perry is that his films are working a slow burn in terms of international audience's growing familiarity with his brand.[9] However, Tyler Perry Productions would have to make some significant changes to the brand if expanding the US and international markets is a true future goal. In addition to improving the overall quality of his production values, Perry will need to consider market saturation, genre filmmaking, and the limits of his skills. That is, a lack of product diversification (genres, talents, etc.) suggests limits to his creative abilities—which is OK; it just means improving the quality of what he is able to successfully produce. As the range of objects of study in this collection evince, Perry is voluminous in his output, releasing at least two properties (feature films, television shows, DVDs, plays, and books) with his name blazoned in the title every year since 2006. Given Perry's precarious relationship between his façade and his edifice, audiences have begun to limit their theatrical viewing, as evinced by his declining box-office dollars. Further, flooding a market with too much of the same "inexpensively" produced products tends to drive that product's value down. Instead of churning out more of the same across all platforms, he might consider product diversification across multiple sectors of market segmentation.

Having parted ways in 2014 with his longtime distribution/production partner Lionsgate means that Perry will have to work harder at speaking the language of individual buyers across the globe, or he will have to better network with the Hollywood machinery which influences everything from block bookings to day-and-date releases to satellite outlets in outposts around the globe. His ability to build relationships with international buyers will continue to grow as long as he can deliver the types of films buyers (who are the cultural gatekeepers to their consuming audiences) feel they can turn a profit on. This may mean making the types of genre films that travel more successfully across segments of other markets as well as abroad. Alternately, it may mean making union films and casting union actors with international name recognition, or paying more attention to the global end-around: striking co-production and co-financing deals with local producers in other regions. All of this only works in the future if Perry is not invested in having his name yoked with each title, given the fact that his presence and his name does not carry the same level of recognition or connotations that it does in the US.

Finally, since it is unlikely that Perry can play Madea indefinitely and cater to the same niche market until he "retires," will we soon see a Perry reboot, rebrand, or new set of self-inventions? Any rebranding initiative or savvy marketing reconstructions would likely begin with a valuation of Perry's current brand, and perhaps a "major identifiable change in positioning and aesthetics that fundamentally redefines the company."[10] To this, I would add that Perry as an entrepreneur will also have to be self-conscious about how his trend toward moralizing, uplift, and shepherding of neoliberal ideology can be reconfigured around transnational approaches to filmmaking that allow for global audiences to find pleasure in cross-cultural identification.[11] This may mean a return to representing Black American culture as set of values, modes of expression, historical underpinnings that can also withstand universalization.

As this collection has theorized and problematized Tyler Perry from a variety of critical perspectives, I have tried to encourage us to think of Tyler Perry's image as central to discussions about celebrity, branding, blackness, consumption, marketing, and (international) distribution. I remain curious about how Perry's success rests with his ability to decontextualize historical paradigms of blackness in order to recontextualize it as a brand full of affect so that it can ultimately be better commoditized. Blackness and representation functioning as such will continue to alter and inform how we remember and document our shared cultural histories.

Notes

This chapter incorporates content from a previously published essay: Leah Aldridge, "Mythology and Affect: The Brands of Cinematic Blackness of Will Smith and Tyler Perry," *Spectator: The University of Southern California Journal of Film and Television* 31, no. 1 (Spring 2011): 41–47.

1. Gerri Hishey, "Tyler Perry's Brand New Day," *Men's Health, Best Life Magazine*, April 2008, 131.
2. "What is Branding and How Important is it to Your Marketing Strategy," About.com, http://marketing.about.com/cs/brandmktg/a/whatisbranding.htm.

3. Sara Banet-Wiser, *AuthenticTM: The Politics of Ambivalence in Brand Culture* (New York: NYU Press, 2012), 20.

4. bell hooks, "The Oppositional Gaze," in *Black Looks: Race and Representation* (New York: Routledge, 1992), 118.

5. Anne Friedberg, "A Denial of Difference: Theories of Cinematic Identification," in *Psychoanalysis and Cinema*, ed. E. Ann Kaplan (New York: Routledge, 1990), 42.

6. Isaac Julien and Kabena Mercer, "De Center and De Margin," in *Stuart Hall: Critical Dialogues in Cultural Studies*, eds. Kuan-Hsing Chen and David Morley (New York: Routledge Press, 2007), 452, 454.

7. Raymond Williams, "Structures of Feeling," in *Marxism and Literature* (New York: Oxford University Press, 1977), 128–35.

8. Timothy Havens, *Black Television Travels* (New York: New York University Press, 2013), 153.

9. See Havens, *Black Television Travels*, for the international syndication path and strategy deployed by Viacom for *The Cosby Show*.

10. Laurent Muzellec and Mary Lambkin, "Corporate rebranding: destroying, transferring or creating brand equity?" *European Journal of Marketing* 40, no. 7/8 (2006).

11. Russell Meeuf and Raphael, "Introduction," in *Transnational Stardom: International Celebrity in Film and Popular Culture*, eds. Russell Meeuf and Raphael (Palgrave Macmillan, 2013), 4.

EPILOGUE

Playing with the Changes

—Miriam J. Petty

My first major programming gambit as a junior faculty member in Northwestern University's department of Radio/Television/Film was the organization of a daylong symposium on the media of Tyler Perry. The symposium took place in November of 2012 and drew a standing room audience to the auditorium of Northwestern's Block Museum. I knew I wanted to organize this symposium as part of the undergraduate course I was teaching that same quarter on Perry and his films, plays, and television shows. And though this would be a serious and extended scholarly engagement with a body of media that had so often been dismissed as either too lowbrow or simply too problematic to warrant such attention, I also knew that aspects of the symposium had to sync with a certain humorous energy and sensibility of Perry's work.

It has always been clear to me that Perry delights in play, spoofing, and parody as a means of engaging with popular culture. His creation of Madea—an amalgam of heroic African American mothers, aunts, and grandmothers from his own life—is one instance of this; his works' endless side references to popular culture (hip hop, films with a Black cult following, R&B hits) or culturally specific Black allusions to Christian church practices is one more; his obsession with bootlegging as both humorous and larcenous is yet another.[1]

Perry's own acts of "bootlegging" in the multiple parodic posters that he created for his 2011 film *Madea's Big Happy Family* provide effective examples of his proclivity for positing Madea as a playful, destabilizing, and disruptive figure. For example, as TreaAndrea Russworm mentions in this book's introduction, Perry created posters to advertise the film, using layouts that spoofed 1970s television sitcom *The Brady Bunch* (ABC, 1969–74), as well as three 2010 films nominated for Oscars in that year's Best Picture category. These parodic posters were the perfect bootleg gag that suggested that Perry hoped to entice (or confuse) potential audiences who might go and see these other, more prestigious films into coming to see *Madea's Big Happy Family* instead.

In this regard, one poster, modeled on the historical drama *The King's Speech* (Tom Hooper, 2010), uses the same orange background and semi-silhouetted images as the original, but replaces Colin Firth's cropped, close-up profile with Madea, mimicking Firth's pose of leaning in close to an old-fashioned microphone. Just beneath her chin is the caption "Do you understand the words that are coming out of my mouth?"—itself a lift of comedian Chris Tucker's memorable line from the 1998 movie *Rush Hour* (Brett Ratner). And beneath this caption is the title *The Queen's Speech: Madea's Big Happy Family* (complete with a crown over the "Q" in "Queen"). In the poster spoofing Darren Aronofsky's psychological thriller *Black Swan* (2010), Madea appears in full whiteface makeup and soft grey wig, a vacant expression on her face. Her light blue glasses complement the dramatic "swan" makeup around her reddened eyes, and her head is topped with a blue-white diamond tiara. Beneath the image is the somewhat enigmatic caption: "Madea is The Real *Black Swan*." Perhaps the most fitting of these three playful posters is the one modeled on Ethan and Joel Coen's remake of the classic Western *True Grit* (2010). Drawing upon this film's own appropriation of the old-fashioned "Wanted" handbill as its prototype (and also playing on the fact that *Grit* principals Jeff Bridges, Josh Brolin, Matt Damon, and Hailee Steinfeld each appeared in individualized versions of the original poster), Madea is posed in full body profile in front of the same weathered wooden backdrop, wearing a flowered dress and earrings, a rifle clenched in her left hand, her lips coolly pursed. The same dramatic "Old West"-style font is used as the original poster, but the *True Grit* tagline "PUNISHMENT Comes One Way or Another" has been replaced by the legend "BREAKFAST Comes One Way or Another." Appropriately, the film's title has been changed to *True Grits*. Given Perry's visual play with Madea in a series of comic mugshots over the years, the *True Grit* wanted poster is nearly predictable, fully consistent with Madea's brand of vigilante justice.[2]

Perry's construction of Madea as iconic has certainly facilitated his commodification of the character. I am reminded of his insertion of

Madea into a version of Andy Warhol's Marilyn Monroe Diptych for one poster from *Madea's Family Reunion* (Tyler Perry, 2006). It is not difficult to see Tyler Perry the megalomaniac in this, especially since *Family Reunion* was only his second film. But there is also something of this and other deployments of Madea that is sheer play, punning, delight in excess, clowning, riffing.

It was this broader and complex sense of play that I hoped to engage by titling the 2012 symposium "Madea's Big Scholarly Roundtable," and by using an image of Madea that conjured up some of the same kinds of visual play to which Perry himself subjects the character ad nauseam. The image that sprang to mind for a scholarly symposium was from the original advertising for Perry's 2003 play *Madea's Class Reunion*, in which a slightly sepia-toned Madea sports a graduate's cap and gown, vintage cat-eye glasses with rhinestones at the corners, and large button earrings. With the help of the Block Museum's communications manager, this image was superimposed over a photograph of the spires of Northwestern's University Hall, under the title "Madea's Big Scholarly Roundtable," for an effect that was nearly as Monty Python-esque as it was Tyler Perry-inspired.

The event poster now sits in my office, where the "scholar's"—that is, Madea's—hint of a smile never fails to remind me of the character's affective power in the midst of the rest of Perry's work that is also so blatantly, even toxically, sexist, class-baiting, homophobic, and heterosexist. As a character who is a kind of walking catharsis for herself, for Perry himself, and apparently, for the millions of African American women who support Perry's plays and films over and over, Madea sometimes musters play and humor as a way of creating narrative closure or offering facile solutions to real, complex problems. Play can often be an easy out and an oversimplification, and during these times I think Tyler Perry's images function at their clichéd worst.

Less frequent but nonetheless powerful are moments when the work around Madea simultaneously and self-consciously demonstrates that play is limited but is also potentially restorative. This includes the times when play becomes a vehicle, even briefly, for the very politics and possibilities that Perry otherwise explicitly forecloses.

To wit: the scene in *Diary of a Mad Black Woman* (Darren Grant, 2005) that Rachel Daniel discusses in this collection, when Madea and

Helen (Kimberly Elise) destroy a walk-in closetful of clothes belonging to the newly installed other woman, pays obvious homage to Angela Bassett's legendary performance as the furious, wronged wife Bernadine in Forrest Whittaker's film adaptation of *Waiting To Exhale* (1995). At Perry's discretion, however, the scene quickly descends into farce. "Rip it!!!" Madea growls, grabbing a gown, and Helen, tentatively warming to this spirit of revenge echoes, "Rip it!" then asks, "But Madea, what's this going to solve?" "Nothing!" responds Madea cheerily, "It's just gonna make you feel better." As the two women toss and tear clothes at full tilt, Madea references queer cult classic *Mommie Dearest* (Frank Perry, 1981) when she dramatically discovers "a wire hanger!!" in the overstuffed closet. The moment also recalls the two of Perry's playful bootleg *Madea's Big Happy Family* posters that position Madea, and Perry by extension, as a "queen" of some sort (of England? of *Swan Lake*?).

I think about Madea as a figure that allows Perry the freedom to cross otherwise uncrossable lines and boundaries, and to play generically, iconographically, intertextually, cross-culturally, visually, intergenerationally, and performatively. Playing in this multitude of ways allows him to bring Madea forth in all of her taboo, ideologically vexed, contradictory glory. Ultimately, the one act enables the other; their interconnectedness is at the core of Perry's significance as contemporary cultural phenomenon.

As I write this, and work on other, related projects, I continue to ponder, what does it mean to both play with and critique Madea, and also, invariably, to send her to "school"?

Notes

1. Bryant Keith Alexander presents an extended discussion of Perry, Madea, and bootlegging in his chapter on Madea in his book *The Performative Sustainability of Race: Critical Reflections on Black Culture and the Politics of Identity* (New York: Peter Lang, 2012).

2. And, of course, the poster is a cultural reference within a reference; the "grits as punishment" meme is one that Perry uses frequently, in an allusion to the sordid past of R&B great Al Green.

Contributors

Leah Aldridge is a PhD student in the University of Southern California, School of Cinematic Arts, Division of Critical Studies. Her research interests include representations and circulation of Black images; diaspora and globalization; independent, documentary, and experimental production; and how race in America impacts television syndication practices. Aldridge has a BA in English Literature/Creative Writing from USC and an MFA in Screenwriting from the University of California, Los Angeles.

Karen M. Bowdre received an MS from the Communication Department at Cornell University and a PhD in Critical Studies from the University of Southern California, School of Cinema-Television. She is an independent scholar who has published on African American media, theatre, and romantic comedies in *Black Camera: An International Film Journal*, the *Journal of American Drama and Theatre*, *Falling in Love Again: The Contemporary Romantic Comedy*, *The Politics and Poetics of Black Film: Nothing But a Man*, and *Cinema Journal*. Her research interests include race and representation, gender, early African American theatre history, adaptation, romantic comedies, telefantasy, and telenovelas. Her book *Shades of Love: African Americans and the Hollywood Romantic Comedy* is forthcoming from the University of Illinois Press.

Aymar Jean "AJ" Christian is an Assistant Professor of Communication at Northwestern University. His book-length manuscript, *Open TV*, will be the first full study on the rise of Web television, incorporating years of documenting and participating in this emerging art form and market. His work on television and new media has been published in the journals *Continuum*, *Transformative Works & Cultures* and the *Journal of Communication Inquiry*, and, in the popular press, in the *Wall Street Journal*, *Indiewire*, and *Slate*, among others. He has produced several video projects, including a Web series, *She's Out Of Order*, nominated for outstanding lead and guest actress at LA Web Fest 2015. He has curated film, television, and video for the Philadelphia Museum of Art and the Tribeca Film Festival, among others. He is a voting member of the Peabody Awards, the International Academy of Web Television, and the Streamy Awards Blue Ribbon Panel.

Keith Corson received his PhD in Cinema Studies from New York University and has taught courses in film studies at Rhodes College, Memphis College of Art, and NYU. His research focuses on film history, African American cinema, media industries, popular music, and the culture of sports. He has contributed book chapters and journal articles on topics including Malcolm X, Sidney Poitier, Ice-T, Bollywood, and sports documentaries. His book, *Trying to Get Over: African American Directors After Blaxploitation, 1977–1986*, is forthcoming from the University of Texas Press.

Rachel Jessica Daniel recently received her PhD in English with a concentration in American Studies, and a Graduate Certificate in Advanced Feminist Studies from the University of Massachusetts, Amherst. Her manuscript, *Resurrection*, investigates political narratives embedded in various forms of contemporary Black evangelical popular culture.

Artel Great is an accomplished filmmaker, social practice artist, and winner of a Film Independent Spirit Award nomination. He is the first Black valedictorian at UCLA film school where he graduated *summa cum laude*. Great earned his MA at UCLA, and he is a PhD candidate at New York University. His research explores the intersection of social justice and modern technologies alongside the cultural politics and intellectual history of African and Black-American film, television, and digital media. Great is a Cinema Research Institute Fellow, and he is the founder of the *Project Catalyst* movie and music app, the first-ever multicultural transmedia entertainment application. His films have been featured in major multiplexes, art-house theatres, film festivals, and museums nationally and internationally, as well as on Netflix, cable, and broadcast television. His *Project Catalyst* app currently serves audiences and filmmakers in more than thirty-five countries around the world.

Brandeise Monk-Payton is a PhD Candidate in Modern Culture and Media at Brown University. She received an MA in Media, Culture, and

Communication from New York University and a BA in Film and Media Studies from Swarthmore College. Her research centers on race and representation in screen media, especially as it relates to theories of performance. She has published journal articles in *Reconstruction: Studies in Contemporary Culture* and *The Black Scholar*. Her dissertation, "Blackness, Celebrity, and the Dark Side of Publicity in Media Culture," analyzes the aesthetics and politics of Black subject formation by examining racialized public relations in an expanded field in the post-civil rights era. Looking across television, film, and digital media, it explores the myriad ways in which blackness alters dominant forms of visibility and visuality, and can thus be mobilized to provide fresh insight into publicity in screen media culture.

Miriam Petty is an Assistant Professor in the Department of Radio/Television/Film and African American Studies at Northwestern University. She writes and teaches about stardom, reception, genre, race, and media, and is especially interested in the history of African American representation in Hollywood film. Her book, *Stealing the Show: African American Performers and Audiences in 1930s Hollywood* (University of California Press, 2016) explores the complex relationships between Black audiences and Black performers in the first decade of Hollywood's "golden age." Petty is currently at work on a book manuscript examining media mogul Tyler Perry's productions and their connections to such African American cultural forms as folktales, literature, and religious practice. An academic with a longstanding commitment to public scholarship, Petty is also an avid producer of public programs; her recent projects include the 2012 symposium *Madea's Big Scholarly Roundtable: Perspectives on the Media of Tyler Perry* at Northwestern University and the 2014 film retrospective *Mama and Papa Lala: 30 Years of Hatch-Billops Films* at Emory University.

Eric Pierson is an Associate Professor and former chair of the Communication Studies Department at the University of San Diego. His work on Black images and audiences has appeared in the *Encyclopedia of African American Business History*, *Screening Noir*, the *Encyclopedia of the Great Black Migration*, and the *Journal of Mass Media Ethics*. His most recent works, "The Promise of Roots" and "The Clinton 12 and Prom Night In Mississippi: Conversations in Integration," appear in *Watching While*

Black: Centering the Television of Black Audiences and *Documenting the Experience: Essays on African American History, Culture and Identity in Nonfiction Films*. Eric holds two degrees from the University of Illinois at Urbana-Champaign, a BFA in Fine Arts, and a PhD from the Institute for Communications Research.

Paul N. Reinsch is Assistant Professor of Practice—Film in the department of Theatre and Dance at Texas Tech University. He is the author of *A Critical Bibliography of Shirley Jackson* (Edwin Mellen) and has written about audio-visual media for *Music and the Moving Image, Film International, Spectator,* and *PopMatters.*

TreaAndrea M. Russworm, a self-proclaimed Afrogeek, received her PhD in English from the University of Chicago. Currently an Assistant Professor of English at the University of Massachusetts, Amherst, she teaches classes on American studies, popular culture, and new media. Her articles and book chapters have appeared in *Teaching Media, FlowTV*, and in the anthologies *Watching While Black* and *Game On, Hollywood!* She is the coeditor of two edited collections, *From Madea to Media Mogul* and a new collection on identity and representation in video games. Dr. Russworm's monograph, *Blackness is Burning*, problematizes the politics of recognition in Black and American popular culture during and since the civil rights era. *Blackness is Burning* is forthcoming from Wayne State University Press.

Rashida Z. Shaw, PhD, is an Assistant Professor of English at Wesleyan University. Her forthcoming book project examines "Chitlin Circuit" theatrical productions and the reception practices of African American spectators. Shaw's scholarship and interviews with "Chitlin Circuit" theatre practitioners have appeared in the journals *Theatre Survey* and *Theatre Topics*, as well as *Time Out Chicago* magazine.

Samantha N. Sheppard, PhD, is Assistant Professor of Cinema and Media Studies in the Department of Performing and Media Arts at Cornell University. She published "Persistently Displaced: Situated Knowledges and Interrelated Histories in *The Spook Who Sat by the Door*" in *Cinema Journal* (Winter 2013). Her essay "Bruising Moments: Affects and the L.A. Rebellion" is included in the book *The L.A. Rebellion: Creating a New Black Cinema* (University of California Press, 2015). Her essay "She Ain't Heavy, She's Madea: The Tyler Perry Discourse and Black Cultural Production" is included in the forthcoming edited collection *Black Cinema Aesthetics Revisited*. She is currently working on a book manuscript titled *Sporting Blackness: Race and Embodiment and Sports Films*.

Ben Raphael Sher is Vice President of Development at X-G Productions and an instructor at UCLA. He received his PhD from UCLA's Cinema and Media Studies program (dissertation title: "Fraught Pleasures: Domestic Trauma and Cinephilia in American Culture"). His work has appeared in various publications, including *The Cinema of Rob Zombie: The Social and Political Philosophy of Horror* (forthcoming from Open Court Publishing Company), *Leonard Maltin's Movie Guide*, *Fangoria*, and the websites for Chiller TV (a division of NBCUniversal) and Shout! Factory. He received the UCLA Distinguished Teaching Award in 2014.

Khadijah Costley White is an Assistant Professor in the Department of Journalism and Media Studies at the School of Communication and Information at Rutgers University in New Brunswick. White researches race, media, gender, and politics with an interdisciplinary lens. Her book manuscript, "Raising the Volume: How the News Media Created the Tea Party," is a multi-platform study that examines the rise of the Tea Party as a political brand in online, print, broadcast, and cable news. Her work has been published in the journals *Thirdspace: A Journal of Feminist Theory & Culture*, *Urban Geography*, *Transforming Anthropology*, and others. She has also served as a contributor and commentator for outlets such as the *New York Times*, *Atlantic*, and National Public Radio. Previously, she worked as a journalist on an Emmy-nominated team at *NOW* on PBS and served as a White House intern on the Obama administration's Broadcast Media team.

Index

12 Years a Slave, xxv, 122, 141
34th Street Films, 3, 4, 11, 17, 19–20, 22
60 Minutes, 77–78, 183
700 Sundays, 42

ABC, 12, 20, 42, 58, 99, 128, 142, 148, 164–66, 177, 233
Abee, Edward, 43
About Last Night, 122
Abrams, J. J., 54, 207
Academy Awards, xx–xxi, xxv, 12, 60
Ackroyd, Peter, 131–32
A&E, 168
aesthetics of testimony, 80–84
affect, xviii, xxiii, xxviii–xxix, 12, 20, 23, 73–74, 80, 82, 88–89, 95–96, 103–4, 111–12, 114, 174, 228, 231, 235
Ahmed, Sara, 84
Akil, Mara Brock, 128, 140, 142
Akil, Salim, 67, 68, 140, 142
Albee, E. F., 33–34, 44
Aldridge, Leah, xxxii
Alex Cross, 21, 69, 207, 229
Allen, Woody, 192
Allison, Dorothy, 96
Almodóvar, Pedro, 201
Als, Hilton, 3, 7, 110
Amblin Entertainment, 205
Amen, 166
American Chopper, 169
American Graffiti, 203, 215
American Marketing Association (AMA), 226
American Theatre Wing, 40
Amos 'n' Andy Show, The, viii, 76, 149, 164–65, 171–72, 180
Anderson, Anthony, 177

Anderson, Lisa Arrindell, 127, 193
Angelou, Maya, 23, 108
Anger Management, 147
Antwone Fisher, 112
Any Day Now, 143
Applegate, Christina, 42
archives of feelings, 96–97, 99
Are We There Yet?, 143, 147
Aronofsky, Darren, 234
Astor Place riot of 1849, 31–32, 33, 44
ATL, 17
Atlanta, Ga., 7–8, 19, 56, 80, 145, 147, 160, 170, 210, 216
Attack the Block, 141
audience: Black, xv, xxix, xxxi, 4–5, 7, 81–82, 131, 136; Black female, 3, 9–10, 22–23, 52–53, 56, 58–59, 61, 64–67, 69, 78, 97, 110, 119–20, 139, 149–50, 181, 188, 192, 227–28, 235; Christian, 3, 7, 52–53, 56, 58, 60–62, 67, 73, 78, 81–82, 84, 125–26, 131, 181, 228; international, 228–30
Aunt Bam's Place, 138
authorship, 184–86
Avengers, The, 54
Aytes, Rochelle, 127, 193

Baker, Josephine, 229
Baker, Roger, 129
Baldwin, James, 98, 174
Bamboozled, 75, 180, 194
Banet-Weiser, Sarah, 227
Baraka, Amiri, 33, 161
Barbershop, 186
Barnette, Neema, 68
Barrett, Malcolm, 17
Barthes, Roland, 102–3
Basketball Wives, xviii

Bassett, Angela, 236
Bastard Out of Carolina, 96
Beacon Theatre, 40, 44
Beaty, Daniel, 47
Beauty Shop, 36, 162
Becker, Christine A., xviii
beef, defined, 181–82
Being Mary Jane, 128
bell hooks, 66, 75, 83, 97, 227–28
Bendix, William, 213
Benson, 166
Berlant, Lauren, xxiv, 124
Bernstein, Ira, 145, 169
Best Man Holiday, The, xxiv
Beulah, 164–65, 171–72
Bill Cosby Show, The, 165
Billingsley, ReShonda Tate, 69
Birth of a Nation, The, viii, 97, 186
Birth of Madea, The, 118
Black, Shane, 20
Black authenticity, 75, 188–89
Black cinema, contemporary, 74–80
Black creative production, 138–51
Black cultural production, xvii, xix, xxi–xxii, xxvi–xxviii, xxxii, 3–5, 8–9, 11–12, 19, 23–24, 74, 153, 229
Black Enterprise Entrepreneurs Conference, 180
Black Entertainment Television (BET), x, 46–47, 64, 69, 128, 142–44, 167
Black exclusion, 164
Black female filmmakers, 75
Black film market, 141–44
Black Film Review, 78–79
Black identity, 187–88
black-ish, 177
Black Masculinity and the U.S. South, 188
Black Movie Awards, xxx, 107, 111
blackness, viii–ix, xvii, xix, xxii–xxvii, xxxi–xxxii, 11, 54, 73, 75–78, 83, 89, 159–60, 163–67, 174–75, 180–95
Black popular culture, xiv, xvi–xxvii, 16, 30–31, 41–49, 109, 126

Black Power movement, 132
Black Swan, 104, 234
Black Voldemort, 21, 22–25
Blaxploitation, viii, 54, 63, 69, 228
Block Museum, 233, 235
"blues cosmology," 87
Bluest Eye, The, 98
Bobo, Jacqueline, 23, 97–99, 109–10
Boondocks, The, 72, 83, 210
Bourdieu, Pierre, xxii, 190
Bowdre, Karen M., xiv, xvi, xxvii, xxxi, 10
Bowser, Yvette Lee, 166
Boyd, Todd, 46, 163, 201
Boyega, John, 141
Boykin, Philip, 40
Brady Bunch, The, 104, 233
brand, xxvii, 3, 5, 11, 14–15, 17, 19–20, 22–23, 44–45, 57, 61–64, 68–69, 78, 119, 135, 145, 149–54, 162–63, 168, 172, 204–5, 210, 225–31
Braveheart, 60
Bravo, 168
Breuer, Lee, 38
Bridges, Jeff, 234
Broadway League, 40
Broderick, Matthew, 42
Brolin, Josh, 234
Brown, James, 182
Brown, Michael, xxi
Brown-Jackson, Teri, 146
Buckingham, David, xxii
Bullins, Ed, 161
Burdine, Warren, 35
Burke, Delta, 43
Burnett, Charles, 185
Burns, Michael, 145
Burns and Allen, 164
Butler, Judith, 130–31, 134
Butler, The, xxiv

Caldwell, John, 15
"call and response," 66, 105, 120, 126
Cantone, Mario, 42

Carlomusto, Jean, 96
Carroll, Diahann, 17, 165
Carsey-Werner, 142
Cartoon Network, 72
Car Wash, 59
CBS, viii, x, xxxi, 43, 76, 77–78, 107, 142, 145, 159, 164–66, 201
centrality, xvi–xvii, xxxi–xxxii, 130, 185, 227
Chaplin, Charlie, 201–2
Chapmyn, James, 162
Cherry, Marc, 146
Chicago Sun-Times, 163
Chism, Tina Gordon, xxviii, 4–5, 16–18, 20–22, 24
"Chitlin Circuit" theatre, xxviii, 7–8, 30–38, 48, 55–56, 58, 69, 74, 83, 120–21, 161–62, 180, 185, 190
Chop Up, The, 46–47
Christian, Aymar Jean, xxx, 19
Christian Broadcasting Network (CBN), 60
Christianity, xv, xxix, 56–62, 84–85, 95, 106, 111, 120, 133, 136, 149, 151, 161–63, 205, 212–13, 217, 225, 233
Cinema Journal, xvi
cinema of alterity, 80–81
cinema of recuperation, 76–77
cinephilia, xxix–xxx, 94–114
civil rights movement, ix, xxiii, 172, 189
Clansman, The, 186
classical era nostalgia, 213–18
"Clean Up Woman," 126
Clybourne Park, 40–41
CNN, 75
Coburn, Carol, 42
Coen, Ethan, xxv, 234
Coen, Joel, xxv, 234
Cohen, Rich, 216
Cohen, Rob, 21, 69, 207, 229
Collins, Patricia Hill, 46
Color by Fox, 14
Colored Actor's Union, 34
Color Purple, The (film), 13, 98, 107–11, 208, 210

Color Purple, The (novel), 23
Combs, Sean, 43, 227
Comedy Central, 169
Constantine, 162
Contemporary Christian radio, 60
Coogler, Ryan, xxiv
Cook, Pam, 217
Cooper, Brittney, 10, 152–53
Coppola, Francis Ford, 203, 214, 216
Cornish, Joe, 141
Corson, Keith, xxix
Cosby, Bill, 47, 143, 165
Cosby Show, The, 42, 47, 142, 166
Costley White, Khadijah, xxx, 19
Cougar Town, 148
Courageous, 60
Cover, 67
Coyle, Jake, 210–11, 213
Crawford, Joan, 98
critics, xiii–xiv, xix, xxviii, 3, 10, 21, 37, 46–48, 52, 56, 62–66, 72–74, 79, 97, 113, 120–22, 128–29, 149, 180, 184–88, 192, 200–201, 209–10, 213, 219, 225
Crystal, Billy, 42
Cukor, George, 56
cultural politics, 4, 23, 25, 140
Curtis, Bryan, 207–9
Cvetkovich, Ann, 96
CW, 143, 167–68

Da Brick, 141
Daddy's Little Girls, 64–65, 127, 133, 163
Dallas, Tex., 57
Damon, Matt, 234
Daniel, Rachel, xxx, 235
Daniels, Lee, viii, xxiv, 4, 11–12, 99, 128, 208–10, 212
Dash, Julie, 185
Da Sweet Blood of Jesus, 182
Davidson, Tommy, 194
Davies, Hannah, xxii
Davis, Angela, 132
Davis, Bette, 98

246 Index

Davis, Cassi, 150, 170
Davis, Kristin, 43
Davis, LaVan, 150, 170
Davis, Ossie, 204
Davis, Sammy, Jr., 161
Davis, Zeinabu Irene, 78–79, 80
Davy, Kate, 129
Deadliest Catch, 169
Dead Zone, The, 169
Dear White People, xvii
Death of a Salesman, 40
Debmar-Mercury, 8, 139–40, 145–48, 169
Debruge, Peter, 210, 213
Dee, Ruby, 19
Dent, Gina, xxvi
De Palma, Brian, 214
Designing Women, 43
Devine, Loretta, 23, 112
Diamond, Lydia, 41
Diary of a Mad Black Woman, xxxii, 6, 9, 45, 52, 62–64, 67, 74, 104, 118, 120–21, 127, 132–33, 145, 161–63, 180, 192, 225, 235–36
Diawara, Manthia, 97, 165
Diff'rent Strokes, 166
DirectTV's Audience Network, 143
Discovery Communications, 147, 169
disguise, xxviii, xxx, 118–36
Disney, 142, 206, 218–19
diversification in film, 54
Dollar, Creflo, 57, 69
domestic trauma, xxx, 94–114
domestic violence, xvi, xix–xx, 46, 58, 95, 99, 105, 107, 113, 120, 127, 160, 193
Don't Make a Black Woman Take Off Her Earrings, 6–7, 135, 150
Do the Right Thing, 74–75, 180
drug addiction, 171–72
Drumline, 17
Du Bois, W. E. B., 191
Dudley, Sherman (S. H.), 33–34
Dudley Theatrical Enterprise, 33
Duke, Bill, 67
Dunye, Cheryl, xv

Dutcher, Richard, 60
DuVernay, Ava, xx

East Side, West Side, 201
Eastwood, Clint, 183–84
Ebert, Roger, 9, 120–22, 163, 210–11, 213
Ebony, 152, 203
Elba, Idris, 127
Electronic Labyrinth THX 1138 4EB, 203
Elise, Kimberly, 62, 120, 236
Elsaesser, Thomas, 107, 109
Emmerich, Roland, 54
Empire, 128
Empire Strikes Back, The, 54
Entertainment Weekly, 122
Esquire, xv
Essence, 13
Ethel Barrymore Theatre, 39
Everett, Anna, 97–99
Everybody Hates Chris, 167
exceptionalism, xxviii, xxxi, 180–195

Facing the Giants, 60
Fahrenheit 9/11, 9
Falco, Edie, 42
Fantastic Four, 186
Fantastic 4: Rise of the Silver Surfer, 186
Farquhar, Ralph, 166
Fechit, Stepin (Lincoln Perry), 45
Feltheimer, John, 78
Fences, 37–39
Fey, Tina, 146
Fighting Temptations, The, 59
Film Comment, 201
Fincher, David, 207
Fireproof, 60
First Sunday, 68
Firth, Colin, 234
Fisher, Frances, 42
Flavor of Love, xxv
For Better or Worse, 6, 13, 143, 146–48, 177, 205
For Colored Girls (film), xxxi, xxxiii, 20, 22, 69, 81, 104, 201–2, 207, 209–14

For Colored Girls Who Have Considered Suicide When the Rainbow Is Enuf, xxxiii, 20, 81, 104, 209
Foreigner, The, 42
Forrest, Edwin, 32
Forrest Gump, 108
Fox, Crystal R., 152
Fox, Robert, 44
Fox Faith, 60
Fox Network, 14, 128, 142, 146, 166–67, 169, 175, 205, 215
Foxx, Jamie, 135, 140, 229
Francis, Terri Simone, 87
Fresh Air, 99
Friedberg, Anne, 227
Fruitvale Station, xxiv
Fuller, Charles, 56
Fuller, Sam, 201
Furie, Sidney J., 107
FX, 147

Gaines, Jane, 97–99
Game, The, 142, 144, 167
Gans, Herbert J., 48
Garrett, Shelly, 36, 55, 162
Gates, Henry Louis, Jr., 120–21, 161
Gates, Racquel, xvi–xvii, xxv
Gatorade, 226–27
Gay, Roxane, 23–24
Gaynor, Gerren Keith, 152
Gem of the Ocean, 42
George, Nelson, 45–46
Gerard, Jeremy, 38
Gershwin, George, 40
Gershwin, Ira, 40
Ghost, 41
Ghost the Musical, 41
Gibson, Brian, 107
Gibson, Mel, 60–61
Gillette, 226–27
Gimme a Break, 166
Girlfriends, 142, 167
Glass Menagerie, The, 42

Glory, 210
Glover, Savion, 194
Godard, Jean-Luc, 184
Godfather, The, 104
Goldberg, Whoopi, xxxiii, 23, 54, 184
Goldstein, Patrick, 3
Gone Girl, 207
Good Deeds, xxix, 62, 84–88, 138
Good Times, 107–9, 111, 165
Gordon, Ed, 72
Gordy, Berry, 113
gospel, 87–88, 162, 168
Gospel, The, 67
Gospel at Colonus, The, 38–39
gospel cinema, xxix, 52–70
Goulding, Edmund, 108
Grammer, Kelsey, 167
Grand Hotel, 108
Grant, Darren, 6, 104, 118, 145, 162, 180, 225, 235
Gray, Herman, xxiii–xxiv, 4, 154, 166, 187
Gray, Macy, xxxiii
Great, Artel, xxxi, 14
Great Gatsby, The (film), 20
Grier, David Alan, 17, 40
Griffith, D. W., viii, 186
Grimstead, David, 32
Gross, Kali N., xxiv
Gross, Lance, 170
Gross, Terry, 99, 101
Guerrero, Ed, 76, 172
Guidry, Gary, 36
Guillermin, John, 54
Gulf, 229
Gunning, Tom, 214

Hall, Stuart, xxv–xxvii, 49, 187
Hamilton, Lisa Gay, 42
Hamlin, Larry Leon, 47
Hansberry, Lorraine, 40–41, 43, 161
Hardy, Rob, 67
Harlow, Jean, 98
Harper, Frances, xix

Index

Harpo Productions, 11
Harris, Fredrick C., xxii
Harris, Steve, 120
Hart, Kevin, 122
Harvey, Steve, 129
hashtags, xx–xxi, xxvi
Hatch, James, 34
Haunted House 2, A, xxiv
Havens, Timothy, 229
Haves and the Have Nots, The, x, 13, 15, 138, 140, 147–48, 151–53, 177, 205
Hawk, Kali, 17
HBO, 42, 141–43, 211–13
Help, The, 208
Hemingway, Anthony, 141, 202, 210, 212
Henderson, Odie, 21
Henson, Taraji P., 6
Hepburn, Katharine, 43
Higgensen, Vy, 36, 162
Higginbotham, Evelyn Brooks, xxii
Hill, Errol, 34
Hines, Gregory, 112
Hitch, 162
Holiday, Billie, 112
Homeboys in Outer Space, 167
Homesteader, The, 16
Honeymooners, The, 164
Hooper, Tom, xxv, 234
Hot Tub Time Machine 2, xvii
House of Blues Atlanta, 145
House of Payne, x, xxxi, 8, 14, 18–19, 138, 140, 143, 145–46, 150–51, 153, 159–77, 180, 205
Howard the Duck, 205
Huffington Post, 134
Hughes, Robert J., 42–44
Hunger Games, The, 148
Huyck, Willard, 205

I Can Do Bad All by Myself, 6, 15, 57, 121, 125–27, 131, 144, 160–61
Ice Cube, 68, 147
I Don't Want to Do Wrong, 138
If Loving You Is Wrong, 7, 13, 177

Ike, Rev., 59
I Know I've Been Changed, 7, 56–57, 144–45, 160
Independence Day, 54
Indiana Jones franchise, 205, 215
Industrial Light & Magic, 203
In Living Color, 166
Inside Man, 182
Iola Leroy, xix
Iron Man 3, 20
I Spy, 165
Iton, Richard, 48
Iyanla: Fix My Life, 13–14

Jackson, Samuel, 183
Jakes, T. D., xxix, 52–70, 145
Jameson, Fredric, 215, 217, 219
Jamie Foxx Show, The, 167
Jarmusch, Jim, 192, 206
Jeffersons, The, x, xxxi, 159, 165
Jenkins, Henry, 5
Jersey Shore, 104
Joe Turner's Come and Gone, 38–39
Johnson, George, 186
Johnson, Je'Caryous, 36, 68
Johnson, Noble, 186
Johnson, Robert, 142
Johnson, Roy S., 203, 216
Jones, James Earl, 40
Jones, Orlando, 134–35
Jones, Quincy, 204
Jordan, Louis, 204
jouissance, 95, 102–3, 109, 111
Jules and Jim, 101
Julia, 165
Julian, Isaac, 228
Jumping the Broom, 67

Kardashian, Kim, 119
Keathley, Christian, 102–3
Keith, B. F., 33–34, 44
Kelley, Peter, xxii
Kendrick, Alex, 60

Kershner, Irvin, 54
Kickstarter, 182–83
Kidman, Nicole, 43
King, Martin Luther, Jr., 189, 191
King's Speech, The, xxv, 104, 234
Knowles, Beyoncé, 227
Kodjoe, Boris, 193
Krasner, David, 34

LaBelle, Patti, 146
Lady Sings the Blues, 107, 111
Lange, Jessica, 42
LA Rebellion, 54, 192
Laugh Whore, 42
Lawd Ha' Mercy, 162
Lawrence, Francis, 162
Lawrence, Martin, 65, 129, 140, 142, 229
Lear, Norman, 107, 165
Lee, Malcolm D., xxiv
Lee, Spike, xv, xxxi, 10, 24, 54–55, 72–79, 141–42, 180–95, 201, 208–9, 211
Left Behind, 59–60
Lemieux, Jamilah, 24
Lemmons, Kasi, xv
Lemon, Don, 75
Leon, Kenny, 43
Levine, Lawrence W., 48
Levy, Eugene, 69
Lewis, Jennifer, 23
Lewis, Norm, 40
Life After Death, 181
Lifetime, 143
Lionsgate Entertainment, x, xv, 6, 8, 11–12, 17–18, 20, 64, 78, 81, 104, 139–40, 145–48, 162, 169, 185, 205, 215, 230
Living Single, 166–67
Logo Network, 143
Long, Tom, 213, 217
Lopez, Jennifer, 140, 227
Lorde, Audre, 95
Lorre, Chuck, 146
Los Angeles Times, 3
Lott, Tommy, 79, 84

Lovely, Patrice, 151
Love Thy Neighbor, 13, 138, 140, 147–48, 150–51, 153, 177, 205
Lubiano, Wahneema, 75, 182, 188
Lucas, George, xxxi, 141, 200–219
LucasArts, 204
Lucasfilm, 204–5, 218–19
Luhrmann, Baz, 20
Luke, Derek, 66
Lull, James, 174
Lumenick, Lou, 210–12
Lumet, Sidney, 201
Lyle, Timothy, 130–31, 213
Lynch, David, 206
Lynn, Jonathan, 59

Mabley, Moms, 136, 161
MacDonald, Audra, 40
MacLachlan, Kyle, 43
Macready, William Charles, 31–32
Madea, vii, xii, xiv, xxxi–xxxii, 3, 6, 12–13, 45, 55, 57–58, 62, 65, 77, 104, 108, 110–12, 151, 160–61, 173, 188, 192–93, 202, 204, 206, 216, 226, 229, 231, 233–36; and false disguise, 118–36; intimate public, 122–26, 131, 133, 135; potential demise, 134–36
Madea Christmas, A, 122, 134, 138
Madea franchise, x, xxii, 8, 69, 84
Madea Gets a Job, 138
Madea Goes to Jail, xxxiii–xxxiv, 66, 121, 126, 130, 132
Madea's Big Happy Family (film), xxxiv, 6, 104, 121–22, 183–84, 233–34, 236
Madea's Big Happy Family (stage play), 6
Madea's Class Reunion, xxx, 101, 104, 107–8, 110–11, 235
Madea's Family Reunion, xiii, xvi, xxx, 107, 109–10, 121, 127, 130, 145, 151, 162, 193, 235
Madea's Tough Love, 135
Madea's Witness Protection, 69, 122, 127, 230
Magnolia Pictures, 61
Mahogany, 113
Make Room for Daddy, 164

Malcolm & Eddie, 167
Malcolm X, 189, 191
Malcolm X (film), 180
Mama, I Want to Sing, 36, 162
Mann, David, 6–7, 125, 151
Mann, Tamela, 6, 125
Ma Rainey's Black Bottom, 37
Marcarelli, Robert, 59–60
Markell, Patchen, xxiv
Markham, Dewey "Pigmeat," 161
Markowitz, Robert, 211
Marriage Counselor, The, 45–46
Marshall, Penny, 59
Martin, 166
Martin, Trayvon, xxi
Marvel, 218
masculinity, 129–31, 134, 150, 188–89
Mayfield, Curtis, 68
Maynard, Ghen, 168
McCauley, Robbie, 56
McClain, China Anne, 170
McGruder, Aaron, 72, 210
McKinney, Demetria, 150, 170
McQueen, Steve, xxv, 122, 141
Means Coleman, Robin, 143, 164, 175
media: convergence, 4–8, 9–10; culture, xv, xxvi, 5, 11, 76, 120, 173, 176–77, 227; empire, viii, xv, xxv, xxxii, 3–4, 6, 58, 73, 81, 130, 135, 139, 160, 175, 200, 219; industry, viii, 13, 24, 73; platforms, xvi, xxi, xxvii–xxviii, 3–25, 44, 118–19, 124, 135, 140, 144, 147, 151, 154, 230; studies, xiii–xxxii, 25, 88
Meet the Browns (film), 6
Meet the Browns (stage play), 6
Meet the Browns (television series), x, xiv, 6, 19, 143, 146, 150–51, 177, 180, 205
Men's Health Magazine, 225
Mercer, Kobena, 228
Merkerson, S. Epatha, 17
MGM, 216
Micheaux, Oscar, xix, 16, 139, 186, 192, 201, 204

Mike Tyson: Undisputed Truth, 141
Miller, Veronica, 15
Millner, Denene, 206
Minnelli, Vincente, 56
minstrelsy, xxxi, 32–34, 45, 47, 75, 159–61, 165, 172, 183, 188, 194
Miracle at St. Anna, 211
Mississippi Burning, 210
Mo' Better Blues, 195
Modine, Matthew, 42
mogul, viii, xvi, xxviii, xxx–xxxi, 3, 12, 15, 80, 138–39, 180, 202–4, 207, 219, 225
Mommie Dearest, 236
Monk-Payton, Brandeise, xxix
Moore, Shemar, 133
Morehouse, Henry Lyman, 191
Morgan, Tracy, 68
Morris, Wesley, 201, 207
Morrison, Toni, 98
Moynihan, Daniel Patrick, 151
MTV, 168
Murdoch, Rupert, 142
Murphy, Eddie, 54, 63, 64–65, 129, 229
My Grandmother Prayed for Me, 162
My.Te.Pe. Productions, 3, 8

Naficy, Hamid, 80–81
National Association for the Advancement of Colored People (NAACP), 19, 143, 146, 165
National Black Theater Festival, 47
National Labor Relations Board, 19, 146
National Managers Protective Agency, 34
National Public Radio (NPR), 99
Native Son, 98
NBC, x, 42, 142–43, 165–66
Neal, Mark Anthony, 168
Netflix, 128
New Hollywood, 214–15, 218
Newton, Thandie, 85
New Yorker, 110, 161
New York Post, 163
New York Times, 6–7, 42, 135, 168

New York Undercover, 166
New York University (NYU), 76, 185
NFL Films, 216
niche, xxviii, xxx, 59, 88–89, 122, 139–40, 166, 227–28, 231
Nicholson, David, 78–79
Nielsen, 142–43, 169
'Night Mother, 42
Noah's Arc, 143
Norbit, 64–65
Norman, Marsha, 42
Norris, Bruce, 40–41
Northwestern University, 233, 235
Not Easily Broken, 67
Nu Metro, 229

Obama, Barack, 146, 191
Obenson, Tambay, 14, 21
Oedipus at Colonus, 38
Omega Code, The, 59–60
Oprah Winfrey Network (OWN), x, 4, 6–7, 12–15, 128, 138–40, 147–48, 151–53, 177, 180, 205, 225
Oprah Winfrey Show, The, 12, 58, 99–101, 103–10, 160
#OscarsSoWhite, xx–xxi, xxvi
O'Steen, Sam, 68
Our World with Black Enterprise, 72–73
Our Young Black Men Are Dying and Nobody Seems to Care, 162
Oz, 143

Palcy, Euzhan, 185
Palen, Tim, 104
Palmer, Keke, 151, 173
Paper Magazine, 119
parables, 85–86, 88
Parker, Alan, 210
Parker, Mary Louise, 42
Parker, Sarah Jessica, 42
Parks, Gordon, 185, 192
Parks, Suzan-Lori, 40, 56, 161
Passion of the Christ, The, 9, 60

Patterson, Robert J., 204
Pawnbroker, The, 201
Payne, Allen, 170
pedagogy, 85
Peeples, xxviii, 4–5, 16–18, 20–22, 23–25
Perry, Frank, 236
Petty, Miriam J., xvi, xxxii
Phillips, Michael, 210
Pierson, Eric, xviii, xxxi–xxxii
Pink, Steve, xvii
Pinkett-Smith, Jada, 194
Pitts, Byron, 183
plagiarism, 147, 148–54
platforms, xvi, xxi, xxvii–xxviii, 3–25, 44, 118–19, 124, 135, 140, 144, 147, 151, 154, 230
Pleasures of the Text, The, 103
Poitier, Sidney, 19, 54, 63, 146, 185, 204
politics of respectability, xxi, xxii–xxiv
Porgy and Bess, 40–41
Potter House, 57–59
Practice, The, 42
Preacher's Wife, The, 59
Precious, viii, 4, 11–12, 23, 99, 101–5, 210, 212–13
Pressley, Nelson, 144
prime-time television, 163–67, 175
Pryor, Richard, 54, 59
public persona, 96–97, 99–106, 110, 113
Puig, Claudia, 210, 212–13
Pulitzer Prize, 37, 161
punctum, 102–3

Queen Latifah, 140, 143

race films, 54, 186–87
Radioland Murders, 205, 215
Raisin in the Sun, A, 40–41, 43
Rancière, Jacques, 164
Randolph, Da'Vine Joy, 40
Rapaport, Michael, 183, 194
Rashad, Condola, 40
Rashad, Phylicia, 23, 42, 85
Ratner, Brett, 234

Reagan-era social policies, 165–66
rebrand, xxvii, xxxii, 225–31
Red Hook Summer, 75
Red Tails, xxxi, 141, 200, 202, 207, 210–11, 215, 217–18
Reeves, Keanu, 162
regionalism, 187–90
Reinsch, Paul, xxxi
representation, xxv–xxvii, xxix, 15, 18, 22, 55, 65, 72–74, 100–103, 105, 107, 110, 112–13, 139, 207–13; Black representation, vii, ix, xiv–xxiii, xxx–xxxii, 4, 9–10, 15, 25, 46, 75–78, 89–90, 98, 125, 128, 142–44, 148–50, 153–54, 160, 165, 167, 174–76, 187, 192–93, 228, 231; politics of representation, 4, 72–74, 77, 80, 109, 149
respectability, xv, xx–xxvii, 86, 151
Rhimes, Shonda, xix, 128, 140, 146
Richardson, Riché, 188–89
Ride Along, 186
Riding Dirty on I-95, xix
Ridley, John, 141, 210
Robbins, Brian, 64–65
Robertson, Dick, 163–64
Robeson, Paul, 229
Robinson, Bill "Bojangles," 161
Robinson, Chris, 17
Robinson, Craig, 17
Roc, 166
Rock, Chris, xvii, 167
Rogue, 143
Rosie Show, The, 13
Ross, Diana, 113
Ross, Tracey Ellis, 177
Royce 5'9", 182
Rubin, Scott, 40
Rush Hour, 234
Russworm, TreaAndrea M., 185, 233

Sanford & Son, x, 165
Santa Barbara Film Festival, 61
Santana, Carlos, 227
Sarafina!, 38
Sarin, Vic, 59–60
Saturday Night Live, 135
Savran, David, 35
Scandal, xix, 20, 128, 142
Schatz, Thomas, 214
School Daze, 187–88, 195
Schultz, Michael, 59
Scorsese, Martin, 214
Screen Gems, 67
Sedgwick, Eve Kosofsky, 95
Seiter, Ellen, xix
Seitz, Matt Zoller, 201, 215
Selma, xx, xxii
Sex and the City, 42, 43
sexual abuse, xix, xxx, 12, 56, 94, 96, 99, 101–4, 106–7, 111–13, 124, 127, 160, 193–94, 225
Shakur, Tupac, 86
Shamos, Jeremy, 41
Shange, Ntozake, xxxiii, 20, 81, 104, 209–10, 212–13
Shaw, Laramie "Doc," 170
Shaw, Rashida Z., xviii–xix
Sheen, Charlie, 147
She Hate Me, 195
Sheppard, Samantha N., xiv, xvi–xviii, 95–96, 110, 126
Sher, Ben Raphael, xxix–xxx, 12
She's Gotta Have It, 180, 192, 194–95
Showtime, 143
Shue, Larry, 42
Simien, Justin, xvii
Sinbad Show, The, 166
Single Ladies, 143
Single Mom's Club, The, xx, 7, 10, 15
Singleton, John, xv
Sirk, Douglas, xv, 113, 201
Smalls, Biggie, 181
Smiley, Rick, 129
Smiley, Tavis, 191
Smith, Anna Deavere, 56
Smith, Jacqueline, xvii–xviii
Smith, Mel, 205
Smith, Michelle, xxiii

Smith, Tasha, 67
Smith, Will, 19, 54, 63, 140, 143, 146, 162, 229
Smith-Shomade, Beretta, xvi, xvii, 142, 173, 194
Snead, James, 82, 177
social media, xx–xxi, 9, 16, 119
Sony, 67, 219
Sopranos, The, 42
Soul Food, 143
South Africa, 64
South Central, 166
Southern Consolidated Circuit (SCC), 33–34
South Park, 169
Sparkle, 68
Sparks, Jordin, 68
Spears, Britney, 227
spectatorship, 72–90, 97–99, 105
Spielberg, Steven, 23, 107, 110, 205, 208, 214, 216
Spivak, Gayatri, 74
Stallybrass, Peter, 48
Star Trek (2009 film), 54, 207
Star Wars, 204, 215, 218
Star Wars franchise, xxxi, 205–6, 212, 218
Star Wars: The Clone Wars, 205
States of Grace, 60
Steel Magnolias, 43
Steinfeld, Hailee, 234
Stempel, Larry, 32
stereotypes, vii, xv, 44–45, 55, 65, 76–78, 89, 118, 122, 149, 152, 165, 174, 181, 187, 189
Ster Kinekor, 229
Sternhagen, Frances, 43
Stewart, Jacqueline, 16, 82, 97–99, 153
Stewart, Nzingha, 20
Stick Fly, 41
Stone, Charles, III, 17
Story, Tim, 186
Stowe, Harriet Beecher, 189
Sturgis, Gary, 127
Summit Entertainment, 148
Sweet, Eli, 182

Sweet Charity, 42
Sweet Sweetback's Badasssss Song, 112

Tag Heuer, 226–27
Talbert, David E., 36, 55, 68–69, 162
Tarantino, Quentin, 183
Taylor, Charles, xxiv
Taylor, Clyde, 78–80
Taylor, Joe (Miss Sophia), 147
Taylor, Tate, 208
TBS, x, xiv–xv, xxxi, 6, 8, 13–15, 138, 140, 143, 145, 147–48, 159, 163–64, 169–70, 177, 180, 205
Telecommunications Act of 1996, 143
Television Critics Association (TCA), 141
television deregulation, 142–43
Telson, Bob, 38
Temptation, 10, 22, 113, 138, 140, 149–50, 229–30
Tennant, Andy, 162
testimony, xxix, 72–90, 193
That's My Momma, 165
Theater Owners Booking Association (TOBA), 33–34, 161
Think Like a Man, 186
Think Like a Man Too, 186
third meaning, 102–3
thirst, xxviii, xxxi, 173–76
THX 1138, 203, 215
Tiddes, Michael, xxiv
Time magazine, 58
TLC (The Learning Channel), 169
Tony Awards, xxix, 35–41, 200
Top Five, xvii
Torres, Sasha, 77
Towering Inferno, The, 54
True Grit, xxv, 104, 234
Truffaut, François, 101, 184
Tucker, Chris, 234
Turner, Ike, 109, 111
Turner, Kathleen, 43
Turner, Miki, 210
Turner, Nikki, xix

Turner, Ted, 142
Turner, Tina, 109, 111
Tuskegee Airmen, The, 211–12
TV One, 72–73
Twilight, 148
Tyler Perry Company, 3, 8, 145
Tyler Perry Presents, xxviii, 4, 11, 16–24
Tyler Perry Presents Peeples, xxviii, 4–5, 16–18, 20–22, 23–25
Tyler Perry Productions, 230
Tyler Perry Studios, xv, 3, 8, 80, 146, 204–5, 216, 219
Tyler: The Tyler Perry Show, 15
Tyler TV, 148
Tyson, Cicely, 19, 23, 204
Tyson, Mike, 141–42

Union, Gabrielle, 85
unions, 18–19, 32, 34, 83, 140–47, 230–31
United Artists, 215
UPN, 14, 142–44, 167, 169, 175
urban circuit theatre. *See* "Chitlin Circuit" theatre
USA Network, 169
USA Today, 3

Van Peebles, Melvin, 17, 112, 192
Variety, 145
vaudeville, 33–34, 44, 161
VH1, xxv, 143, 168
Viacom, 143
Vimeo, 182
Von Gunden, Kenneth, 214

Waiting to Exhale, 111–12, 236
Walker, Alice, 23, 110
Wall Street Journal, 42
Wal-Mart, 128
Warhol, Andy, 235
Warner, Kristen, xvii–xviii, xxii
Warner, Malcolm-Jamal, 47
Warner Bros. Domestic Television (WB), 14, 143, 163, 167, 169, 175

Warner Bros. Studios, 203, 219
Warren, Michael, 125
Washington, Booker T., 191
Washington, Denzel, 43, 54, 112, 140, 229
Washington, Kerry, 17, 20
Washington Post, 144
Watching Race, xxiii
Watkins, Mel, 45, 161
Wayans, Damon, 194
Wayans, Marlon, 142
Wayans, Shawn, 142
Wayans Brothers, The, 167
Wayne, John, 213
Weber, Bruce, 42
Welcome to Sweetie Pie's, 13
West, Cornel, 191
"What's Beef," 181
What's Love Got to Do with It?, 107–9, 111
Whedon, Joss, 54
Which Way Is Up?, 59
White, Allon, 48
White, Brian, 85
Whitfield, Lynn, 23, 193
Whittaker, Forrest, 236
Who's Afraid of Virginia Woolf?, 43
Why Did I Get Married?, 6, 15, 68, 140, 163
Why Not? With Shania Twain, 13
Willemen, Paul, 100–101, 103
Williams, Katt, 68
Williams, Spencer, 8
Williams, Tennessee, 42
Williams, Tyler James, 17
Williamson, Adrian, 162
Willis, Sharon, 74
Wilson, August, 37–39, 42, 56, 161
Wilson, Darren, xxi
Wilson, Flip, 129
Wilson, Janelle L., 217
Winfrey, Oprah, xv, 11–15, 19, 23, 57, 64, 99–101, 106, 108, 110, 138, 146, 177, 184, 189–90, 201, 219, 225
Wings, 213
Within Our Gates, xix

Woman Like That, A, 68
Woman Thou Art Loosed (film), 57–59, 61, 67
Woman Thou Art Loosed (stage play), 57–58
Woman Thou Art Loosed: On the 7th Day, 68
Woodard, Alfre, 23
Woods, Tiger, 226–27
Wright, Betty, 126
Wright, Richard, 98
Writer's Guild of America, 18–19, 141
Writer's Guild of America West, 146
Wydro, Ken, 36, 162
Wynter, Sylvia, 80

Yearwood, Gladstone L., 79, 88
Yorkin, Bud, 165
Young, Damon, 128
Young Indiana Jones Chronicles, The, 205

Zacharek, Stephanie, 204
Zimmerman, George, xxi
Zook, Crystal Brent, 14
Zucker, Jerry, 41
Zwick, Edward, 210

www.ingramcontent.com/pod-product-compliance
Lightning Source LLC
Chambersburg PA
CBHW030337240426
43661CB00052B/1665